LOGIC AND SYSTEM

LOGIC AND SYSTEM

A STUDY OF THE TRANSITION FROM "VORSTELLUNG" TO THOUGHT IN THE PHILOSOPHY OF HEGEL

by

MALCOLM CLARK

MARTINUS NIJHOFF / THE HAGUE / 1971

PRINTED IN THE NETHERLANDS

TABLE OF CONTENTS

PREFACE

This book will examine one of the oldest problems in understanding what Hegel was trying to do. What is the place of the *Logic* in the Hegelian system? That is, how did Hegel see the relation between "pure thought" and its origins or applications in our many forms of experience?

A novel approach to this old question has been adopted. This book will study Hegel's account of what he regarded as the closest "illustrations" of pure thinking, namely the way we find our thought in language and the way philosophical truths are expressed in religious talk. The preface will indicate the problem and the approach. The introduction will examine three recent works on Hegel and suggest how they invite the sort of study which is proposed here.

There was a time when Hegel was read as the source of all wisdom, a time also when he was treated only as an occasion of ridicule. Both are now past. The attitude of metaphysicians is more cautious, that of their opponents more receptive. Each side is better prepared to allow those who hold an assured place in the history of philosophy to speak for themselves and reveal their achievements and their limits.

In this atmosphere there is special reason, on both sides, for the study of Hegel. No one has made such extreme claims for metaphysical thought and developed it so extensively and systematically. No one has demanded more from posterity in the criticism of such thought.

In one sense, Hegel's position may be stated quite briefly. For him, to be a metaphysician is to recognize that thinking is not finally distinct from that about which we think. What is "there" is there only as experienced, and our many ways of experiencing culminate in the pure thought of the philosopher. Philosophy is not "about" a foreign reality. Philosophy is reality. Better expressed, philosophy is the way we gradually master or see through the many oppositions we find or assume. These are not simply denied. Our life is made up of them. But they remain "within" the final "identity" of thought and its object, "overcome" by it. Absolute knowledge is absolved from dependence on anything merely outside it. The philosopher starts with the totality "abstractly" experienced and ends with the totality "concretely" known.

In another sense, Hegel's position is impossible to state. All the words in the above account draw their meaning from use at stages of the way far short of the final one they describe. *Within, overcome, identity* itself, all are but crude metaphors carrying a wide range of meanings and a rich train of images. It is only in following the complete way which Hegel prescribes that his student can hope to understand the final stage and formulate it in less inadequate language.

Hence, any study of Hegel is condemned, by Hegel's own norms, to a certain one-sidedness. Unless it try to retrace the full way, it must view his system from some particular stage or stages. So far, however, as it is conscious of its own position within the whole, it should – again by Hegel's own standards – go some distance toward overcoming this bias.

Hegel's position brings with it a consequence that may, perhaps with gross over-simplification, be stated as follows. All thinking is confronted sooner or later with an obstacle that cannot be mastered, with an "unintelligible". Philosophical systems may be classified crudely according to where they set, or accept, this obstacle. The philosopher who advances slowly but surely on a "foreign" reality starts with what he can most easily handle and moves toward that which is and remains beyond his grasp. A philosopher who claims to start with the totality may use a similar model to record his progress. Yet a certain insight into Hegel's thought can be gained by seeing it as drawing the consequences from a resolute refusal to treat the unintelligible as a "beyond", as a merely "residual unknown": the firm rejection of any *Jenseits* is the mark of Hegel's philosophy and temperament. However, the corollary – and this Hegel never admitted in such direct terms – is that the unintelligible must be faced at the beginning. Indeed, if the suggestion is allowed, Hegel made this the "principle of explanation" in his philosophy. The very fact of beginning so deliberately with the totality involves certain basic paradoxes, in the "light" of which all else, all within the whole, is "explained".

Perhaps this is caricature. And perhaps such a project sounds absurd. Yet nonsense is relative, and it is not easy to say what anyone is doing in "explaining", least of all a philosopher. At any rate, those who approach Hegel for the first time must be struck by an air of paradox about his system in its entirety and in its parts. We may, then, in trying to indicate the approach this study of Hegel will make, offer a short account of the paradox of his system as it confronts anyone who examines it afresh, free from the weight of commentaries.

Hegel's system consists of three parts. The first he calls "Logic"; the second, "Philosophy of Nature"; the third, "Philosophy of Spirit" – though a basic ambiguity is suggested by the fact that he also refers to these as "the Idea", "Nature", and "Spirit". The reader of the Logic learns early in the game that he is studying no merely formal logic, no classification of thought-categories that are applied to reality. The Logic deals with "objective thoughts". It follows the self-constitution of that all embracing thought which is reality itself: "Logic therefore coincides with metaphysics, the science of things in their thought." (Enc. § 24). The categories which are the affair of the Logic compose the stages by which thought passes from its most abstract forms to the culmination of philosophical thinking, the Absolute Idea, which "alone is being, imperishable life, self-knowing truth, and the whole of truth... the only object and content of philosophy." (WL, II, p. 484)

Yet a few pages later, the perplexed reader finds that "thought passes out of itself into its other in Nature." The efforts he made throughout the Logic to realize that he was experiencing, not a thought opposed to reality, but thought constitutive of reality, now seem to have been in vain. He has passed "out" of this thought to the most elementary forms of nature, thus to begin a long pilgrimage through the realms of physical and chemical processes, of vegetable and animal organisms, to the gradual reappearance of consciousness with which the third part of Hegel's system opens. Only at the end of the Philosophy of Spirit, after human experience has been traced in its profusion of individual and collective forms, does the reader regain, at the final stage of Philosophy, the thought of the Logic which had already been achieved in the first part of the system.

Hence the basic paradox of Hegel's system: logical thought is at once the whole of philosophy and but a part of it. In Hegel's own terms, logical thought contains its other. That is, true philosophical thought *contains* all reality and is not simply opposed and applied to it. Nevertheless, thought contains reality as its *other*, not merely as a "confused thought", but as that which reduces the system of pure thought to one part of a greater whole.

Again language, sunk in the metaphors of space and time, comes to confound the search for the meaning of this paradox. Yet it may be asked if language does not itself, as often suggested by Hegel, aptly illustrate what he means. Thought informs sounds and sights to make them intelligible. They are its "incarnation"; without them it cannot be. But the union is no simple one. Thought must always struggle for expression in a resisting language of space and time. Language remains an "other", in relation to which thought is less than the whole.

This illustration offers the student a position, as yet scarcely exploited, from which he may seek a renewed understanding of the meaning which finds formulation in the paradox of Hegel's system. If the problem is to interpret a system whereby Logic is both the whole and one of the parts, this question may be re-phrased as that of a philosophical thought which both creates and presupposes a spatio-temporal language as its "other". In Hegel's own terms, the question becomes one of the transition to thought from what he called *Vorstellung*, the language or "picture-thinking" which is the immediate other of genuine thought.

Hence, though any study of Hegel be condemned to a certain one-sidedness from the necessity of adopting a particular position, there may be hope for fruitful re-examination of his central problem through an investigation of his doctrine – explicit and implicit – of the relation between thought and its language. So the title of this book refers to the paradox of the system, the sub-title to the approach which has been chosen.

Until Hegel slipped for a time to the periphery of philosophical interest at the end of the last century (and somewhat later in England and Italy), the "transitions" of his system – particularly that from Idea to Nature – formed the subject of much controversy. Most of it was a reflection of its age and draws little response today. In the choice of a fresh approach, the interests of an age are no less clearly shown. Yet it was Hegel himself who taught that the philosopher can no more escape from these than an individual from his own skin.

The brief statement of Hegel's position, made on the opening page, is taken in this book as fundamental to any interpretation of his thought – whatever the commentator himself thinks of this supreme metaphysical claim. Hegel's is the philosophy of a final totality, of an identity which treats all oppositions as interior to itself. To maintain that Hegel, of set intention rather than from failure, accepted any final duality that admits a reality simply "outside" this identity would be to emasculate his philosophy, to withdraw from it that which assigns it to its historical position and gives it its greatest interest for adherents and foes alike.

However, this is not to concede that Hegel's philosophy must then be treated as a dogmatism which gives a description of all reality simply from the standpoint of this final identity. To interpret lower stages merely from a higher is to achieve a purely "abstract" identity, which Hegel emphatically rejected. His introduction of a "Phenomenology" to German Idealism marks his realization that, if the stages are to be understood only from the result, the result must no less be seen from the stages. There is a wealth of experience and of problems in his dictum that "the beginning is the result". Hegel's claim was to have raised the lower standpoints to a higher, without loss of anything proper to them. Indeed, as will be seen later, he explicitly rejected the "domination" of opposition: reconciliation is as much a respecting of duality as a simple removing of it.

So Hegel's interpretation of a final totality is not easy to grasp – or to criticize. A long familiarity with the dualities that appear and are overcome along the way is needed before one can pose the question of that duality which remains "within" the final identity. This study will offer some preparation for posing this question by examining that section of the way where the opposition of thought and language recurs within their fundamental identity.

The embarrassment of language came home acutely to the author in preparing this book for publication. Originally composed as a doctoral dissertation, it remained for years in typescript awaiting a free period in which it could be thoroughly rewritten. However, time for this did not come. The author was pleasantly surprised to receive many requests for an unpublished manuscript and to hear it quoted at philosophical conventions. So the decision was made to present it as originally written. It is hoped that those who are interested in the problem it tackles will allow for the inelegance and innocence of a doctoral work.

Since many of those who show this interest will be more at home in German than in English, most quotations have been left in their original language. In particular, for reasons that will be given later (pp. 26-7 below), no attempt has been made to offer an English equivalent for the key term *Vorstellung*. Where italics are present in a quotation from Hegel, they come from Hegel himself. However, his frequent use of such emphasis has not been rigorously followed.

The bibliography at the end is preceded by a list of the editions of Hegel's works that have been used, together with the abbreviations given in the footnotes. With minor exceptions, the most critical edition has always been consulted. Where only a page number stands in the footnotes, the reference is always to the last work cited. Where reference is to another page of this book, the number is followed by the word "above" or "below". An appendix has been added, giving an outline of the categories of the Logic and Encyclopaedia that are discussed.

Of the professors at the University of Louvain who helped in this study, I owe a special debt of gratitude to Joseph Dopp and Alphonse De Waelhens. I should also like to thank Professor Louis Dupré, of Georgetown University, for his insistence that the work be published as it is and that the ideal of a total rewriting should be set in an un-Hegelian *Jenseits*.

INTRODUCTION

Philosophy is a fulfilment and not a mere striving. Yet he has certainly not reached it who does not, in his thinking, ever experience the frustration of inability to raise to thought the images that incorporate thought. The scandal of the history of philosophy is not that so many contradictory answers have been given. It is rather that thought has never been able to rise to the point where truly contradictory answers can be held.

If it is permissible in a work on a philosophical system to admit the difficulty of beginning, it is doubly so in a study of Hegel. For him the beginning is the result. Hence the entry "into" his thought and the task of writing "about" it must induce a painful consciousness of inadequacy. Externality is clearly false, but it is no less futile to seek a mere internality: that of repeating what has already been said much better by the philosopher himself.

If inadequacy be inevitable, it is at least easier to hide behind that of others. Expression for the problem to be discussed will therefore be sought by reference to three recent works on Hegel.[1] That they come from very different philosophical climates is not entirely unintended. It is hoped that a certain unity of attitude may all the better be revealed.

At the centre of the question what is meant by the history of philosophy stands the fact that each of those who can be held responsible for a true event in that history awaits, and will await, a successor who can assimilate or criticize his thought as a whole. So is it certainly with Hegel. The task of understanding which Hegel imposed on his posterity has by now been carried at least beyond the stage where one can simply accept or reject him. Rather has he now become a source to which the thought that is contemporary will turn for help in its attempt to formulate its problem. And as this problem varies, so will that vary which in sought, and found, in Hegel.

---

[1] J. Hyppolite, *Logique et Existence:* Paris, 1953.
Theodor Litt, *Hegel: Versuch einer kritischen Erneuerung*: Heidelberg, 1953.
G. R. G. Mure, *A Study of Hegel's Logic*: Oxford, 1950.

I. THREE CONTEMPORARY STUDIES OF HEGEL

a. J. Hyppolite

No attempt to understand present concern with Hegel can avoid consideration of the work of Hyppolite. His annotated translation (1939-41) of the
Phänomenologie des Geistes marks the rise in France of Hegelian studies of
considerable extent and vitality. It is, however, rather his monumental
commentary (1946) to that work, the first to be attempted, that can claim
most credit for present application to the earlier writings of Hegel, for the
effort to find in him a spirit more akin to contemporary phenomenological
interests than the traditional presentation of his "System" would suggest.

A first reaction might be that little more than verbal analogy is here involved. What passes today under the name of Phenomenology is an attempt
to go beyond the positions and questions of classical metaphysics, and
"return to things themselves", to render explicit man's original experience. It
may well be asked how inspiration for these purposes is to be found in a
work of Hegel that seems to run counter to them in its basic conception. It
happens – indeed, against its author's first intentions – to bear the title of a
"Phenomenology". But its "description" of the forms of human experience
presupposes Hegel's whole ontology. The philosopher understands "at the
beginning" the dialectical nature of absolute spirit, and simply retraces the
course by which it manifests and constitutes itself in experience.

In an article on the meaning of phenomenology in Husserl and in Hegel,[2]
A. De Waelhens tries to go beyond the over-simple statement of this contrast
and suggest that, despite their fundamental difference, the problem of the
relation between these two conceptions of phenomenology is profound and
fruitful. He sees in Husserl a notion of consciousness basically similar to that
treated by Hegel, in that it does not "possess" contents but is an interiority
which exteriorizes or manifests itself. And this manifestation, though it be
presented by Husserl as that which an "unbeteiligter Zuschauer" describes,
can not escape the involvement of the phenomenologist in his "description",
nor can this situation avoid the essentials of a dialectical development. That
is, the notion of an absolutely presuppositionless phenomenology can not be
maintained – and has in fact been largely abandoned.

Hence the contemporary interest of a study of Hegel's "Phenomenology".
For there the awareness of presuppositions, of a knowledge always beyond
that of the particular experience, is never absent. It comes with the celebrated
distinction between passages that are "für sich" (for the subject immersed

---

[2] *Revue Philosophique de Louvain*: avril 1954, pp. 234-49.

in his experience) and those that are "für uns" (for the philosopher who reflects upon the experience from a position that grasps the whole course of experience).

Yet the value of such a study for modern phenomenology is limited. The radicality of Hegel's presupposition, his claim of an achieved totality, is unacceptable. For non-Hegelian phenomenology, the direction of consciousness to another (that is, "facticity") is an absolute, a constitutive of experience which can not be overcome; and this denies us any standpoint that can boast its possession of a final totality. In this is the basic opposition – and perhaps the only radical opposition – between the two conceptions of phenomenology. Hegelian phenomenology, it may be said, forgets its own origins.

This article is cited as indicating that the renewed concern for Hegel's "Phenomenology of Spirit" and his earlier writings rests not merely in the depth of experience that he brilliantly, if enigmatically, presents; nor in the purely historical question of studying the origins of his system; but also, and perhaps fundamentally, in the ontological problems of contemporary thinkers. These may be stated in many ways: they may question the relation of phenomenology and ontology, of "regional" ontologies and "general" ontology, of experience and thought. They are, at root, problems that can be sought at all points in the history of philosophy. But of the classical systems, it may be that none incorporates them so clearly as that of Hegel. Unfortunately, the clarity seems too frequently to appear in over-confident answers that belie the depth of the question posed.

It is the relation of phenomenology and logic (that is, ontology) in Hegel that Hyppolite makes the subject of his book, *Logique et Existence*.

Comment s'opère le passage de la Phénoménologie au Savoir absolu? Cette question est la question hégélienne par excellence, et l'objet même de cet ouvrage est de tenter de la poser en confrontant les diverses attitudes de Hegel à son égard.[3]

The "attitude" with which Hyppolite chooses to introduce the question, and which in many ways persists throughout the book,[4] is the position Hegel adopts to the development of a philosophical language. His ontology is, in its claim, not a thought "about" being but a logic, the self-manifestation of being in intelligible language. That is, for Hegel there can be no ineffable, no "beyond" to all words that try to express it: "Ce discours que le philosophe fait sur l'être est aussi bien le discours même de l'être à travers le

---

[3] *Logique et Existence*, p. 31; cf. also *Genèse et Structure de la Phénoménologie de l'Esprit*, pp. 565-70.
[4] "La vie humaine est toujours langage": *Logique et Existence*, p. 12.

philosophe."[5] Yet Hyppolite adds immediately: "Ceci suppose d'abord une explicitation d'une philosophie du langage humain éparse dans les textes de Hegel."

That is, the rejection of an ineffable beyond language is, in a sense, only the displacement of ineffability. It ceases to be an unattainable ideal beyond all accomplished identity of meaning and expression. Yet it reappears under many guises at the heart of this achieved identity.

L'évolution dialectique . . . est bien dualiste *aussi*, mais ce dualisme n'est pas comme chez Spinoza le parallélisme du Logos et de la Nature qui ne se rencontrent jamais, il est le dualisme de la médiation. La Nature et le Logos sont à la fois contraires et identiques.[6]

It is in this "dualism of mediation", this "speculative identity" which reconciles duality without suppressing it,[7] that the originality and paradoxes of Hegel's thought are to be found. In terms of a philosophical language, the duality to be reconciled is one whereby words reveal, on the one hand, a merely particular "immersion" in finite experience that falls short of metaphysics; and, on the other hand, a merely abstract grasp of that which goes beyond this particularity, a "talking about" the absolute. The reconciliation is, for Hegel, no future ideal. Yet any presence which enforces identity at the expense of the true diversity which is here manifested would be a lapse into one of the extremes, into the abstract formalism of a "talking about". Hegel's effort to produce a human philosophical language which will reconcile the extremes of immersion and formalism is far from banishing the ineffable. His attempted synthesis of "le discours de l'expérience et le discours de l'être. . . pose au sein même de l'hégélianisme de nouveaux problèmes, peut-être insolubles.'[8]

[5] p. 5.

[6] p. 211; cf. *Genèse*, p. 581.

[7] *Logique et Existence*, p. 74.

[8] p. 44. The effect of this unachieved "dualism of mediation" on the history of Hegelianism is well suggested by Léon Brunschvicg in *Le Progrès de la Conscience*, II, p. 396:

"A travers les deux mondes on peut dire que Hegel est encore aujourd'hui le prince des philosophes, au sens où Aristote l'était pour le moyen âge; c'est le maître de la scolastique contemporaine, le grand professeur des professeurs. Il leur fournit tour à tour deux instruments: philosophie de la logique et philosophie de l'histoire, dont le néo-hégélianisme reconnaîtra la dualité (en cela il sera néo-hégélianisme et non plus hégélianisme), mais qu'il cherchera du moins à rapprocher par des combinaisons qui se prêtent à une infinité de nuances. De même que les milles manières de doser le raison et la foi ont donné aux théologiens, classiques ou romantiques, la facilité de se créer un système quelque peu original, sans cependant sortir du cadre de la tradition, de même il suffit à un hégélien d'incliner davantage, ou vers l'intemporalité de la logique ou vers la succession du devenir, pour se différencier de ses voisins sans renoncer à la commodité d'un répertoire exhaustif en compréhension et en extension."

(quoted by H. Niel, *De la Médiation dans la Philosophie de Hegel*, p. 347)

The problems raised by the particularity of experience and the formalism of thought are not solved by an extended affirmation of their concrete reconciliation. There is a sense in which Hegel's philosophy may be said to be a far-ranging awareness and statement of the problem rather than a "solution" of it. As Hyppolite says of the relation of Logos and Nature, in their contradiction and identity: "On peut reprocher à Hegel d'énoncer seulement la difficulté, mais non pas de refuser de la voir."[9]

Hence Hyppolite's own study is but a presentation of the many attitudes Hegel takes toward the question of the transition from phenomenology to absolute knowledge. The question itself remains at the end of the book:

La difficulté maîtresse de l'hégélianisme est la relation de la *Phénoménologie* et de la *Logique*, nous dirions aujourd'hui de l'anthropologie et de l'ontologie . . . Hegel a cru dans la *Phénoménologie* pouvoir comprendre la réflexion humaine à la lumière du savoir absolu (le pour-nous de l'ouvrage), et il nous semble que le principe de cette compréhension est contenu dans la signification de l'ontologie hégélienne, mais il a cru pouvoir manifester le devenir-savoir-absolu de la conscience humaine, comme si ce devenir était une histoire. L'histoire est bien le lieu de ce passage, mais ce passage n'est pas lui-même un fait historique.[10]

It would go beyond present purposes to pursue here an examination of Hyppolite's study of the relation between Phenomenology and Logic. Our aim, in quoting from his work, is only to elicit a problem in a manner that becomes somewhat less abstract through its many aspects. It will therefore be sufficient merely to mention some of the ways in which Hyppolite sees the relation of Phenomenology and Logic as the living question which underlies the apparently formal structure of Hegel's system.

The transition to absolute knowledge imposes itself at the end of the Phenomenology; ostensibly, that is, before one has started to think the system itself. Within the system, the transition that appears most decisive and most questionable proceeds in the reverse direction: from the Absolute Idea (i.e. the culmination of the Logic) to Nature. This has been reckoned by some to be a purely artificial construction. Yet, Hyppolite maintains, the thought underlying it may be counted as touching the decisive point of Hegelianism.[11] For the transition means that:

Nous ne pouvons pas sortir du Logos, mais le Logos sort de soi en restant soi . . . L'Absolu soulève la pensée, qui ne serait que pensée, au-dessus d'elle-même en l'obligeant à se contredire; il fait de cette contradiction le moyen spéculatif de réfléchir l'Absolu lui-même.

[9] *Logique et Existence*, p. 75.
[10] p. 247.
[11] p. 131.

This reveals, thus, the "paradox" of the system which we have chosen as the point of entry for this study:

On ne peut parler de la place de la Logique spéculative dans le système sans se contredire, car en un sens cette Logique est tout, elle est l'être de tout ce qui est, en un autre elle est une partie du système qui se prolonge en une philosophie de la nature et de l'esprit.[12]

If it is difficult to set oneself in the Phenomenology and then explain one's passage to absolute knowledge, it is no less difficult to give oneself to the self-developing thought of the Logic and then account for a sheer otherness "outside", and for the passage to this as Nature.[13] Yet the difficulty is at heart the same, for the two transitions are two aspects of Hegel's basic philosophical insight. The beginning of philosophy is neither an experience that is simply opposed to the pure thought of absolute knowledge, nor the latter as simply opposed to the former. It is that which embraces both: "spirit", "das Ganze". Yet this is a true beginning only so far as it has made itself the result. That is, it must no less be grasped as the culmination of a path that must make the transition from "mere" experience to thought, and of a path that must make the transition from "mere" thought to experience.

In his concluding remarks, Hyppolite suggests that the Logos is to be understood, not as the "essence" of the world, but rather as "l'élément où l'être et le sens se réfléchissent l'un dans l'autre."[14] The final identity of the system is achieved in the comprehension of all diversity as "reflected dualities" at its heart. Hegel's philosophy is a vigorous rejection of any "second world", but it poses the problem of a series of profound dualities: of beginning and result,[15] of negativity in thought and negativity in experience,[16] of logic and phenomenology.[17] It is true that all such dualities can be interpreted only in the light of the final unity. Yet it is no less true that the latter, if it is not to become abstract and formal, demands a constant rethinking and re-experiencing of these dualities.

---

[12] p. 92. So he elsewhere discusses "le paradoxe . . . selon lequel Hegel réduit la philosophie à la Logique et en même temps dépasse cette réduction.' (*Genèse*, p. 580) Similarly, R. Kroner speaks of the Logic as "die ganze Philosophie als Moment ihrer selbst." There is a relation such that the Logic rules the system and the system rules the Logic. (*Von Kant bis Hegel*, II, p. 509).

[13] *Logique et Existence*, pp. 213-4.

[14] p. 246.

[15] pp. 79-80, 84-6.

[16] p. 136.

[17] p. 72.

b. *Theodor Litt*

The preceding "Essai sur la Logique de Hegel" may, for all its learning, leave the reader somewhat sceptical about the value of interpretation and criticism of Hegel. The "circularity" of his thought, where every statement finds its truth and its contradiction, deprives both interpreter and critic of any solid hold. Each finds himself condemned to the task of playing variations on a theme.

It is a first merit of Theodor Litt's attempt at a critical renewal of Hegel's thought that he has sought a method of exposition that remains within the system yet avoids the sterility of repetition, by reversing the direction and proceeding from the most concrete definitions of the absolute to the most abstract. Far from being a violence to Hegel's thought, this is the complementary thinking of the system implied in its circularity and often explicitly demanded by Hegel himself. "Das rückwärtsgehende Begründen des Anfangs und das vorwärtsgehende Weiterschreiten desselben fällt ineinander und ist dasselbe."[18]

This direction of thought, however, which is presented (second Book) merely as an alternative form of exposition for the Philosophy of Spirit, becomes (third and fourth Book) the basis for a critical approach to the Philosophy of Nature and the Logic. For this is the direction Hegel's own thinking took in its development. And the question is thus posed of the validity of the transition in that thinking when he passed from the world of experience of his "Jugendschriften", which later became the basis of the Philosophy of Spirit, to the realms of Logic and Nature and the system that unites the three. That is, we must ask:

Vertragen es die Grundbegriffe, die in der Selbstbesinnung des Geistes ihren Ursprung haben, in die Sphären übertragen zu werden, die nach Hegels eigener Feststellung dem Erwachen des Geistes voraufliegen? Muss sich nicht bei dieser Übertragung ihr Inhalt so sehr abwandeln, dass nur das Festhalten an dem *Wort*, welches den Begriff bezeichnet, den Schein der Übereinstimmung hervorruft, die Sache selbst dagegen die begriffliche Zusammenfassung Lügen straft?[19]

Here can be seen a formulation of the problem similar to that of Hyppolite. Firstly, by reversing the direction of exposition, Litt emphasizes that the systematic transition from Logic to Nature and Spirit is fundamentally one with the passage from human experience to absolute knowledge.[20] Secondly, the question of the validity of such a passage is posed in terms that likewise raise the problem of the bearing of language on thought.

[18] WL, II, p. 503.
[19] *Hegel: Versuch einer kritischen Erneuerung*, p. 207.
[20] Cf. p. 6 above.

Or one may compare this criticism to that made by contemporary pheno-menology,[21] that Hegel's thought sins by forgetting its own origins: the totality that is demanded for its validity is excluded by the nature of the experience with which we "start". Litt presents the Philosophy of Spirit as a self-reflection that avoids passing outside human experience and human thinking to any self that would stand beyond and against it.[22] But the passage to a like- developing Philosophy of Nature which Hegel's "will to system" demanded now contradicts his own principles:

> Solange wir die Selbstbesinnung als eine Leistung ansehen, die der Geist nur als im Subjekt "Mensch" sich verkörpernder vollbringen kann, solange müssen wir die Annahme eines Subjekts, das Natur und Geist in seiner Identität vereinigte, verneinen. Halten wir umgekehrt an dieser Annahme fest, so kommt das der Statuierung eines Subjekts gleich, das, weil nicht in die Schranken menschlicher Selbstbesinnung eingeschlossen, recht eigentlich "übermenschlich" heissen müsste.[23]

In his critical summary at the end of the book, Litt returns to this point in alleging that the illegitimate totality of the system amounts to a "Wieder-herstellung des Anderen". Absolute spirit, rather than actualizing itself in the particular, becomes inevitably a "logisches Gefüge,"[24] a true freedom, but foreign to the particular subject,[25] a mythological "Selbstmystifizie-rung".[26]

If the transition from Spirit to Nature may suggest that the same words incorporate different ideas and the same movement expresses different subjects, so the transition to Logic raises the question of the autonomy of logical thought. The Logic is presented as a self-movement of thought which develops its full content, its meaning, not from illustration in the world of sense-experience, but purely from itself. It is "das Reich der Schatten, die Welt der einfachen Wesenheiten, von aller sinnlichen Konkretion befreit."[27] This freedom is, however, scarcely to be accepted without qualification by those who have made the effort to understand any part of the Logic from its own development rather than from its "illustrations" in other parts of Hegel's philosophy (which Litt follows Hegel in calling his "Realphiloso-phie"). Litt develops this objection, summarizing the many ways in which the dependence of the Logic on the Realphilosophie is manifested.[28]

[21] p. 3 above.
[22] E. g., *Hegel*, p. 86.
[23] pp. 210-11.
[24] p. 302.
[25] p. 293.
[26] pp. 219-20.
[27] WL, I, p. 41.
[28] *Hegel*, pp. 244-51.

If one abandons the perhaps over-simple view of a Logic that can start and develop in total independence, so must one at least re-think the sense in which the Logic is the beginning of the system. If, however, one follows the suggestions[29] that it could just as well come at the end, the other parts being "sublated" (aufgehoben)[30] into it – "so ist das Logische die allgemeine Weise, in der alle besonderen aufgehoben und eingehüllt sind"[31] – then we come back to our previous doubts of the legitimacy of such a transition.

As Hyppolite here spoke of the Logos that passes out of itself while yet remaining itself,[32] so Litt suggests that the Logic brings us "dieselbe Ineins-bildung des die Weltentwicklung leitenden Logos und der diesem Logos sich fügenden Weltwirklichkeit, die auch der zweite und der dritte Teil des Systems aufzuzeigen bestimmt waren."[33] That is, under the expression of a system of three parts, each passing "over into" another, must move a thought which Litt prefers to characterize as "zweigleisig", a mutual deter-mination and development of Logic and Realphilosophie, of ontology and phenomenology. Whether one can then truly speak of a "kritische Erneu-erung" of Hegel's thought would seem to depend on whether such can be found in him or must be forced upon him.

c. G. R. G. Mure

In the first part of *Logique et Existence*, that dealing with language and logic, Hyppolite acknowledges his debt to the books on Hegel by G. R. G. Mure. Writing in a philosophical climate where the question of language, as a philosophical barrier or ideal, is a primary consideration, Mure naturally shows a more explicit concern for this aspect of his Hegel interpretation than would a French or German philosopher. It is, however, among his merits that, rather than simply measure his author by foreign standards, he goes to greater pains than the others to develop his criticism within and from the author's own thought.[34] For philosophy, he rightly holds, must of its nature be self-critical.

Thus, in his *Study of Hegel's Logic*, he gives in his opening chapter a summary of Hegel's own theory of verbal language. Whereas for many philosophers a discussion of the relation of thought to language might seem external to their system, this is an explicit part of Hegel's. Language is for

---

[29] pp. 234-42.
[30] Cf. p. 11, note 37 below.
[31] WL, II, pp. 484-5.
[32] Cf. p. 5 above.
[33] *Hegel*, p. 251.
[34] Cf. Hegel's own views on philosophical criticism: WL, II, pp. 217-8.

him the point of the dialectic at which nature and incipient consciousness rise to thought; conversely, it is the point at which thought passes into alienation in nature, into those expressions of itself without which it can not be present to itself.

Hegel treats of language in the Philosophy of Spirit, at the stage of "Vorstellung". As it will be the task of this study to consider at length what is meant by this term, it is sufficient here to emphasize its position at the transition from nature and sense to thought. That is, a study of Hegel's doctrine of Vorstellung – of the complementary transitions from language to thought and from thought to language – must be basically a study of the transitions of Hegel's system, in their two fundamental "aspects", as encountered in the preceding studies. The basic philosophical problems that Hegel presents all too metaphorically in the transitions of his system are far from finding solution in this part of his Philosophy of Spirit. Yet they do find a more detailed re-expression:

Between passive and active, particular and universal, sense and thought there may be chasms which philosophy can never finally cross, but the demand that they be bridged is of the very essence of philosophical thinking, and Hegel – though of course with Kant's help – came far nearer to fulfilling it than Kant. His dialectical treatment of spirit may restate the question, but so does any fresh solution of a philosophical problem which does not manipulate it into nonsense. [35]

Mure's interpretation of Hegel can not be suggested unless we try here to indicate very briefly his critical approach to dialectical movement in general. In a previous book,[36] he sought to introduce Hegel in relation to Aristotle's formulation of the philosophical problem. There, Mure compared the dialectic to the informing of matter, where the matter informed is always a proximate matter, that is, itself an information of matter. So is each phase of the dialectic a proximate matter to the phase above it. The total concrete attitude of subject to object, which constitutes any phase, becomes the object or content of the proximate higher phase, which accordingly exhibits a fresh attitude of subject to object. Thus, in so far as any given stage is abstracted from the total process, the subject will there stand to itself at a lower level as to an object; but, lessening the abstraction, the "object" is no less a subjective attitude to a further level. That is, the subject exists at two (or more) levels "at once". Illustrations are particularly evident in practical experience: thus, desire can be raised to will but never so as to avoid some persistence of desire at its own level, against which will stands to some extent

---

[35] *A Study of Hegel's Logic*, p. 7.
[36] *An Introduction to Hegel* (1940).

as mere caprice. But it is Mure's claim that such "imperfect sublation" is no less the mark of theoretical experience.

One may raise the question whether such a view runs counter to Hegel, so that the adjective "imperfect" is a criticism, or whether it is an interpretation of the Hegelian notion of sublation.[37] Can one maintain that a phase can be, not merely "annulled", nor merely "raised", but also "preserved", without implying some preservation *as* a lower level? Mure's own answer would possibly be that his notion of imperfect sublation is an interpretation of Hegel at some levels of the Logic, a criticism at others.[38]

For the moment it is sufficient that certain applications of this notion be made. Firstly, the charge that Hegelian phenomenology sins by forgetting its own origins can perhaps be qualified. If one discounts Hegel's over-confident manner of speaking, there would perhaps be reason to suggest that his notion of phenomenology would well involve a depressing consciousness of origins: the ground from which it springs is always with it, and the experience that sinks deep into nature must still be preserved in philosophy. Correlatively, the highest experience must "already" be present, albeit abstractly, at the "earliest" stages. Hence the "already constituted totality" need not be quite the abomination it is pictured, and a more sensitive interpretation of Hegel's attempt to think a multiple "standpoint"[39] may yet have something to say on the relation of phenomenology and ontology.[40]

Secondly, in regard to the specific question of language and logic, the important teaching is that language dialectically precedes thought. Thus, in Hegel's terms, language is raised to thought in such a way that it is no less preserved than annulled; or in Mure's terms, language is transcended in thought but at the same time survives to express it, in some sense opposed to it. It is not true that thought exists naked and selects a language as one would a garment; certainly not that a quasi-mathematical language can be

[37] The German word "Aufhebung" has no English equivalent that carries the various senses which Hegel sees as essential to his notion of a dialectical synthesis (cf. WL, I, pp. 93-4). Hence this study will follow the custom of translating it by the artificial term "sublation": a translation introduced by Hutchison Stirling's classical study of the "Secret of Hegel" (1865).

[38] Cf. p. 13 below.

[39] This is clearly a spatial image, but it is Hegel's; whether his frequent reference to "Standpunkt" and cognate pictures does find its ground in thought remains to be seen.

[40] Hegel might perhaps make against many contemporary thinkers the charge he directed at Kant, of "viewing spirit as containing the features merely of a phenomenology, not a philosophy, of spirit" (Enc. § 415). That is not, in itself, to deny that a "direction to another" may always be preserved: it is rather to charge that the lower forms of "direction" are made to characterize more developed phases. It is the task of philosophy to pursue the question of the "other" of thought; not, however, to "explain it away".

invented which would serve as a perfect garment.[41] Nor, however, is it true
that the level of Vorstellung (and "under" it the whole life of sense and nature)
can be so perfectly raised to thought that we need have no worry about
fitting clothes. Were such the case, then the notion of a purely autonomous
Logic, rejected by Litt, would still hold. Entirely fabricated technical terms
would have sufficed for "naming" the categories (for their meaning would
come completely from within) and Hegel's intense effort to draw gleams of
reason from words, in their etymological and metaphorical senses, would not
have been necessary.[42]

The caution necessitated by consciousness of the imperfect elevation of
language to thought governs Mure's study of Hegel's Logic, to which the
above considerations were merely a preface. If the task of expounding Hegel
belongs finally to Hegel himself, then that of his commentator is "not to
translate Hegel into ordinary language but to show more clearly than Hegel
has thought worth while how he has developed ordinary language."[43]
Above all, it is a task of pointing out the multiple and varying standpoint
that he must hold who will think with Hegel. For the Logic is unintelligible
unless one sees it as an effort to think the totality, and to think it as always
present but increasingly concrete. The mental gymnastics prescribed are
severe. One's final criticism of Hegel may rest with his notion of totality; but
it must be thought to be criticized.

At the end of his study, Mure adds four chapters in which he tries to
formulate more clearly the critical approach that has been suggested above
and to make it the basis for an assessment of the value and limits of the
dialectical method as such. His criticism, if at times it seems to move in an
element strange to Hegel, is explicitly identified as an approach to the traditional Hegelian questions:

Did Hegel stuff his Logic with alien material? Do the categories, in his view, gain
or lose by phenomenal manifestation? Is the transition from Idea to Nature a mere
tour de force, a quite illegitimate attempt to bridge the chasm between thought and
sense? Does the conception of the super-triad, Idea-Nature-Spirit, accordingly set a
mere sham finish on the system?[44]

If philosophic thought is essentially self-critical, one's approach to a philosopher must always be from within the "nucleus" of his thought. For Hegel
this means basically an appreciation of the position whereby human experience is that in which absolute experience constitutes and manifests itself.

[41] Cf. WL, I, pp. 211-2; Enc. § 259.
[42] Cf. WL, I, p. 10.
[43] *Study*, p. 25.
[44] pp. 294-5.

The dialectic of human experience which develops to philosophic thought is at the same time the single absolute activity which constitutes itself in self-manifestation. The function of a critic, Mure holds, is therefore to draw out the implications of the system by rethinking the contradictions fundamental to human experience, for "if the system is flawless, we shall find that in fact the Absolute alone has been our topic, and that the truth of our criticism was already contained in the system."[45] That is, the contradictions, when fully experienced, must lead the "critic" to a level of thought from which the necessity of these contradictions is revealed in the manifested life of thought. The beginning becomes the result and the result the beginning. The absolute appears in, and justifies itself by, finite experience, in such a way that the latter is raised to, and justified by, the absolute. But the system will show itself so far short of being flawless as the critic, "for all his perseverance in grasping the way of learning as a moment in spirit's activity, cannot wholly escape lapse to a lower level where it appears as a finite thinking, the exposition of which has to be complemented with an equally abstract exposition of spirit as absolute thought merely innocent of finitude."[46]

That the first sketches of such a criticism which he offers lead toward the latter conclusion, toward the "perhaps insoluble" problem of "mere immersion and formalism" that Hyppolite indicated,[47] follows clearly from Mure's understanding of dialectic as "imperfect sublation". Again, however, it is suggested that his merit comes largely in his attempt to ground his very objections in Hegel's own Logic.

For it is, he holds, in the Logic of Essence (i.e. the second of the three books of the Logic) that the movement and self-limitations of "imperfect sublation" are thought. It was in this sense that it was hazarded above[48] that Mure might consider his idea of imperfect sublation an interpretation of Hegel in this part of the Logic, but rather a criticism of the first and third books of the Logic as respectively prior and posterior to a verifiable thinking. The complicated movement of Essence, which has to be thought from the standpoint of each of the coupled categories and at the same time as a single movement of spirit, is the logical thinking of that human experience which finds itself at once at two levels: "the unessential is transcended in the essential and at the same time survives to subserve, eke out, and express the essential."[49] In relation to the profoundly experienced thought of the second

[45] p. 300.
[46] p. 44.
[47] Cf. p. 4 above.
[48] p. 11.
[49] *Study*, p. 342.

book of the Logic, the third, with its movement of pure preservation, may justify too well Hegel's own description of it as a mere "play".[50]

d. Summary

With these quotations it has been hoped to evoke the terms of a problem in a manner which, by its many aspects, would be somewhat less abstract than a direct stement. For, though they write with different backgrounds and with different emphasis, the three authors may be interpreted as holding certain basically similar attitudes toward Hegel and as looking for an analogous "critical renewal".

All hope for a deeper interpretation of the thought underlying the transitions of the "System". Hyppolite sees the fundamental Hegelian question as that of the passage from Phenomenology to Logic, one that is in history but not historical. Litt, by reversing the direction of exposition, sets the point of his critical approach on the transition from a Philosophy of Spirit to Nature and Logic. Mure proposes that the value and limits of the dialectical method must appear in the development of a criticism of human experience into the self-manifestation of a "flawless" or less than flawless absolute experience.

Each sees this transition as correlative to the passage from the Idea to nature and finite spirit. Hyppolite asks for an interpretation in terms of the basic contradiction, of a Logos that can pass out of itself while remaining itself. Litt questions the development of Logic into "Realphilosophie". Mure asks whether an adequate dialectical thought could enter into our experience, or whether this latter must ever remain split into a finite thinking and an exposition of absolute thought merely innocent of finitude.

All centre this double movement on a question of the place of the Logic in the System. Is it autonomous, drawing its meaning from within, or does it depend on experience outside its own realm, or are these two opinions in some way reconcilable? If the Logic can come neither simply at the beginning nor at the end, how can one think its place and its movement as a mutual development with "non-logical" experience? What is the relation of the pure categories to those that are phenomenally manifested?[51] How is one to interpret "circularity" and "beginning" in the system?

In the presentation of each author, we have tried to show a connexion

---

[50] Enc. § 161 Zusatz (though, as Mure points out, Hegel here means "unimpeded activity").

[51] To say "schematized" would indicate a historical aspect to the question, due regard being had to the great difference between the interpretation of categories in Hegel and Kant.

with questions posed by contemporary Phenomenology: how can the totality (that is, ontology) be present in an experience that is essentially marked by a lack of totality? Or, more precisely, granted that totality is "virtually" present, what meaning is to be developed for this qualifying adverb?

Finally, it was seen that both Hyppolite and Litt indicate a formulation of the question in terms of the problem of logic and language. Our thought exists in the language that is one with our finite, everyday, historical experience. How can it then pass from the limitations of that position to a "discourse of being itself"? Similarly, in Mure's study, the possibility of developing an approach to Hegel's interpretation of his system through his own theory of language was indicated.

2. THE SITUATION OF THIS STUDY

a. The Purpose

This study will set its purpose in a further thinking, or at least formulation, of the problem which seems common to these three works. As suggested in the preface – and encouraged by the implications of the three authors – an approach to the problem will be attempted through a study of Hegel's conception of the relation of language to thought: that is, of the transition from "Vorstellung" to "Denken".

In that the term "criticize" commonly bears a negative meaning, this purpose is best expressed as an effort to "understand" that thought of Hegel which is conveyed in the transitions of his system. Yet the substitution of the word "understand" in no way dissipates the embarrassment of writing on a philosopher. Understanding and criticism are not easily separated. The dilemma remains of a false externality and a fruitless interiority, of a standpoint that must be both within and outside the movement of thought that is interpreted.

It is thus appropriate that a point of departure has been sought in Hegel's treatment of the problem of language and thought. For it is the gist of Hegel's teaching that a problem, if it be true, is not to be "solved": it is to be thought, but not thought away. And it is thought in its truth so far as the problem is recognized in the very thinking of the problem. The dilemma of a critic, in his need to be both within and outside the thought of his author, is therefore not to be solved: it is rather to be realized in re-thinking the author's own thought in its interiority and exteriority to itself. This, for any author, is his conception – explicit or implicit – of thought's struggle to find itself in that language which it both forms and presupposes, which is both within it and outside it. Though this may, in the study of many philosophers, lead to no easy reconciliation with their explicit formulation of the concern of philosophy, it is this presence of thought to itself only in the alienation of its expression which dominates Hegel's conception of philosophy.[52] To see how this underlies the apparently formal construction of his system is the aim of this present attempt at understanding.

It will be apparent that of the three authors quoted in this introduction, it is Mure whose suggestions of an approach to Hegel have been most influential in the direction this study had adopted. Hegel may have suffered more than he gained by his introduction to English philosophy at the end of the last century. Yet there remains something to be said for one who approaches philosophy with the conviction of a metaphysician and the taste of a positivist.

b. The Title

In choosing a title which asks about the place of the Logic in the System, it is thought to put into relief three words, for which it will be our task to win a closer meaning.

Firstly, any contemporary attempt to be at home with a metaphysician must consist largely in an understanding why his thought should exist in the form of a system. With Hegel is this all the more necessary, for there are few philosophers in whom the "will to system" is more evident; and this tendency, useful as it may be in many realms of achievement and knowledge, is today commonly regarded as at variance with philosophical experience as such.

Hegel would certainly have denied the incompatibility.[53] That which remains in metaphor or hides in the ineffable must, for him, fall short of philosophy, for this can exist only in adequate self-expression. Systematic formulation is, in his view, not external to thought but rather that which makes "philosophical experience" possible. "Das Wort System bedeutet bei Hegel keine seinem Inhalte äusserliche Form; Hegels System will nicht bloss ein wissenschaftliches Ganzen sein; vielmehr ist der Geist sich selbst System und das System sich selbst Geist."[54]

Nevertheless, no serious commentator, however much inspiration he finds in Hegel, will deny that his "Geist" is often a form foreign to its con-

---

[52] "Expression" is here understood in its broadest sense, yet always as "touching" thought in a Vorstellung of thought.

[53] E.g., cf. Enc. § 14.

[54] Kroner, II, p. 299.

tent, that he offers ripe examples of metaphysics falling to the "ontic". Whether Hegel himself was as blissfully unaware of this as is usually implied is a question that itself presupposes a full investigation of his doctrine of Vorstellung and thought. He was certainly aware that the very idea of "Geist", which constitutes his system and marks his advance on Schelling, though it finds its "Sitz und Boden im Denken", is itself no less a Vorstellung than "Fürst, Gericht, usf."[55] It must, then, fall within our scope to suggest an approach to the question of Hegel's attitude to the perfectibility of his system.

Secondly, emphasis is placed by the chosen title on the word "Logic". It might be questioned why, of the three elements which compose the system, the Logic should be designated rather than the Philosophy of Nature or of Spirit – why, indeed one should so select any of them rather than speak neutrally of the transitions in the system. For if only the Whole be the True, than the truth of Hegel's thought is finally to be looked for, or rejected, only in the Encyclopaedia as a flawless totality. So for Kroner, all Hegel's thought is there contained in a living unity, such that it develops "frei und notwendig zugleich aus und zu dem absoluten Geiste, der ihre Substanz ist."[56]

Others are less impressed by the life or the unity. And if we regard Hegel's thought more in terms of the books he wrote, there is certainly a sense in which "das Haus, in dem der Geist wohnen kann' (*ibid.*) is, even for Hegel himself, not so much the Encyclopaedia as the *Wissenschaft der Logik*. Without rising to the charge that the former merely sets a "sham finish" to incorporate the latter with extensive empirical investigations, one may possibly see Hegel's Logic as the work to which all his other studies stand as preparatory inquiries or illustrative commentary.

Whether the triadic system is to be judged a true unity or an artificial construction must form the verdict, and not the presupposition, of this study. Yet even in accepting the unity, there would remain a sense in which the Logic should be given a certain pre-eminence. For the pure "Denken des Denkens", which the Logic claims to be,[57] must – for Hegel, at least – be the entirety of experience, even though, as "nur Denken", it is but a moment of experience. This is precisely the paradox of the system, with which we have started, and it can not fairly be judged – or stated – until we have considered the expression given to it, by the Encyclopaedia, of a thought that is by itself only in being opposed to itself as Vorstellung, and the expression given to it, by the Logic, of a thought that is the essential only in being a mere essential

[55] RB, p. 113.
[56] Kroner, II, p. 503.
[57] Enc. § 19.

opposed to itself as unessential. Indeed, whatever one's ultimate verdict on Hegel's attempt, no consistent thought can perhaps conclusively avoid the problem of a logic which is the whole of philosophy and yet only a moment of it.

Finally, though the title has been left in the uncommitted ambiguity of "Logic *and* System", the most important word is that which relates the two that have been discussed. "And" states merely that language was not formed for such expression. More definite, and perhaps more suggestive, would have been a phrase indicating a relationship of position, though this would still fail to translate the thought of a part that is yet the whole. To ask for the *place* of the Logic *in* the System would at least imply that solicitude for the "Standpunkt" of thinking which has been imposed. Neither Hegel nor his critic enjoys a privileged position, and his thinking must finally be an understanding of the situation in which it is exercised.[58] For Hegel, experience is ultimately the thought of experience, and every place "in" the system is a different manner of apprehending this identity in a no less evident opposition.

c. The Method

He who would study the system of Hegel precisely as system faces the strange circumstance that almost all that has been written on it comes from generations of commentators. The passages in which Hegel himself discusses the transitions of the system triad are short and yield no key to their interpretation. Indeed, the question where such a "key" could come from is at the centre of our problem. Even if the Logic can be understood purely from itself, how can the transition *from* the Logic be understood from within the Logic? In fact, can the system triad itself be understood on the model of any triad within any of its parts? To point out that for Hegel the reverse must be closer to the truth is still not to arrive at a source of interpretation.

Clearly the interpreter can hope for no more privileged approach than Hegel himself. At the close of his Phenomenology, he writes of the "correspondence" between the moments of pure thought and the forms (Gestalten) of phenomenal existence.[59] Neither is richer nor poorer than the other, and the task of the philosopher is to recognize (erkennen) each in the other. To judge from his writings and lectures, this was the task Hegel pursued throughout his life. "The force of mind is only as great as its expression; its depth

---

[58] E.g., WL, I, pp. 14-15: "Insofern also das subjective Denken unser eigenstes, innerliches Tun ist, und der objektive Begriff der Dinge die Sache selbst ausmacht, so können wir aus jenem Tun nicht heraus sein, nicht über demselben stehen, und ebensowenig können wir über die Natur der Dinge hinaus."

[59] Phän., p. 562.

only as deep as its power to expand and lose itself when spending and giving out its substance."[60] His was no idle contentment with an achieved logic but an interest, which perhaps no other philosopher has matched, for the expression of pure thought in nature, psychology, society, history, art, religion, and the history of philosophy itself. Whatever one's final verdict on the balance of insight and construction, a just assessment of his thought must see it inseparably as a wide factual experience seeking understanding in a logic and a logic seeking understanding in this experience.

Hence a study of Hegel's system, if it is to be true to his own method, can neglect neither side. However it narrow its way of approach, it must examine what Hegel has said both in the element of thought (fundamentally, the Logic and the Encyclopaedia) and in those realms of experience which form the bulk of his collected works. Each side constitutes an interpretation of the other.

With this at least as an ideal, the present study is divided into two parts. The first is concerned principally with the Encyclopaedia and the Logic, the second with the Lectures on the Philosophy of Religion.

A preliminary justification for the approach that has been chosen, through the question of language (Vorstellung) and thought, has been made throughout the preface and introduction. The value of this approach can be determined only in the sequel. The first chapter will give a cursory view of Hegel's use of the terms, and the second will examine his treatment of the dialectic of Intuition, Vorstellung, and Thought in the Encyclopaedia. A logical expression for this movement at the transition to thought will be sought in the third chapter.

More justification is required here for the selection of the Lectures on the Philosophy of Religion as the principal matter for the second part. Of the many fields of experience to which Hegel gave his attention, religion offers the most evident advantages for the purpose of this study.

Firstly, religion is for Hegel the stage of experience immediately prior to the final stage of pure thought in philosophy. Hence if one is to interpret pure thought in its illustrations, there is reason for choosing the proximate illustration.

Secondly, it is in religion that Hegel sets the level of experience to which the form of Vorstellung is proper. Thus, his lectures are in large part concerned with a concrete presentation of that relation of Vorstellung to thought which formed the approach adopted in the first part.

Finally – and the main reason for the choice – those sections of the Lectures dealing with "Absolute Religion" constitute a rich source for an interpreta-

---

[60] Phän., p. 15.

tion of Hegel's system. For it is there that Hegel tried four times in his final years[61] to express at some length the triadic form of his system in its proximate illustration in the "vollkommene Religion". Yet it is a source that has apparently not been exploited for this purpose. For those who have written on Hegel's philosophy of religion in any detail have done so primarily in the interest of identifying his notion of religion or theology with their own, or of measuring the distance between them.[62]

Hence the second part of this study will consider briefly the historical development of Hegel's system (Chapter IV), and then examine the expression he gave it in the element of Vorstellung (Chapter V). The material from the Lectures will be correlated with the pertinent parts of the Phenomenology.

It is freely to be admitted that the Lectures on the Philosophy of Religion do not form a work published by Hegel, so that citations from them are to be interpreted with caution.[63] This is, however, a disadvantage that is shared by all the other Lectures. And it must not be forgotten that the Lectures are to serve us, as they served Hegel himself, in the function of an illustration. That is, if Hegel's notion of the inevitable circularity of philosophical thought is likewise to be imposed upon his critic, then our examination of the Encyclopaedia and the Logic in the first part must form as much a conclusion as a preparation for our study. The final chapter (VI) will thus be a result that is no less a return to the beginning.

[61] 1821, 1824, 1827, 1831.

[62] The work which comes closest to interpreting the system from the philosophy of religion is that of E. Schmidt on *Hegels Lehre von Gott* (1952), but his interest is still mainly a religious one and the approach we have proposed is not envisaged by him. J. Möller's study of Hegel's philosophy of religion (*Der Geist und das Absolut*: 1951) is also of value but gives only twenty pages to a summary of the Lectures.

Of the works on particular aspects of the philosophy of religion, two stand out. Ogiermann's study of *Hegels Gottesbeweise* (1948) touches the fundamental metaphysical questions, but his problem is only indirectly that of the system. Asveld's exposition of *La Pensé Religieuse du Jeune Hegel* (1953) is a thorough study of the early years, but the author has shown great restraint in regard to any reference to the system or the developed expression of Hegel.

Hessen's account of *Hegels Trinitätslehre* (1922) is disappointingly meagre, and a reappreciation of the central doctrine of Hegel's philosophy of religion in terms of contemporary thought could well be supported.

[63] The edition of Lasson, which will be used, distinguishes Hegel's manuscript (for the course of 1821) from those sections compiled from the notes of students (for 1924 and 1827: no record survives of the course of 1831). The degree of correspondence between these notes is an indication of their trustworthiness (cf. RB, p. 318). But the mere combination of different texts leaves much to be desired in a professedly critical edition and Lasson's pedagogical interests often motivated his editing. For a criticism of this edition, consult *Zeitschrift für philosophische Forschung* (11) 1957, pp. 122-3.

PART I

"VORSTELLUNG" AND THOUGHT

CHAPTER I

THE DESCRIPTION OF VORSTELLUNG

I. THE MEANING OF MEANING

The difficulty of beginning, of formulating a "first" question, has already sufficiently been exposed. If Hegel's thought, or metaphysical thought as such, presents itself as a flawless whole, then any entry into it from outside brings an acute consciousness of the problem of communication. And this, as a relation between author and reader, finds its original statement in the prior question of self-communication. Words, we say, "come to mind" to carry and to constitute our thought. If they did no more than carry a thought that is achieved apart from them, the problem of communication – with oneself and with others – would be merely a technical one. If they were a perfect incarnation of thought, a simple identity with it, then there would be no problem, no struggle of thought to find itself in its expression.

It is the naive adoption of one or the other of these suppositions that accounts for the success of communication in everyday life. Truth exists there in words issued ready from the mint to be taken up and used.[1] Better, they are rubbed by myriad hands to rough meanings which serve the barter of daily life and enable those who would speculate beyond this to hide the uncertainty of their exchange.

The exact sciences have achieved their precision of communication by the technical perfection with which they have developed this "commercial" construction of meaning. Firstly, they have explicitly adopted the standpoint of an observer who is involved only in the act of manipulation. Secondly, they have developed an exact rate of exchange, a frame of reference in relation to which all elements derive their meaning as a measured position.

The ideal of exactitude is imposed no less upon philosophy. But the philosopher is denied attainment of this ideal through any construction that is an abstraction from experience. He can accept no pre-established measure

[1] Phän., p. 33.

of meaning, for it is his task to return to that originality of experience from which the measure itself must derive its meaning. And this return is the struggle of thought to "enter into" its very inability to reflect perfectly upon itself, that is, the struggle to think and express the fundamental experience that true meaning is at once the identity and the difference of thought and its expression.

Hegel's attempt to penetrate this "at once", without the falsification of a construction in terms of one of the extremes, will form the theme of this whole study. A beginning may be made at a point where he explicitly poses the question of meaning. In his effort to define the aim and scope of a philosophy of religion in relation to philosophy and to religion, he maintains:

Wir müssen zuerst betrachten, was *Bedeuten* selbst bedeutet, und die Bedeutung der Idee aus der Bedeutung selber deuten. Wenn wir fragen: "was bedeutet dies oder jenes?", so wird nach zweierlei gefragt, und zwar nach Entgegengesetztem. Erstlich nennen wir das, was wir meinen, den Sinn, den Zweck, den allgemeinen Gedanken jenes Gegenstandes, den wir vor uns haben, jenes Ausdrucks, Kunstwerkes usf.; nach dem Innern fragen wir. [2]

That is, in order for us to be able to pose a question, something must be present to us as questionable. The further determination which we seek would be expressed in an answer as a predicate, to which this only partially known is a subject. If we ask, for example, what a plant is, then "plant" is, as questionable, present to us as a mere name or as a presupposed meaning, a "Vorstellung", which is in need of comprehension. [3] If we ask what "this" is, then "this" is at first present to us as a merely designated object, grasped only in the most general categories of "being". Or if, as Hegel continues the above passage, we ask what God is, we are asking for a "logical" comprehension that goes beyond the immediate sense of the totality with which we start: "Nach dem Begriffe, dem Wesen Gottes wird gefragt; die Vorstellung haben wir wohl."

Clearly one will need to determine what is to be meant by "logical", "concept", "essence". But even prescinding from this, the analysis remains partial. For the question of meaning is equally a movement in the opposite direction:

Anders ist es mit dem zweiten Sinn der Bedeutung. Wenn wir von reinen Gedankenbestimmungen anfangen und nicht von der Vorstellung, wenn als die Bedeutung des Gegenstandes sein Begriff als logischer angegeben ist, so kann es sein, dass

[2] RB, p. 30.
[3] WL, II, p. 266; cf. Enc. § 169.

sich der Geist in diesem reinen Gedanken nicht zu befriedigen vermag, nicht darin zuhause ist, sondern fragt, was das bedeute . . .Was uns fehlt, ist die Vorstellung; wir verlangen ein Beispiel des Inhaltes, der vorher nur im Gedanken gegeben wurde . . . Durch das Beispiel wird er uns deutlich, der Geist ist so erst in diesem Inhalte sich gegenwärtig.[4]

If one accept that interpretation of the Logic, criticized by Litt,[5] according to which its self-development should render unnecessary all reference to the world in which "examples" or "illustrations" are found, then one may assume that this second movement of the search for meaning is merely that of common thinking and should find no place in a thought that has been raised to a philosophical level. True thought, it would be said, should have no need of the element of Vorstellung to be at home with, or present to, itself.

That Hegel is not here describing a weakness of lesser minds, but is intending the movement of thought itself, is implied by the identification that follows immediately of this process with the life of the Absolute Idea:

Diese zweifache Bedeutung der Bedeutung deutet uns die Idee als der innere Begriff, der reine Gedanke, der aber ebenso zur Entäusserung seiner fortgeht, sich Beispiele seiner selbst gibt und darin das Wesentliche bleibt und für sich selber durch das Beispiel seiner wird . . . Gott stellt sich nur vor und stellt sich selber vor sich: dies ist die Seite des Daseins des Absoluten.

Further, this identification would seem to dispel the notion that Hegel is giving a purely psychological description of two thought processes that may occur independently, such that we may at one time be engaged in the first, at another time in the second. As the life of absolute spirit is inseparably an externalization of itself into existence and a return to itself from existence, so the process of human thought is an expression of itself in its Vorstellung, which is *eo ipso* a raising of Vorstellung to thought.[6] The formulation of a true question in a language that it finds is a raising of the language (and of the full experience with which it stands) to the originality of the thought. Each is renewed in the other.

Yet complementarity does not mean indifference, and Hegel concludes the passage quoted above with the following sentence:

Doch ist zugleich in dem Worte Beispiel schon die Äusserlichkeit als nur beiher Spielendes, der reine Gedanke aber als das Substanzielle anerkannt.

---

[4] RB, p. 31.

[5] Cf. p. 8 above.

[6] Cf. Hegel's review of Göschel's *Aphorismen über Nichtwissen und absolutes Wissen*, where he considers the author's treatment of "das Herüber- und Hinübergehen von der Vorstellung zum Begriffe und von dem Begriffe zur Vorstellung". (Berlin, pp. 318 ff.)

For Hegel, "das Substanzielle" means the essential element,[7] and "Beispiel" that which is opposed to it as unessential.[8] Hence one is warned to avoid conceiving the double movement of meaning as an exchange between independent moments. What Hegel proposes in this movement is that the essential nature of thought, its presence to itself in its meaning, exists only in an inner opposition of itself as "mere" essential to itself as unessential. True meaning is the identity of the identity and the difference of thought and its expression.

For Hegel's final attempt to think this movement we must wait until we are in a position to seek it in the Logic. First, it will be necessary to investigate further what he meant by Vorstellung. The rest of this chapter will introduce the general characteristics he ascribes to it.

2. THOUGHT AS VORSTELLUNG

The question what Hegel meant by a term is seldom to be answered in the form of a definition. For his approach to the problem of philosophical language was to determine meaning from position in the dialectic of thought and experience. A glance at the categories of the Logic will show the same names occurring several times; that is, the meaning of a category comes from its place in the Logic rather than from a definition designated by a certain name.

The difficulty is multiplied in regard to the term "Vorstellung" by the fact that it is a medium between sense and thought, and correspondingly between a mere subjectivity and a true objectivity. Added to that is the circumstance that it is a much handled word which Hegel uses loosely as well as technically. Hence the need for caution with quotations and for a derivation of its exact sense from its place in the dialectic of Subjective Spirit (Chapter II).

Hegel speaks indiscriminately of "die Vorstellung" and "das Vorstellen". In a paragraph of the Encyclopaedia where he compares it to thought, he points out that the latter may be seen as an agent, an activity, and the product of this activity.[9] So Vorstellung is used for a faculty, an activity, and its product (assuming the position of common sense which would distinguish the three). The translators of the *Wissenschaft der Logik* admit that difficulty arose at each occurrence of this word.[10] They have rendered it as sensuous representation, image, imagination, presentation, idea, general idea, ide-

---

[7] E.g., RA, p. 160: "Der Grund, das Substanzielle ist die Natur der Sache."
[8] E.g., Phän., p. 80: "Diesen Unterschied des Wesens und des Beispiels . . ."
[9] Enc. § 20.
[10] W. H. Johnston and L. G. Struthers, *Hegel's Science of Logic*, I, p. 27.

ation. This variety, the relation of the terms to the empiricist tradition, and particularly the failure to convey the literal sense of the German ("setting-before"), must excuse the refusal to translate it in this study.

a. "Das mittlere Element"

The philosophy of Leibniz impressed Hegel as forming, in certain respects, an attempted reconciliation of the empiricism of Locke and the rationalism of Spinoza.[11] Thus, the "perceptions" of the monad preserve the multiplicity and changeability of sense, yet achieve the unity, self-determination, and totality of thought.[12] Hegel took it upon himself, in this commentary, to translate "perceptio" by "Vorstellung". And his own doctrine of Vorstellung he customarily introduces by assigning it the position of a transition stage to thought from those lower levels which are variously described as intuition,[13] feeling,[14] or sense.[15] That is, on the one hand, external existence and all intermediate stages of cognition and appetition become present to thought through their sublation into the transitional stage of Vorstellung, such that Hegel can speak of Vorstellung as "die Bestimmtheiten des Gefühls, der Anschauung, des Begehrens, des Willens usf., insofern von ihnen gewusst wird."[16] On the other hand, it is through its return to Vorstellung that thought can be present to itself in the multiple forms of its there-being. Vorstellung is thus the medium in which "einerseits die äussere Realität selber als innerlich und geistig existiert, während das Geistige andererseits in der Vorstellung die Form des Äusserlichen annimmt und als ein Aussereinander und Nebeneinander zum Bewusstsein gelangt."[17]

Hence, so far as we are to ascribe properties to the stage of Vorstellung, we must say that it shares with sense a spatio-temporality and a mere multiplicity of its elements, but is distinguished from sense by an interiority and universality capable of giving expression to even the most elevated speculative thought.[18] It may be described as a picture-thinking, but as one in which the pictures are recognized for such, as carrying a meaning not simply to be identified with them.[19] For the Vorstellung is 'auf dem Wege der Abstraktion.'[20]

---

[11] Gesch. Phil., XIX, pp. 449, 454.
[12] pp. 458-9.
[13] E.g., RB, p. 116.
[14] E.g., p. 68.
[15] E.g., Enc. § 20.
[16] § 3.
[17] Ästhetik, p. 585.
[18] E.g., Enc. § 20, Ästhetik, pp. 932-3.
[19] RB, p. 110.
[20] p. 285; Ästhetik, p. 666.

The stage of Vorstellung is therefore the first at which one may speak of objectivity,[21] for it is here that the intuition is recognized as such.[22] In this respect, also, we can understand it only as a transition-point between the immediate unity of subject and object at lower levels[23] and that true separation of objective from subjective that demands the attainment of philosophical thought.[24] Vorstellung is thus described as neither a merely inner image (Bild) nor a merely outer existence (Dasein), but a synthesis of the two which is thereby set before the objective appreciation of the intellect (vorgestellt).[25] It is here that a realization first arises of a distinction between a spatiotemporality proper to the subject and to the object, and thought experiences its "guilt" in a dawning awareness of its need and inability to find itself in its expression. But a discussion of this growth of objectivity and of the possibility of true transition must await the following chapter.

For the present it is sufficient to stress that Vorstellung must be seen both as thought and as the "other" of thought. "In der Logik wird es sich zeigen, dass der Gedanke und das Allgemeine eben dies ist, dass er Er selbst und sein Anderes ist, über dieses übergreift und dass nichts ihm entflieht."[26] Vorstellung is the form proper to religion, and it is Hegel's constant argument that religion has "den innersten Sitz im Denken"[72] and presents the same truth as philosophy.[28] Yet Vorstellung is equally a level of experience below that of thought, such that the task of philosophy may be expressed as that of making the transition from Vorstellung to thought.[29] The paradox is one whereby we can first at the stage of Vorstellung say that a certain expression "has a meaning", and indeed an absolute meaning; yet that this, precisely in its absoluteness, is a mere development towards its meaning. The question of development within fulfilment will recur frequently during this study and is fundamental to any interpretation of the "achieved" system. Here we can but make a first beginning by considering further how Hegel describes those characteristics of Vorstellung which give occasion to the "Trieb der vernünftigen Einsicht."[30]

---

[21] RB, pp. 107, 286.
[22] Enc. § 449 Zusatz.
[23] E.g., RB, p. 96.
[24] E.g., BN, p. 517.
[25] Enc. § 454.
[26] Enc. § 20.
[27] RB, p. 193.
[28] E.g., Enc. Vorrede, p. 12; Gesch. Phil., XVII, p. 108; RB, p. 299; Berlin, pp. 72-81.
[29] E.g., Enc. §§ 1, 20.
[30] RB, p. 294.

b. Contingent and Abstract

That which accounts for the difficulty of philosophy, Hegel points out, is the need we feel to measure our meaning in relation to familiar Vorstellungen, which constitute for us a fixed ground on which we can stand and feel at home.[31] What philosophy demands is not a suicidal renunciation, but rather a flexibility whereby our "Weltvorstellung" is constantly renewed as a developing thought is verified in it. Yet this demand, so lightly spoken, carries with it the full pathos of thought, for it seems of the essence of Vorstellung that it should sustain us with the familiarity of sheer fact rather than with the necessary connexion proper to thought.[32] "So kommt in unserm sinnlichen Wahrnehmen die Welt als Autorität an uns; sie ist, wir finden sie so, wir nehmen sie als Seiendes auf und verhalten uns dazu als zu einem Seienden."[33]

We saw above that Hegel proposes the philosopher the task of recognizing pure thought in the forms of phenomenal existence, and the latter in the former;[34] that is, of understanding his logic in his factual existence and fact in his logic. But from the position of Vorstellung as a middle ground, it follows that this ideal brings forth a constant unrest, in which "das Sinnliche und Allgemeine durchdringen sich nicht innerlich."[35] The result is that the natural innocence of sense gives way to the responsibility of an awareness of relations and purposes, but these remain purely external.[36] Identity is recognized, but rather than being an organic identity in difference,[37] it is that which may be exemplified in the "association of ideas".[38] A totality is grasped, but one formed by a contingent collection of elements or predicates, connected by a mere "also".[39]

It is the false independence of externally related experiences or thoughts to which Hegel applies the term "abstract". Though there are variations in his use of the terms, he customarily means by concrete and abstract, not empirical and universal, but that which finds close illustration in "living" and "lifeless". The concrete is, as the etymology implies, that which grows to an inner unity of its many elements. To think or experience abstractly is, in the image he supplies in the Phenomenology, to grasp a culture by erecting

---

[31] Enc. § 3.
[32] E.g., RA, p. 16; RB, p. 61.
[33] RA, p. 204.
[34] Phän., p. 562; cf. pp. 18-9 above.
[35] RB, p. 116.
[36] Phän., p. 532.
[37] RB, p. 294.
[38] Enc. § 398.
[39] RB, p. 113; Enc. § 20.

the scaffolding of its outward existence, neglecting the reality that environs and inspires it: it is to observe some beautiful fruit without the tree that bore it, the earth and elements which formed its substance, or the climate and seasons which controlled its growth.[40]

Hence the familiar "Weltvorstellung", to which we turn for our meaning, is for Hegel, as a "Sammlung von unendlich vielen Zufälligkeiten", an abstraction at which he cannot rest who would grasp the original human experience; and this is the task which philosophy sets itself in the "Beschreibung und Analyse des Ganges des Geistes".[41] For experience is falsified so far as it draws its understanding from a fixed object; that which we must truly call experience is the dialectical process out of which a new object – and hence a new Vorstellung – arises.[42] The abstract elements cannot be left in their familiar independence, but must be experienced in their organic unity. And it is this which constitutes the transition to thought.[43] For "die logische Vernunft selbst ist das Substanzielle oder Reelle, das alle abstrakten Bestimmungen in sich zusammenhält und ihre gediegene, absolut konkrete Einheit ist."[44]

c. Space and Time

For Hegel, the attribution of spatiality and temporality to Vorstellung[45] is not merely based on the comparison one would commonly make between image and thought. It is rather to be seen as the condition which renders thought or experience abstract, in the above sense. For it is in so far as our thinking is spatial and temporal that we are able to hold its elements apart in an abstract independence.[46] This act of withdrawal from the process which is experience is a setting-before us (Vorstellung) of experience as a past or future event; or if it be seen as present, it is such merely in opposition to these constructions of past or future. "Das Jetzt des Genusses zerrinnt in der Vorstellung. . . teils in Vergangenheit, teils in Zukunft. Der Geist aber ist sich schlechthin gegenwärtig."[47]

This identification of Vorstellung with a spatialized time, with the dissipation of thought into a "nebeneinander" and "nacheinander", must occupy our attention in the following chapter. Here we can merely stress the ab-

---

[40] Phän., pp. 523-4.
[41] Enc. § 50.
[42] Phän., p. 73.
[43] WL, I, p. 142; RB, p. 153.
[44] WL, I, p. 29.
[45] E.g. Berlin p. 14: "In Allem dieser Weise der Vorstellung ist eine Fremdartigkeit, Äusserlichkeit, in Zeit und Raum."
[46] RB, p. 297.
[47] RA, p. 215.

stract nature of a meaning that retreats from the experience of thought to the "misology" of a ready-made world.[48] For thought can, according to Hegel, come to itself only in that process which it reveals in its self-contradictions.[49] But this self-realization is frustrated in all attempts to impose a final, static state of non-contradiction by interpreting conflicting elements as "different respects"; for the contradiction is thus merely displaced, moved from reality to the privileged position of an external reflection.[50] And this attitude of formal thinking "lässt den widersprechenden Inhalt, den es vor sich hat, in die Sphäre der Vorstellung, in Raum und Zeit herabfallen, worin das Widersprechende im Neben- und Nacheinander aussereinander gehalten wird."[51] The responsibility of thought is shirked in the diplomatic constructions of language.[52] "In der Vorstellung hat alles ruhig nebeneinander Platz."[53]

By such constructions the problem of meaning is readily "solved". For they establish a fixed world whose fabric allows each particle to be defined by its "distance" from another.[54] "Now" has its meaning as a point between a measurable "before" and "after". Red has its meaning in its contrast to yellow and blue.[55] Yet this drawing of meaning in terms of another is the essential mark of the finite, whereas thought is fundamentally an understanding of itself from itself.[56] Thought as Vorstellung is thus a retreat from its true meaning, and its being in time and space is that which constitutes its finitude.[57]

Again, it is to be stressed that the ideal proposed is no mere renunciation of Vorstellung and of the whole realm of experience that is present in it.[58] Philosophical thought must no less find its origin and illustration in the vast riches of spatio-temporal existence than interpret them.[59] But this double process is vitiated so far as either side becomes a static model for the other.

[48] Enc. § 11.
[49] E.g., WL, I, p. 38. Hegel's doctrine of contradiction will be discussed in Chapter III.
[50] WL, II, p. 40.
[51] p. 496.
[52] These notions will be developed at greater length in the second half of Chapter III, where Hegel's treatment of the different types of "reflection" will be examined.
[53] RB, p. 117.
[54] The emphasis must here be placed on the word "fixed". For, as pointed out above (p. 26), it is Hegel's approach to the problem of philosophical language to determine the meaning of any category of thought from its position in the dialectic of thought; yet this dialectic is an organic movement, a "concrete" whole, where each member is as much a presence of the whole as a relation to other members.
[55] Enc. § 42 Zusatz.
[56] § 28 Zusatz.
[57] § 51.
[58] E.g., RB, p. 104; RA, p. 224.
[59] Cf. pp. 18-9 above.

The words in which Hegel expresses his thought – "an-sich", "ausser-sich", "Reflexion". . . – all are drawn originally from a certain construction of experience, and no development of thought can totally free itself from inadequate verifications. But they become "mere" Vorstellungen so far as they retain a fixed verification at a certain level of experience and are "employed" as a model of explanation for other levels rather than rising to repeated "newness" with the dialectical process.[60] In this Hegel supplies the criterion with which his own thought must be measured in its abstractness or concreteness.

d. Meaning as "Meinung"

In the following chapter we shall trace the course by which thought is gradually weaned from the subjectivity of "its" world and exposed to the objective reality of "the" world. Yet it must not be supposed that this is a passage from a personal to an impersonal realm.[61] Personality is for Hegel a recognition and communication of that which is concretely universal.[62] This is true "individuality" and is opposed alike to an abstract universality and to that particularity whose meaning is purely "Meinung" ("mine") in that it deserts the common ground of thought.[63]

This is not to deny that common activity may be based on "Meinung". All may respond in the same way to a red traffic-light, but no one can communicate to another his experience of red. A complete science may be based on meanings that are to be reduced finally to simple designations, but it remains "das Bodenlose, das nie dazu kommen kann zu sagen, was es meint, weil es nur meint und sein Inhalt nur Gemeintes ist."[64]

It will be clear that the meaning proper to Vorstellung tends toward "Meinung" so far as it is a mere designation of elements in a pre-established world and an explanation of one simply in terms of another. Vorstellung is a "gemeinsames Meinen". It is the way in which truth may be offered to all men.[65] Hence the transition from Vorstellung to thought is from subjective to objective and from a mass to a personal existence.

In his earliest writings, Hegel expressed no great optimism in this regard: "Die Philosophie ist ihrer Natur nach etwas Esoterisches, für sich weder für

[60] Phän., p. 73; cf. p. 30 above.
[61] Cf. Hyppolite, *Logique et Existence*, p. 17: "Le Moi qui se vise unique est bien plus près d'un On."
[62] E.g., WL, II, p. 503; Enc. § 63.
[63] E.g., RB, p. 40.
[64] Phän., p. 235.
[65] E.g., Enc. Vorrede, p. 12; RB, p. 69.

den Pöbel gemacht, noch einer Zubereitung für den Pöbel fähig."[66] The Phenomenology represents a modification of this view, but his final lectures still stress that speculative thought is "das Esoterische".[67] For it has but one presupposition: "bei keinem subjektiven Standpunkt aufzuhalten."[68] Yet this is the most exacting of commandments, and it is these halts which form the stages in the history of philosophy.[69]

That which constitutes a "subjective standpoint" is an attempt to grasp the whole of experience in terms of a fixed principle which is an abstraction from that whole. It is an explanation from one situation at the expense of the others, the imposition of our categories rather than an understanding of the self-division of the whole.[70] The philosopher is therefore called upon to overcome "die Eitelkeit und Besonderheit des Meinens" and take upon himself "einen wahrhaften Ernst um die Sache".[71] For the supposed pride of philosophy is rather an ascetical rejection of the vanity of particular meanings – of the "private worship of one's own divinity"[72] – and a seeking of that humility whereby one's thought is "in die Sache vertieft"[73] and submits itself to the "Durchlaufen der Bewegung der Sache".[74]

This ideal was Hegel's from his earliest meditations. The way in which he finally sought its attainment, in philosophical thought and in a system and method designed to lead to it,[75] was not always his. A brief summary of the efforts that led to his system will be given as an introduction to the second part of this study (Chapter IV). Here it may simply be noted that from his first essays he rejected the abstract thought of Rationalism in favour of a return to the original unity of human experience from which all its contradictions spring. Though he followed the Romanticism of his day by seeking a principle of reconciliation in organic and aesthetic categories, it is in terms of religious doctrines that this search is most commonly and most profoundly expressed in his surviving writings.[76] In the Trinity, the Eucharist, and

---

[66] PK, p. 185.
[67] Gesch. Phil., XVIII, p. 238.
[68] RB, p. 182.
[69] Enc. § 14.
[70] E.g., RA, pp. 13-14, 29-30.
[71] Recht, p. 6.
[72] p. 139; cf. GW, pp. 384-5.
[73] Enc. § 23.
[74] Beweise, p. 122; cf. Hegel's comments on the "Anstrengung des Begriffs", Phän., p. 48.
[75] Enc. Vorrede, pp. 3-4.
[76] This is not to deny the value of Lukacs' work in emphasizing Hegel's early interests outside the strictly religious sphere, and in pointing out the bias of German commentators of the Jugendschriften; cf. also Hyppolite, Etudes sur Marx et Hegel, p. 83.

particularly in the Gospel of love, Hegel thought to have found those formulations in which the fundamental unity could best be grasped.

This was for him at first a realm beyond reflective thought. It was only in
inspired terms that man could speak of the divine.[77] But Hegel's period at
Jena, the six years that preceded the Phenomenology, constituted a rejection
of this position as a refuge in intuition from the obligations of philosophy;
and to his final lectures in Berlin he would counter all attempts to achieve the
task of thought by the invocation of any principle that merely affirmed its
attainment. For it is, he constantly maintained, only in thought that one can
hope to avoid the partiality of a subjective standpoint and submit to the
"Bewegung der Sache". Thought is "Bei-sich-sein".[78] To seek the originality
of any human experience is to seek a final "bei-sich" in which thought can
neither be excluded nor subordinated. But the only experience which can be
submitted to the presence of thought without thereby stepping outside itself
to an understanding from an alien standpoint is thought itself. Thought
alone enters into itself by thinking itself. And Hegel's Logic represents for
him the concrete process by which this entry is to be attempted.

In the terms in which he was finally to express himself, the philosopher's
aim must be a thought of experience which is finally grounded in itself and
draws its meaning from itself, "die Wahrheit *als* Wahrheit, in der *Form* der
Wahrheit – in der Form des absolut Konkreten."[79] For him experience must
ultimately be the thinking of experience. Form and content are one.

It is in relation to this doctrine of the true identity of form and content
that Hegel's conception of Vorstellung as a form of experience immediately
below that of thought must be understood.[80] For even where Vorstellung
rises to the true content of philosophy, as in religion, the form remains inadequate to it. There, speculative truth is still in the element of "Meinung",
and hence short of the final "bei-sich" where thought is the form as well as
the content.[81]

---

[77] E.g., Nohl, p. 305.

[78] Enc. § 23.

[79] RB, pp. 292-3.

[80] A further examination of Vorstellung in relation to the form and content of experience will occupy us in the first half of Chapter V.

[81] An appreciation or criticism of the conception of philosophy that is involved would
go beyond the aims of this study. Yet it is of interest to notice, in passing, that there are a
few texts of Hegel which seem to question this complete supremacy of thought; for
example, in the introduction to the Logic, Hegel concedes that the philosopher must
choose to enter into the nature of thought as such, which initial decision may be looked
upon as "eine Willkür" (WL, I, p. 54). Similarly, in the Encyclopaedia, he sets the beginning of philosophy "in dem Entschluss, rein denken zu wollen" (§ 78). Such concessions,
however, are rare and scarcely influence the traditional interpretation of Hegel in this
matter.

It must be remembered, as pointed out above,[82] that Hegel supplies, with this doctrine, the criterion with which his own thought must be measured. If the ultimate nature of experience is thought, it is not the "mere thought" of common sense, but a concrete thought in which the breadth and depth of experience must be verified. So far as Hegel fails, or achieves his goal too cheaply by the diplomacy of construction, then he must submit to the judgment that his philosophical thought remains at the level of Vorstellung, that it is a form foreign to its content.

Yet, before judging, one must beware of an over-simple understanding of the criterion. To regard thought and Vorstellung as stages, one simply above the other, is itself to bow to the spatialization of Vorstellung, to observe the two terms as a permanent "nebeneinander" rather than to enter into the nature of their process. Thought can, for Hegel, attain its final concreteness, its "Bei-sich-sein", only through a self-alienation in which it is "mere thought" as opposed to the particularity of its expression as Vorstellung. The process involved has up to now been seen in the inadequacy of Vorstellung opposed to thought. We must now turn briefly to the complementary movement, viewing the inadequacy of thought in its opposition to Vorstellung.

3. THOUGHT AND VORSTELLUNG

In our study of the Logic, we shall see how the struggle of thought to pass from "Being" to "Essence" leaves the latter constantly affected with the former.[83] It is a primary lesson of Hegel's dialectic that progress by opposition is always to a complementary abstraction that remains fundamentally at the same level of inadequacy. To deny "categorically" an opponent's views is to affirm that one stands on the same metaphysical ground. Where the distance is too great, the luxury of denial is no longer possible. The history of philosophy supplies a commentary to this dialectic, though Hegel's historical position may have made his own lectures on this subject an abstract exposition.

a. Transition to Formal Thought

The lesson is experienced by every thinker who would pass "from" the images that both incorporate and bemire his thought. The attempt to pass from the illustrations of thought to "thought itself" finds itself to be a

---

[82] pp. 31-2.

[83] Chapter III. In the first book of his Logic, Hegel treats of "Being" as the immediacy of thought. The second book examines the sophistication of thought that comes with the reflection of immediacy into the dual categories of "essential" and "unessential".

passage from one form of illustration to another. Just as Vorstellung itself was constituted as a "Kampf gegen das Sinnliche", so is the first appearance of thought a merely abstract universality determined by its negative relation to the levels of experience still immersed in sense.[84] The struggle against the contingency of independent experiences in their spatio-temporal separation achieves only the equal but opposite errors of abstraction. "Ein Reich einheitloser Empirie und reinzufälliger Mannigfältigkeit steht einem leeren Denken gegenüber."[85] Complementary to the "diskrete absolute harte Sprödigkeit" of the former is the "einfache unbiegsame kalte Allgemeinheit" of thought,[86] and the abstract "nebeneinander" of spatial position is matched by the abstract formality of a thought whose elements stand "gegeneinander gleichgültig".[87] The arbitrariness of meaning by designation is turned into a no less capricious thought based on abstract identity and, beside it, abstract difference.[88] It is a thinking which offers unlimited possibilities of alternative formulations, for it has "keinen Halt, keine Substanz".[89]

Thought takes a self-complacency in its first grasp of its "Bei-sich-sein", such that it feels a "Gleichgültigkeit gegen die Besonderung, damit aber gegen seine Entwicklung."[90] Whereas meaning in Vorstellung tended to be a mere verification at a pre-determined level of experience, here there is a search for a pure interiority of meaning which shuns all attempt at verification. Hegel illustrates this with an understanding of history in terms of the eternal will of God, a principle of explanation which is set comfortably in a realm where it is "unbegreiflich und unerforschlich".[91]

The result is that one is equally far from the meaning of "die Sache selbst". The particularity of a designation "below" it has been replaced by a formal signification "above" it. This is what common sense condemns as a mere thinking *about* reality: "Bei der Reflexion hingegen habe ich nur subjektive Gedanken über die Sache, nicht die Sache selbst."[92] As we shall see in the chapter on the Logic, "Reflexion" is for Hegel the basic movement of thought in its concreteness, but this comes only as the result of a dialectic that must pass through a merely external reflection. And it is this form of re-

---

[84] RB, p. 115.
[85] GW, p. 404.
[86] Phän., p. 418; cf. pp. 185-6.
[87] WL, II, p. 317; cf. Phän., p. 91; Enc. § 114: ". . . nur neben-oder nacheinander durch ein *Auch* verbindet."
[88] WL, II, pp. 26-7.
[89] Phän., p. 462.
[90] Enc. § 12.
[91] RB, p. 114. So, in his article on Hamann, Hegel accuses him of the 'Pantheismus der unechten Religiosität, dass alles Gottes Wille sei": Berlin, p. 257.
[92] RB, p. 143.

flection with which we are here concerned, a sense of the term which Hegel sets in apposition to "Meinung".[93] For it is such thought that supplies each with the ability to make his own construction of reality, his private system, from the infinite repertory of possible combinations.[94]

b. "Verstand" and "Vernunft"

It will be clear that what has here been described as formal thought is what Hegel terms "Verstand"[95] in opposition to "Vernunft"; and it is in this sense that he can say that "die Vorstellung trifft hier mit dem Verstande zusammen."[96] Yet one must beware, again, of picturing Verstand and Vernunft as levels of thought, such that one can pass simply from one to the other. The characteristics of the former remain present in any thinking of the categories proper to the latter. As Kroner points out, the thought of Vernunft, if it is not to be an empty infinity, must no less regard "das Abstrakt- oder Diskret-sein der Kategorien, ihre Getrenntheit voneinander" than their concrete self-development.[97] In more practical terms, the Logic remains a task to be achieved, a book to be thought.[98]

Similarly, the multiple standpoint proper to any task of thinking can not be wished away from the thought of the Logic. Even retaining the distinctions that Hegel sets between Phenomenology and Logic, one can scarcely deny that the Logic itself exhibits the dual movement of "für sich" and "für uns" that is celebrated in the Phenomenology. "Daher gibt es also auch in der Logik zwei Bewegungen: die Selbstbewegung der Momente und die Bewegung des denkenden Selbst."[99] The Notion that first logically appears fully to itself in the result is present at each prior step as a "für uns", "hinter dem Rücken". "Dies ist der phänomenologische Anteil des dialektischen Fortschreitens: hinter dem Rücken des Seins ist der denkende Geist tätig."[100]

It will be our task throughout this study to gain a closer understanding of what is involved in this phenomenological aspect of logical thought. It is fundamental to Hegel's philosophical insight that the "Bewegung der Sache" is no simple linear movement from a beginning to an end. The

---

[93] WL, I, p. 54; cf. p. 21: "die Ungeduld der einfallenden Reflexion".

[94] Cf. p. 4, footnote 8 above.

[95] E.g., WL, I, p. 26: "Der abstrahierende und damit trennende Verstand, der in seinen Trennungen beharrt."

[96] Enc. § 20; cf. RB, p. 293.

[97] Von Kant bis Hegel, II, pp. 420-1; cf. Hyppolite, Genèse, p. 565.

[98] Cf. Kojève, Introduction à la Lecture de Hegel, p. 424.

[99] Kroner, II, p. 423; cf. Hyppolite, Genèse, pp. 565-70.

[100] Kroner, II, p. 425. So Hyppolite speaks of "ce caractère phénoménologique de la Logique hégélienne": Genèse, p. 568.

result reveals itself as the true beginning and as presupposed from the start.[101] Thought is equally a positing and a presupposing of itself.[102] Consequently, the necessarily linear exposition of thought and system will involve the appearance of a "petitio principii"; the Phenomenology will seem simply to presuppose the Logic, and the Logic the Phenomenology.[103] Yet what is sought is a truth to that concrete experience of the mutual presupposition of thought and its expression, a process which yields to no simple formulation, and to which we hope here to find an approach in the double movement of "Vorstellung" and "Denken".

c. The Return to Vorstellung

We have seen the inadequacy of Vorstellung and the need to seek the pure interiority and "self-accountability" of thought. Yet this has shown itself at first to be a "mere" interiority, a flight from verification to the false security of an arbitrary system of concepts. Hence it is realized that the desire for the familiarity of Vorstellung was not entirely vain, for it is this instinct which induces the onward movement of the dialectic.[104] This is a search for that which is fully concrete experience, that with which we are truly in contact.[105] If philosophical thought be seen as abandoning its stake in the familiar world, it is only in order to return to a profounder experience of it.[106] The transition from Vorstellung to thought is itself but an abstraction of the concrete movement which includes no less a return from thought to Vorstellung.

In this light we may look again at the passage quoted at the start of this chapter, Hegel's discussion of the double movement in the question of meaning. Hegel continues his analysis there by stressing that the thought of the Idea consists in its pure self-development, but that it is *because* of this self-development that the Idea must produce itself, give itself determinate existence in Nature.[107] That is, the transition of thought to its forms of

---

[101] Cf. WL, I, p. 56.
[102] Cf. pp. 97-9, and 113 below.
[103] Cf. Hyppolite, *Genèse*, p. 567; and p. 167 below.
[104] Enc. § 87.
[105] § 7.
[106] Cf. Fichte, *Sonnenklarer Bericht*, Einleitung § 4: "Ich erkläre sonach hiermit öffentlich, dass es der innerste Geist, und die Seele meiner Philosophie sei: der Mensch hat überhaupt nichts, denn die Erfahrung, und er kommt zu allem, wozu er kommt, nur durch die Erfahrung, durch das Leben selbst. Alles sein Denken, sei es ungebunden, oder wissenschaftlich, gemein, oder transzendental, geht von der Erfahrung auf, und beabsichtigt hinwiederum Erfahrung."
[107] RB, p. 32.

phenomenal existence is the condition of its own true development, in a purity that draws only from within. It is therefore a false image which presents the Logic as achieving itself and *then* passing over into Nature. Rather is every stage of logical thought a certain manner of exteriorization into, and return from, Vorstellung and Nature. The transitions "within" the pure thought of the Logic and the transition "from" the Logic cannot be held in abstraction from each other.

How this is further to be thought, and how it may be interpreted as conveying the experience with which we are truly "in contact", must form the topic of the following chapters. Before approaching the explicit formulation of the system in the second part, we shall need to examine further, in Chapter II, this self-alienation which is the price thought must pay for a deeper presence to itself. We shall see how Hegel tries to re-think rational psychology as a process of "Erinnerung" through a repeated recognition, overcoming, and reinstatement of that duality of meaning which has been introduced in this chapter: thought understands itself only in a dialectic that moves between the equally abstract extremes of particular designation and of formal thinking "about" experience.

Yet if this movement is to be grasped as more than a somewhat imaginative rejection of opposite vices for a virtue that sinks to mediocrity, it must be traced to its source in Hegel's Logic. It is there that the critic must finally witness the struggle of Hegel's own thought to find itself in the language he both formed and presupposed. Chapter III, therefore, will study parts of the Logic of Essence, on the ground, to be justified only in what follows, that it is there that Hegel came closest to thinking the thought that is present to itself only in the opposition of a "merely essential" to its "Beispiel".[108]

It would be a gross understatement to describe the way which Hegel proposes, and which we must follow, as obscure and tortuous. Yet it is only through a detailed attention to this way that its goal may appear as a true "Aufhebung", and not as an abstract identity which merely glosses over the repeated predicaments of thought in its groping for self-communication.

---

[108] Cf. Mure, *Study*, p. 96 (footnote): "The reader will see that the dialectic of show, indeed the dialectic of Essence generally, is well illustrated in the paradox of language which we discussed in Chapter I. Thinking posits language as its reflection and expression, but language is logically prior to thinking, and is therefore posited as presupposed."

CHAPTER II

THE PLACE OF VORSTELLUNG
IN THE PHILOSOPHY OF SPIRIT

I. MEANING AND PLACE

The previous chapter has given some general indications of Hegel's use of the term "Vorstellung". It is, on the one hand, a functional "picture-thinking" which, immersed in the particularity of space and time, is inadequate to the self-possession of thought. Yet it is not simply "below" thought as a level which can be passed and forgotten. The first efforts to rise beyond it produce a merely formal thinking which, in its abstract universality, must pass through a reincarnation in the particularity of Vorstellung before claim can be made to a higher level in the true experience of thought. That is, the Hegelian dialectic of particularity, universality, and individuality is here represented as a complementary movement of passage from Vorstellung and return to Vorstellung, in the search for philosophical meaning. Vorstellung is the "other" of thought, and yet is "interior" to it.

In this chapter the same movement, and a further understanding of it, will be sought in a more detailed study of a section of Hegel's Philosophy of Spirit. This, the third part of the Encyclopaedia, is divided into Subjective, Objective, and Absolute Spirit (cf. appendix of categories). The first traces the "return" of spirit to itself from nature, so far as this return manifests itself in the progressive self-consciousness of the individual subject. It is Hegel's re-thinking of rational psychology, his "genetic description" of thought as the culmination of a dialectic of feeling, perception, appetite and other forms of consciousness that occupy the traditional psychology. Objective Spirit considers thought so far as it is embodied in human institutions; that is, so far as it both expresses and finds itself in law, morality, the state. Absolute Spirit is constituted by those forms of the human spirit which, for Hegel, pass beyond the limits of subjectivity and objectivity that affect the previous two realms: namely, art, religion, and philosophy itself. A discussion of what is here meant, and of how one can reach an "absolute" experience which yet has further development, will be attempted in Chapter V.

This chapter is thus concerned with the first realm, Subjective Spirit, and with those sections of it which treat of Vorstellung, its origin from "lower" stages of consciousness and its passage into thought. In particular, Hegel assigns Intuition (Anschauung) as the stage prior to Vorstellung, and divides the latter into Recollection (Erinnerung), Imagination (Einbildungskraft), and Memory (Gedächtnis); it is in Imagination that the explicit origin of verbal language is placed.

Thus, whereas the previous chapter sought the meaning of Vorstellung by examining certain of its characteristics, this chapter will try to follow Hegel in his derivation of meaning for Vorstellung, language, and thought from the *place* that they occupy in his dialectic. As suggested above,[1] the reader in search of the meaning of a philosophical term would be referred by Hegel, not to definitions nor to isolated descriptions, but to the place where the term appears in the dialectic of the Logic or Realphilosophie.

Fichte would have called this a "deduction".[2] Hegel has no fixed name for this development of partial levels toward a concrete totality: he uses indiscriminately the words "Deduktion", "Konstruktion", "Bewegung", "Totalizierung", "Integration". The critic of the Philosophy of Spirit may be inclined to term it a construction passing for a deduction: that is, to say that Hegel has simply arranged psychological states in an approximate order of approach to self-consciousness and has then related them by an artificial dialectic.

That there is a considerable degree of arbitrariness even in the works for which Hegel claims the greatest rigour of thought, is accepted by every commentator. Nor does Hegel himself, for all the confidence of his customary expression, deny the provisional character of his achievement – at least in its details. He writes, for example, upon the completion of the first part of his Logic:

Es ist keine Kleinigkeit, im ersten Semester seiner Verheiratung ein Buch des abstrusesten Inhalts von 30 Bogen zu schreiben. – Aber injuria temporum! Ich bin kein Akademikus; zur gehörigen Form hätte ich noch ein Jahr gebraucht, aber ich brauche Geld, um zu leben.[3]

In distinction to Fichte and Schelling, who started an often radically altered exposition of their thought with each major publication, Hegel always wrote

---

[1] p. 26.
[2] E.g., the *Wissenschaftslehre* speaks of the deduction of Vorstellung, of sensation, of intuition, of space and time.
[3] Briefe, I, p. 393.

and lectured with the form of his whole system in mind. This does not imply, however, that his own final understanding of what the form itself meant was always unambiguous. Nor does it imply that the details were always more influenced by the whole than by Hegel's casual reading. A close attention to all stages of his dialectic as if they were the only possible realization of his theme – especially if it be coupled, as in some commentators, to a desire to suggest corrections – is to miss the point of Hegel's vast effort.

Though one may well emphasize the arbitrary aspects of the structure, it would be superficial to say that Hegel does no more than to present what he obtained *a posteriori* as though it were a formal *a priori* deduction. Hegel's method can, indeed, best be seen as an attempt to avoid these two extremes as equal "abstractions" of the true origin of meaning. Neither mere designation of given experiences nor deduction by purely analytic thought processes will, as such, lead to philosophy; for this must do justice to both sides of the dilemma of human meaning.

In introducing his Logic as the exposition of the true method of philosophy, Hegel maintained that philosophy had hitherto derived its method either from the systematic structure of mathematics or from the empirical sciences, which offered merely an indiscriminate mixture of given material and of ideas.[4] The method he proposed was a denial of neither the given material nor the ideas, but consisted in replacing the thoughtless mixture with a process proper to thought itself, such that the given would be raised to the idea, and the mere idea be particularized in the given.

To what extent his method, in fact, relapsed into the two extremes of mere arrangement and formal deduction is a question that may be posed at any stage of his dialectic. Yet before turning to a particular part of the Philosophy of Spirit, it is well to emphasize at least the ideal of philosophical meaning which Hegel set himself. Meaning is, for him, to be drawn neither from particular experiences nor from any mere system of concepts. It is finally that experience itself of the process by which these two abstract extremes negate each other and are raised to a synthesis, or "con-crete", that is new in the sense of original: "ein neuer Begriff, aber der höhere, reichere Begriff als der vorhergehende".[5] It is that from which the extremes originate and find their true meaning.

This doctrine, baldly stated and removed from the technical Hegelian sense of the terms, is one in which all theories of meaning may in the end concur. On the one hand, an empiricist theory, that meaning lies in the designation of experiences and that the signification of words is in their use,

[4] WL, I, p. 35.
[5] p. 36.

must admit some totality, some frame of reference or field of possibility, which cannot be reduced to the particular experiences which are set in it. Nor can such a theory finally deny some dialectical relationship between the particulars and the abstract totality, such that the fullest meaning would imply an approach toward a concrete unity of the two.

On the other hand, a theory that would attempt to put meaning ultimately in innate ideas either must allow that these have some verification in at least possible particular experiences (thereby deriving meaning also from this source), or it must reduce the "ideas" to particulars and find itself attempting an empiricist theory of designation.[6]

The authors quoted in the introduction questioned the ability of human language to carry a philosophical thought which presents itself, not as a discourse by the philosopher on being, but as "le discours même de l'être à travers le philosophe".[7] This was offered as a criticism of Hegel and must remain an insuperable obstacle to the final achievement of his philosophy. Yet the aim of the present study is to examine Hegel's thought of the identity-in-difference proper to philosophy at one stage of the way that leads to its final realization, namely the stage where language passes into thought. And here it is, as will be seen, this very unity of word and meaning in a persisting opposition that is the origin of the movement of the dialectic.

How the "Aufhebung" of this standpoint in the totality may "preserve" it as well as "annihilate" it[8] is a problem for the second part of this study. For the present, it is sufficient to emphasize that Hegel's dialectic starts, both in the Phenomenology and in the Logic, with the most abstract, and hence most "limited", experience. His method is the attempt, without ever setting himself simply outside the limits of human experience, to allow the limits themselves to bring to light their own transcendence, to express and explain themselves.

The limits to be considered in this chapter are among the profoundest of human experience. Man knows and expresses his meaning. Indeed, his humanity lies in the assurance that he knows what he says. Yet the detailed verification of this assurance reveals an apparently irreconcilable duality in his meaning. At one level, the words he uses "point" to particular elements in his experience; their meaning is immersed in the sheer "this" of designation. At another level, they form a grammatical and logical whole, where meaning comes without immediate reference to experiences; one may often say, for example, that the answer to a question depends simply on agreed definitions

---

[6] As Hegel often points out, to be purely "in-sich" is to be purely "ausser-sich "(e.g., Enc. § 258).

[7] pp. 3-4 above.

[8] Cf. WL, I, pp. 93-5.

of the terms.[9] A true grasp of one's meaning would demand that these two levels coalesce; yet the sheer particularity of designation remains always to some extent merely complemented by a dogmatic "talking about" experience.

Language separates one from his thought in the very act by which it makes thought possible. For Hegel, however, this duality – and the scepticism it engenders – was no final impasse for philosophy, but a positive beginning. It may be seen as the origin of that movement by which the philosophical meaning which is truly, though "eccentrically", present must start on the way that passes through "the seriousness, the suffering, the patience, and the labour of the negative".[10] Without sharing Hegel's sanguine hopes for a successful outcome, the reader can at least afford to follow some distance along the path by which meaning seeks the "Sache selbst", where abstract thought finds its fulfilment in particularity,[11] and the particular finds its freedom in the idea.[12]

2. THE DIALECTIC IN NATURE AND SPIRIT

Before an examination is made of Hegel's doctrine of language and thought as revealed by his treatment of Vorstellung in the Philosophy of Subjective Spirit, certain notions fundamental to the movement of the dialectic at this point will briefly be considered.

It is in the dialectic of Subjective Spirit that Hegel set the pedagogical beginning of his system. For the second, or antithetical, phase of Subjective Spirit bears the name "Phenomenology of Spirit" and traces, in much abbreviated form, the initial sections of Hegel's earlier work of that name. As will be seen later,[13] this book was written by Hegel as an introduction to his system, indeed was originally intended as its first part. The work set for itself "die Aufgabe, das Individuum von seinem ungebildeten Standpunkte aus zum Wissen zu führen".[14] And the unformed standpoint at which the beginner is to start is that of sense certainty, "das Diese und das Meinen".

There is some justification, therefore, for the suggestion that an understanding of the Encyclopaedia may still begin at this point, where the reader is naturally "at home" and needs no initial effort to set himself at a level of experience above or below that of "common sense". The way forward

---

[9] "Allerdings kann man sich auch, ohne die Sache zu erfassen, mit Worten herumschlagen": Enc. § 462 Zusatz.
[10] Phän., p. 20.
[11] RB, p. 31.
[12] Enc. § 384.
[13] p. 143 below.
[14] Phän., p. 26.

through the rest of Subjective Spirit would thus follow the gradual recognition that is forced upon an individual that the human spirit is essentially a subject in relation to its object, and that the subject becomes progressively richer, more concrete, as it expresses and finds itself in its object. Using the Aristotelian terms suggested by Mure,[15] the attitude of subject to object at any phase is the proximate matter to which the subject at the next phase is the form. Or in terms of the foregoing pages, the subject is always, on the one hand, immersed in particular experience (so far as constituting the proximate matter) and, on the other hand, making a formal construct of that experience (so far as being a fresh attitude of subject to that matter as object). But the philosophical (rather than merely empirical) thought of the subject is the very recognition of this unity and duality which leads to a fresh attitude of subject to itself as a more concrete object. Philosophical meaning is still drawn from two sources, but both the particularity of the "Meinen" and the formality of the universal have come closer to that ground from which both finally draw their meaning.

If one thus begins at the level of naive consciousness, it may be asked how the stages prior to this are to be understood, that is, nature and the phases of conscious life still below the distinction of subject and object. This question raises the whole problem of the interpretation of Hegel's Philosophy of Nature: whether it is truly a study of nature or of our knowledge of nature.[16] Into this problem there is no need here to enter. Yet the fact that the particularity of Vorstellung is expressed in terms of its immersion in space and time makes a brief glance in the direction of nature advisable before confronting the dialectic of Vorstellung itself.

a. Soul and Nature

The stages of spirit prior to consciousness are called by Hegel the realm of "Soul" or "Anthropology". It is a realm which, as it recedes from thought, becomes increasingly impervious to thought. Here especially the problem of different levels or standpoints becomes acute. For it follows from the view of the method presented above that the philosopher can never simply describe what stands as an object before him. He must be at the level of that which he describes as well as transcend it to look "down" on it. But whereas it is relatively easy to be "at" and comprehend the levels of consciousness, it is

[15] Cf. p. 10 above.
[16] E.g., cf. Hoffmeister, *Goethe und der deutsche Idealismus* (1932), p. 65: "Hegels Naturphilosophie ist keine Metaphysik der Natur, wohl aber eine Metaphysik der Naturwissenschaft und der Naturphilosophie, d.h. eine Metaphysik des gesamten menschlichen Wissens von der Natur."

impossible so to comprehend without distortion the phases that are prior to any clear distinction of subject and object. Even to name them (instincts, sensations, feelings, etc.) is to falsify, for they are named from a stage that has already emerged from them. Hence the constant danger of falling from a philosophical comprehension to merely empirical construction.

Hegel clearly yielded to the danger, but not without interesting results. He accepted unconscious modifications – and even activities – in the soul, and had he lived a century later, he would doubtless have devoted much of this section to the findings and theories of "depth psychology".

The difficulties of comprehending philosophically the levels of "soul" become more marked in continuing the backward glance to nature, to the levels of being which are prior even to these first obscure movements of a return to self. Hegel, whose advance on Schelling may be seen as a progress from a philosophy of nature to one of spirit, expressed no great confidence in his ability to think nature philosophically. "Jene Ohnmacht der Natur setzt der Philosophie Grenzen, und das Ungehörigste ist, von dem Begriffe zu verlangen, er solle dergleichen Zufälligkeiten begreifen – und wie es genannt worden, konstruieren, deduzieren."[17] And this limit to philosophy in nature he explains by saying that the philosopher is not so interior to Nature that its divisions can develop internally: he must presuppose, i.e. impose, a system of classification not taken from experience (ibid.). That is, philosophical comprehension falls to empirical construction.

As our concern, however, is simply with spatiality and temporality, it will be sufficient to consider merely the opening paragraphs of the Philosophy of Nature which supply the bare principle of nature as the exteriorization of the Idea[18] and as the antecedent for all return of spirit to itself.

b. Space and Time

A casual reading of the texts in which Hegel describes the transition from Vorstellung to thought may imply no more than a facile conjuring away of the characteristics of space and time that are proper to images. Hegel's understanding of space and time themselves, however, is considerably more complex, and this section will suggest some of its features.

Consideration of Hegel's doctrine of space and time can err in the direction of a too narrow or of a too wide treatment. It would be inadequate to confine one's attention to the opening paragraphs of the Philosophy of

---

[17] Enc. § 250.

[18] i.e., "das ganz abstrakte Aussereinander" rather than "das vereinzelte Aussereinander" (Enc. § 253).

Nature, for – as will be indicated – the abstract space and time of nature are but particular manifestations of profounder realities that may, and do, bear the same name. It would, however, be equally false to Hegel to present his whole philosophy as a treatment of human "temporalities", on the model of contemporary thinkers. One has always the right to find analogies and cover them with a common name; but to depart too far from the terminology of a philosopher is to lose him.

The Double Character of Time

Hegel agrees with tradition in speaking of pure thought as "timeless".[19] Yet pure thought reaches its culmination in the Notion (der Begriff), and Hegel seems to identify the Notion with time itself.[20] In the final chapter of the Phenomenology, where Hegel reflects from the standpoint of Absolute Knowledge over the process that leads to it and constitutes it, he distinguishes between the self-constitution viewed from this position and from any of the levels that lead to it.[21] In the Notion that knows itself as Notion, the moments "appear" prior to the whole as complete; that is, the way of learning (für sich) is truly identical with the process which is the whole (an sich). But at any level on the way, the whole (as still abstract) is prior to the moments, an empty totality that needs to be filled "from outside". That is, Hegel adds, "die Zeit ist der Begriff selbst, der da ist, und als leere Anschauung sich dem Bewusstsein vorstellt."

Time, therefore, is not merely a finite entity or form which affects pure thought from outside. Time *is* the Notion itself in a state of self-externality. It has, then, a double character. Firstly, it is the mark of finitude and externality from which thought must free itself, the *other* of thought. Secondly, it is the very process of thought toward this freedom, the other *of* thought. Thus, Hegel continues the above passage by saying that so far as the Notion grasps itself, it supersedes its time character. No less, however, is time the "destiny and necessity of spirit", which compels it to this movement of overcoming its externality.

The same double character appears in Hegel's discussion of time at the

---

[19] An extended "illustration" of the timelessness of pure thought is presented by Hegel in the first "element" of absolute religion, which treats of God "outside time in the element of the pure thought of eternity" (RA, p. 66). Cf. Chapter V below.

[20] Hegel's metaphysics could not treat the space and time of nature as ultimate facts, simply other than thought and spiritual phenomena. He could understand them finally only in terms of a whole which exists in all these forms. With primary reference to thought, he normally calls this whole "the Notion". But he is equally entitled, with reference primarily to nature, to name it "Time". (cf. p. 61 below).

[21] Phän., p. 558.

beginning of the Philosophy of Nature.[22] All finite things, Hegel states, are in time, and only that which is without process is without time. Yet this latter can be either by defect or by excess. The lowest – mere abstract, unliving universality – is without process, and a relative escape from time can be found in mere duration.[23] But also the highest is not in time: "das in sich Konkrete, das Gesetz, die Idee, der Geist". For this is not a moment within a process; it is process itself. And time is presented as "der Prozess der wirklichen Dinge". It is thus at once that which makes the finitude of things and the very process by which this finitude is overcome. The latter is termed "die Zeit als Zeit".[24] The former is called "die natürliche Zeit",[25] time "als erscheinend".[26]

The Appearance of Space

It is one of the purposes of this whole study to ask what meaning can be given to the "transition" from the pure thought of the Logic to the space and time of nature. At present we shall simply consider how Hegel describes the space and time of nature as they appear from the Idea. It is space that constitutes the first category of nature.[27] Hegel describes it as "vermittlungslose Gleichgültigkeit",[28] a completely abstract "Aussersichsein".[29] He speaks of space also as a sheer "Nebeneinander", a term that recurs frequently later for the fixation of Vorstellung and Verstand in contrast to the organic development of reason.[30] Yet even the image of static points is in advance of what is here thought, for Hegel emphasizes that there can not as yet be even this degree of opposition. It is a stage of continuity as much as discreteness. If one is to think of "here's", they can in no way determine each other. Hegel approves Kant's treatment of space as a pure form, but only in the sense that all determinations are yet to come to it – or rather, from it.

Hegel warns the reader of the difficulty of finding an image for this sheer externality of the Idea. It is not the empirical spatiality of objects but the most rudimentary experience of being "ausser-sich", that pure immediacy and particularity which Hegel seems to imply at the opening of the Pheno-

---

[22] Enc. § 258 and Zusatz.

[23] "Das Mittelmässige dauert und regiert am Ende die Welt . . . denn die Wahrheit stellt sich nicht an ihr als Prozess dar." (*ibid*).

[24] Enc. § 258 Zusatz.

[25] *ibid.*

[26] § 257.

[27] Though it is of interest to note that in his earliest lectures on the philosophy of nature, at Jena, Hegel made time the first category.

[28] For comments on Hegel's concept of "indifference", cf. p. 77 below.

[29] Enc. § 254.

[30] E.g., cf. WL, II, p. 496 and RB, p. 117.

menology as prior even to the "here" and the "now": "der Einzelne weiss reines Dieses."[31] It is prior to all designation, yet is the condition of possibility of a meaning that is to come first by a mere "Zeigen".[32]

Without pressing the comparison, much of what is here suggested may be found in Sartre's description of the "en-soi". This he treats negatively in *L'Être et le Néant*[33] by removing all determinations as derived from "conscience": it is underived, inexplicable, neither affirmative nor negative, active nor passive. In *La Nausée* is described, more "positively", the experience of the brute, opaque existent that is "de trop". It is unnamable; it escapes time.

The Appearance of Time

So also for Hegel is space "abstract existence below time".[34] The escape, however, is an abstraction that is immediately negated in experience of spatiality. More correctly, space negates itself: "Wir gehen nicht so subjektiv zur Zeit über, sondern der Raum selbst geht über."[35] That is, it is false to follow the dialectic of space as one would the development of an object. This would be merely "Negation an einem Anderen". The experience which is implied is that in which space, at however rudimentary a level, negates itself for itself. "So für sich gesetzt ist [diese Negativität] die Zeit", for "die Zeit ist die Negation der Negation, die sich auf sich beziehende Negation."

Hegel offers little help to his reader, but his meaning seems to be that the experience of space can realize its own "dimensionality" (e.g., the designation of discrete points) only by "reflecting" into a dimension other than its own. And this Hegel regards as the passage from the "ruhige Nebeneinander" of space to the "unruhige für sich" of time.

The new experience is therefore of space-time, or "natürliche Zeit".[36] This is the possibility of tracing a spatial whole. Yet the profounder possibility which has been realized in this dialectic is that of nature's first crude "return to itself". And this inner process of space is "die Zeit als Zeit".

If then one is with caution to suggest the fundamental experience of temporality that Hegel indicates, it would be lacking all subtlety to propose mere "flux". The passage of natural time is but a "spatial fixation" of that profounder time which is the repeated negation of every such levelling. Again

---

[31] Phän, p. 80.
[32] p. 85.
[33] pp. 30-34.
[34] Enc. § 258 Zusatz.
[35] Enc. § 257 Zuzatz.
[36] Cf. p. 48 above.

Sartre[37] offers great riches in his descriptions of that concrete phenomenon which is "l'en-soi entouré de ce manchon de néant que nous avons designé du nom de pour-soi."[38] The Time which for Hegel is "das Sein, das, indem es ist, nicht ist und indem es nicht ist, ist"[39] may well, in the dialectic of human experience in the Philosophy of Spirit, have offered more than acknowledged inspiration for the trials of the "pour-soi", which "est ce qu'il n'est pas et n'est pas ce qu'il est."[40]

c. Place

As mentioned above,[41] Hegel approves – with explicit rejection of all interpretations due to subjective idealism – Kant's treatment of space and time as pure forms of experience. Each is termed "das unsinnliche Sinnliche und das sinnliche Unsinnliche". Neither is an object of experience, yet there can be no experience which is simply outside them. Philosophical thought will transcend them only so far as it can pass through the moments "in" the process to become identical with the process-less process itself.

Hence the first experience that we can be expected to verify is neither pure spatiality nor pure temporality but their synthesis. For in his lectures on Logic, Hegel states that the thesis (Sein) and antithesis (Nichts) are but empty abstractions of the synthesis (Werden).[42] And the synthesis of space and time is place, "die gesetzte Identität des Raumes und der Zeit und ebenso der gesetzte Widerspruch."[43]

Yet here again the double character of time is suggested, for it is time, rather than place, which Hegel terms "das angeschaute Werden".[44] Place, we may say, is not merely the sublation of time as an abstract moment; it is also a place *of* time as the fully concrete Notion. Hence the opening triad of the Philosophy of Nature is the archetype for all further stages of nature and spirit on the way to the culmination in philosophy. Each synthesis is a certain fixed spatialization of the process of time, a place in experience, a "situs", situation, standpoint.

As pointed out in Chapter I,[45] the view that the Logic achieves itself and

---

[37] No glib comparison of the two thinkers as metaphysicians is hereby intended. The differences are evident.

[38] *L'Être et le Néant*, p. 716.

[39] Enc. § 258.

[40] *op. cit.*, p. 33.

[41] p. 48.

[42] Enc. § 88 Zusatz.

[43] § 261.

[44] § 258.

[45] pp. 38-9 above.

then passes over into nature is itself a merely spatial image. Rather is every stage of logical thought a certain manner of exteriorization into, and return from, Vorstellung and nature. In these terms, Hegel's system of Logic, Nature, and Spirit is the affirmation that everything is a particular situation in logical thought and spatio-temporal experience. Philosophy is the culminating (and totalizing) identity, but its need for expression in words is a reminder of Hegel's claim (at least) that it should be a concrete identity which respects as much the differences along the way as the partial identities.

It is now our purpose to attempt some understanding of the situation that Hegel describes toward the end of Subjective Spirit, where the identity-in-difference of thought and spatio-temporal language becomes explicit.

3. INTUITION (ANSCHAUUNG)

a. The Place of Intuition

Language appears at the level of Vorstellung, which is the antithesis to which intuition is thesis and thought is synthesis (cf. appendix of categories). The "genetic description" of language must therefore start, at the latest, with some consideration of intuition.

The remarks already made about the general movement of the dialectic in the Philosophy of Spirit, and perhaps also the comments on space and time, will warn against an over-simple interpretation whereby the stages of spirit can be set in a series similar to that of the cardinal numbers, each precisely summing up its predecessors and not overlapping its successors. That is a spatial form which neglects, not merely the particularities of Hegel's "Darstellung", but also the evasiveness of the inner process of temporality. Thus, Hegel himself points out[46] that intuition could well be assigned (though with qualifications) to the stage of "consciousness" (Bewusstsein), which has apparently been passed in arriving at "Spirit" (Geist oder Psychologie). And it is clear that many of the stages of consciousness which precede intuition (for example, those dealing with the recognition of other selves) involve elements posterior to intuition.

Hegel himself describes intuition in relation, not to the immediate predecessors, but to the central theme of Subjective Spirit, the sublation of "Seele" and "Bewusstsein" into "Geist". In passing, however, it is worthy of mention that the prior position of the dialectic of selves, by suggesting that at least rudimentary phases of appetite and "interpersonality" are presupposed by intuition, reminds us that, though we are in the realm of theoretical rather

[46] Enc. § 449 Zusatz.

than of practical spirit, every step of our dialectic has its moment of will. Intellect and will are the mutually developing sides of the concrete process of "freier Geist",[47] and it is always an abstraction to speak of one as though separate from the other.[48] Hence it is totally false to regard the dialectic of intuition, Vorstellung, and thought as a "psychological" process merely "in the mind".

Hegel introduces intuition as a partial reconciliation of the two first phases of Subjective Spirit. The thesis, "Soul" (or "Antropology"), embraces those stages of incipient consciousness (if not subconsciousness), where subject and object are still in the undifferentiated identity of feeling, sensation, habit. Hegel repeats there his customary polemic against the popular conception that "there is more in feeling than in thought". Feeling is rather the state of "selbstische Einzelheit". When a man deserts the notion of the thing itself and appeals to his feelings, he sets himself apart from the community of reason.

The antithesis, "Consciousness", marks the other extreme, in which there is a mere opposition of subject to object. The former fails as yet to recognize itself in the latter.

Hence, intuition may be seen as a first tentative reconciliation. On the one hand,[49] the objective state of consciousness regains the identity of feeling. On the other hand,[50] the sheer immediacy of the latter is transformed by a mediation in which the intellect sets the previously unseparated content of sensation "outside" itself, "wirft ihn in Raum und Zeit hinaus, welches die Formen sind, worin sie anschauend ist."

We have, thus, some right to speak, no longer with implied quotation marks, of an object of experience. We can speak, no longer merely of a "this-experience", but of a true distinction between "this" and "that". And this objectivization comes with the "throwing into" space and time. When Hegel, in the Encyclopaedia, starts his résumé of the process of the "Phenomenology of Spirit",[51] he admits that the "here and now" with which he began that book belong properly to intuition rather than to the earlier stage at which he there stands.

But space and time, as we have seen, are no simple entities which can serve to characterize a phase of spirit. All experience, even that prior to intuition, embodies them. Rather is any level of experience a particular "situation" of time. Hence instead of simply explaining intuition "by" space and

[47] § 443.
[48] § 445.
[49] Enc. §§ 446-7.
[50] § 448.
[51] Enc. § 418.

time, we have rather still to determine what spatialization of time, what "situs", is verified at the level of intuition.

b. The Totality of Intuition

On several occasions Hegel emphasizes that the characteristic of intuition lies in the double movement by which the immediacy of feeling attains the objectivity of consciousness and the sheer separation of the latter gains the identity of the former. Intuition marks the "Trennung und Einheit des Subjektiven und des Objektiven. . . die doppelte Tätigkeit des Aufhebens und des Wiederherstellens der Einheit zwischen mir und dem Andern."[52]

This is, indeed, the double movement which guides the self-constitution of spirit from the "beginning". The "Weg des Geistes" is the double determination, to find something as "seiend" and to posit it as "das Seinige".[53] The subject can find itself only so far as it has expressed itself: it can express itself only so far as it thereby returns to itself.

This is the double movement which will govern the dialectic of thought and language, and which can not be forgotten in any interpretation of the system itself. Yet it is here, in intuition, that it first becomes "für sich", a conscious predicament of experience. Hegel speaks of intuition as the intellect's first awakening to itself,[54] and he adds that – in this sense, at least – Schelling was able rightly to speak of intellectual intuition.[55] Awakening means a passing from mere connexionless images to a rudimentary totality, in which and from which the elements receive their objectivity and meaning.[56] So is the experience of intuition "eine Totalität, eine zusammengehaltene Fülle".[57]

Thus, the task of understanding the situation of intuition may be seen as that of grasping the nature of the totality in which the "this here and now" receives its objectivity and meaning. If the Phenomenology passes from an indeterminate "this" to the most elementary meaning of a pointing at a "this here" and a "this now",[58] so we may suppose that the totality of intuition is the "frame of reference or field of possibility" which makes possible this first meaning by designation. And the supposition is maintained by the

---

[52] § 448 Zusatz.
[53] Enc. § 443; cf JL, pp. 184-5.
[54] Enc. § 450.
[55] § 449 Zusatz.
[56] § 398.
[57] § 449 Zusatz.
[58] Phän., pp. 79-86.

empirical experience which Hegel chooses to name this stage of the dialectic, "Aufmerksamkeit".[59]

c. Attention (Aufmerksamkeit)

Hegel, in presenting a Vorstellung of what he means, relates attention to the sense of wonder which Plato and Aristotle set as the beginning of knowledge.[60] It is the awe with which the subject, in and by grasping an object as object, "finds", as in the archetypal experience of Adam, that this is "flesh of his flesh".[61] It is the originative stage of the "Bildung des Geistes",[62] in which the double movement of spirit shows itself as a "sich-Hingeben an die Sache" that is the effort of the subject to free himself from other things, from a mere "Hinausgehen über Alles", and no less from his own particular self, "seine die Sache nicht zu Worte kommen lassende, sondern vorschnell darüber aburteilende Eitelkeit."

Any concrete act of attention would, however, include elements that involve a more determinate totality than is to be had at this stage. Attention is no more than the first reflection on itself of the sheer externality of sensation, and this reflection is the "noch ganz formale inhaltlose Allgemeinheit" which is the Notion in "die doppelte Form des Raumes und der Zeit."[63] It is simple designation in that empty possibility of space and time which is filled by a mere endless repetition of the "this here and now". It is "unmittelbar in diesem äusserlichseiende Stoff in sich erinnert und in ihrer Erinnerung in sich in das Aussersichsein versenkt."[64]

Thus, the double movement of spirit is at a situation where it is coextensive with a world by being at a point in the world. Spatial terms, which will embarrass thought as it comes more to itself, are here entirely appropriate. The whole burden of spirit is to bring forth a filling for this empty world.[65] But the mere interplay of continuity and discreteness can merely propagate it, never fill it. The popular interpretation of impressions coming from without and of a subject merely pointing from within may fatigue but can never exhaust. If philosophical meaning is to pass on the way of its "Bildung", towards a truer totality that no longer reduces "the" world to "its" world,[66]

[59] Enc. § 448.
[60] § 449 Zusatz.
[61] § 440 Zusatz.
[62] § 449 Zusatz.
[63] *ibid.*
[64] Enc. § 449.
[65] § 442.
[66] Cf. § 403.

spirit must turn into itself, to a new "dimension". Time must pass from the repetition of a spatial level to that reflection on the very experience of that level, which annihilates it and raises it.

4. VORSTELLUNG

a. Recapitulation

Before we consider those sections where Hegel explicitly treats of Vorstellung, language, and the transition to thought, it may be well to pause briefly to ask, not so much where we are in the Philosophy of Spirit, as what the reader of this work is meant to be doing.

The passage from one category of spirit to another may be called a "deduction"; but the word has been avoided here, for it is certainly not a deduction in the sense of Euclid or even of Spinoza. Nor could it be termed, without qualification, a "description", for this would fail to convey the necessity that Hegel claimed for the developing process. "Explanation" would also fall short, for this implies an understanding of one thing in terms of another, whereas the process is itself an attempt to overcome this in the direction of a truth that accounts for itself.

The peculiarity of Hegel's genetic "description" or "explanation" of spiritual phenomena is well exhibited in his "Phenomenology of Spirit". There the reader must adopt a dual standpoint: that of the person engaged in the experiences described (für sich), and that of the "philosopher" who has "already" completed the process and understands it as a "self-accounting" totality (für uns). Even in holding that this is no more than a disguised ontology, a phenomenology only by courtesy of the printer, one may well admit that the complicated interplay of these two standpoints gives a massive impression of the strenuous effort involved: that is, of thinking human experience in a way that gives due weight to the particularities of finite levels of experience and also to that metaphysical claim to totality which must (in some form, at least) appear as soon as the experience is thought.

In contrast, the bald confident structure of the Encyclopaedia may suggest the single standpoint of one who, though perhaps in his youth he passed through many of the stages, now – in the recollection of old age – reduces them to grey shapes to be manipulated into system.[67]

The question of the relation between "Phenomenology of Spirit" and

[67] The very term "recollection" may, however, imply a greater depth to the experience if it can be taken in Hegel's own sense (see below, pp. 57-60).

"Philosophy of Spirit" is complicated and unsolved; for it depends, not only upon a study of the history of Hegel's writings, but upon an interpretation of the system as a whole. Originally, the Phenomenology was intended simply as an introduction to the Encyclopaedia. But it developed, in the course of writing, from a phenomenology of consciousness to a phenomenology of spirit.[68] The latter, as has been seen,[69] repeats the "introduction", the phenomenology of consciousness, as the second phase of Subjective Spirit.

The problem may then be to say which "science" absorbed the other. Hegel himself seldom referred later to his "Phenomenology of Spirit", regarding the Encyclopaedia as the definitive formulation of his philosophy. Yet one may well follow Hyppolite in seeing the Phenomenology as "un moment qui risque d'absorber en lui tout le reste".[70]

Whatever may be thought of this, and of the profounder questions involved, the section of the Philosophy of Spirit we are considering is especially adapted to "absorption" in the dual standpoint of the Phenomenology. For the part of the way which is termed "Vorstellung" is that in which the thinker comes to awareness of the intimate duality of his position. As language is sublated into thought, the new-won meaning is seen to be an unsteady combination of "Meinung" (bound to the particularity of experience and its language) and of a thought which remains a formal "thinking about" that experience.

If the earlier and later sections of the Philosophy of Spirit may invite the criticism that they are a formal explanation "from above", it is this very criticism which sets the reader *in* the movement of the dialectic at this point. For it is in these sections that Hegel reflects "on" and "into" this basic dilemma of all human thought.

b. Transition to Vorstellung

The experience of which Hegel invited us to think to illustrate the stage of intuition was that of the "this" set in a totality of space and time which makes it a "this here and now". That the experience itself becomes the very "criticism" which sublates it is the burden of the opening pages of the Phenomenology.[71] In the terms of the Encyclopaedia, this transition is expressed in the statement that the identity-in-difference of the subjective and objective sides of intuition, merely "an sich" at that level, now becomes "für sich". "Erst, wenn ich die Reflexion mache, dass ich es bin, der die Anschauung hat, erst dann trete ich auf den Standpunkt der Vorstellung."[72] We come thus to a stage at which explicit self-criticism is the process of its resolution. Intellect becomes the "für-sich-seiende Dialektik" of its various levels.[73]

Hegel also expresses this process by saying that intuition now becomes the "Konkrete des Stoffes und ihrer selbst'.[74] The word "concrete" is here implicitly opposed, as it is frequently in the dialectic of Vorstellung, to "synthesis". The distinction may be etymologically explained as the difference between a unity that grows from its inner being and one imposed from without.[75] The unity between subjective and objective sides in intuition is merely "an sich", "äusserlich", "put together". It "grows together" only so far as it becomes "innerlich", so far as thought enters into itself and passes from "ein ruhiges Nebeneinander" to that true opposition in which true identity can appear.

It is the "Erinnerung" of intuition which gives the name to the first appearance or phase of Vorstellung. But before broaching it, Hegel gives a salutary warning[76] that the very division of Vorstellung into phases which have an air of independence is itself the product of a mind held by the limitations of Vorstellung. The true philosophical grasp, he continues, will think the organic development of intellect in those phases. And this way of intellect through the whole course of Vorstellung is the effort "sich-selbst anschauend zu setzen",[77] the double movement of giving utterance to its merely subjective inwardness and of returning from its expression to itself.[78] But, he warns, the result will always, at this level, turn out to be mere "Synthesen", for it is only in thought that the concrete immanence of the Notion is to be expected.

c. Recollection (Erinnerung)

The effort that Hegel makes to draw the gleams of reason out of words at their "common-sense" level[79] is a realization of the very strife of thought in Vorstellung, which at this point is the explicit struggle to reflect on its

---

[72] Enc. § 449 Zusatz.

[73] § 450 Zusatz.

[74] § 450.

[75] Cf. pp. 29-30 above.

[76] Enc. § 451 Zusatz.

[77] § 451.

[78] So that the purpose of the transition "from" intuition is the return to the unity of intuition, no longer at a level close to "feeling", but in the self-positing of thought.

[79] Cf. p. 12 above.

struggle. And it is here that we find one of his happiest choices of names for categories. The reflection into itself of thought, which here becomes conscious and critical of itself, and whose central theme becomes the passage from the outwardness of the space-time of intuition to the temporality of the reflecting subject, finds thoughtful "illustration" in the process of recollection and an apt name in "Erinnerung".

Temporality of the Subject

This passage, which we may say "inwardizes" the original intuition toward the originality of the intuition, is immediately posed by Hegel as a question of the "proper" temporality of the subject. "Als die Anschauung zunächst erinnernd, setzt die Intelligenz den Inhalt des Gefühls in ihre Innerlichkeit, in ihren eigenen Raum und in ihre eigene Zeit."[80] And it is thus that the resulting "image" (Bild) is freed from its "abstract particularity against another" and taken up into the subject, "the first form of universality" that offers itself.[81]

For language itself shows the temporal character of that reflection which enables the subject to know that he "has" an intuition. In the use of "have" for the perfect tense of a "Zeitwort" we reveal that the original intuition is in the past but that the originality of the intuition, the "image" as in our own being, is a present – and a profounder presence than the content as coming from outside in the original intuition.[82] And this presence is not a mere ability to have before us at any external time what was at a particular point in that time. It is a "Beschäftigung" with events which confers on them a "duration" independent of that which is "merely given", a duration that is rather an expression of our interest.[83]

What, then, is the "proper space and proper time" of the subject? As suggested in the treatment of intuition,[84] no phase of spirit can be characterized simply by reference to space and time as to self-evident entities. Each phase of the dialectic is a fresh understanding of a certain spatialization of time. Each stage of the dialectic of Vorstellung is thus a further grasp of that "inwardness' of the subject to which the intuition is raised.

The first stage is that of a *mere* inwardness. The subject is no longer in the simple state of attention to a "this here and now" in opposition to others. He has become conscious of the experience itself as a particular rendering

[80] Enc. § 542.
[81] § 453.
[82] Enc. § 450 Zusatz.
[83] § 452 Zusatz.
[84] pp. 52-3 above.

possible of – and being rendered possible by – a totality of other such particulars. He has risen from "this" to "thisness". He can no longer find, in a mere repetition of attention and designation, the "Befriedigung" of meaning and knowing what he means. Yet this "first form of universality" appears as an error at the other extreme. It is at first a purely abstract totality, innocent of verification. The "image"[85] is in a simple union with the intellect, isolated from the original experience, so that it shows the arbitrariness and contingency always the manifestation of immediacy.[86] While free from deriving its place in external space and time, the image has won no determined situation in the life of the intellect. The dilemma comes to us historically in questions about the place of images that are "bewusstlos aufbewahrt" and about the nature of the intellect as a dark pit in which is stored a world of infinitely many images.[87]

Verification: The Synthesis of Vorstellung

The question about the place of ideas is not foolish, however, if place itself be understood, not from without as a point in external space and time, but from within as a human situation.[88] Philosophy merely follows the course of human "Bildung"[89] in taking the false questions we pose and, by asking what we really mean, converting them into true questions.

Here, the search for meaning in a pure interiority reveals its own futility. For isolation from the exterior deprives it of its character of interiority, and the original duality reappears. The intellect, like the seed and the fruit, passes "zur Rückkehr in seine Einfachheit, wieder zur Existenz des Ansich-seins".[90] And the true "inwardizing" of "Erinnerung" is no less a return to the externality of the intuition: "Die eigentliche sogenannte Erinnerung ist die Beziehung des Bildes auf eine Anschauung."[91]

The return, however, is not merely to the stage of "meaning by designation" which had been left. In common terms, when a recollection is verified in a further experience, this latter is no longer a mere particularity. It is recognized by the intellect as "already its own". The verification is thus a double process. A merely inward image is externalized, and the experience is raised by subsumption under the universalized form of the image. Ex-

---

[85] The word suggests purely psychological theories, but one should give Hegel the credit of at least making the effort here, as he explicitly states, to surpass such a meaning.

[86] Enc. § 452.

[87] § 453.

[88] Cf. pp. 50-1 above.

[89] And no less of the therapeutic synthesis known as psycho-analysis.

[90] Enc. § 453 Zusatz.

[91] § 454.

perience is deepened, renewed. Whereas, in attention, it was merely a "Kenntnis von der Sache",[92] it is now "Erkenntnis".

It is this double movement of verification, the synthesis of mere signification and mere designation, that Hegel identifies with the true sense of the term "Vorstellung":

> Diese Synthese des innerlichen Bildes mit dem erinnerten Dasein ist die eigentliche *Vorstellung;* indem das Innere nun auch an ihm die Bestimmung hat, *vor* die Intelligenz *gestellt* werden zu können, in ihr Dasein zu haben.[93]

That is, when we speak of Vorstellung, we are referring to that effort of thought to rise to expression of itself, which is the uniting of an abstract signification (merely inner "image") and an experience (Dasein) which is deepened (erinnert) as the signification seeks its verification in it. But the union remains a "Synthese", a putting together from without. The signification is not fully verified in the experience, it remains abstractly outside. Nor is the experience fully subsumed under the signification. So that the "meaning" of thought as Vorstellung remains split in two "standpoints". But again it is the very consciousness of this limitation that opens the way to a profounder "Erinnerung" of thought. The inward reflection of thought (das Innere) has in its nature the disposition, tendency (Bestimmung), in and through the very limitations of the spatialization of a "setting-before", to realize itself concretely in the intellect.

The way is the difficult dialectic of the two levels of the synthesis toward that concrete experience where each is fully actual in the other.[94] It is finally the thought of the Logic of Essence. But before seeking the question there, we must follow – though briefly – Hegel's further presentation of it in the Philosophy of Spirit.

d. Imagination (Einbildungskraft)

Recapitulation

It has been emphasized several times that a meticulous attention to each stage of the dialectic as though it were the only possible link in a formal deduction is a misinterpretation of Hegel's effort. Though it is difficult to be

---

[92] § 448 Zusatz.

[93] § 454.

[94] "Anschauung, Erinnerung usf. sind vereinigungen derselben Momente; aber es sind Synthesen: erst in der Phantasie ist die Intelligenz als Einzelheit, d.i. als konkrete Subjektivität, in welcher die Beziehung auf sich ebenso zum Sein als zur Allgemeinheit bestimmt ist." (Enc. § 457).

certain, in any detail, what his intention was, it was clearly not a formal deduction of nature from logical categories, nor of spiritual phenomena from nature, nor of all the stages within any realm. The metaphysician who would so understand his task would no more be able to start than a runner who conceived his activity in terms of the paradoxes of Zeno. As suggested in the introduction,[95] these are chasms which can never be crossed, in the sense of starting with the particular and proceeding to the universal, starting with sense and proceeding to thought, and so for all the other dualities of philosophy.

It is, however, the claim of metaphysics and the assurance of common sense that the "chasms" are crossed. Hegel owes his place in the history of metaphysics for taking this claim at its most serious. His was not the task of starting with any part and advancing to another. He started with the "achieved totality" of experience and constructed a detailed – though not unchangeable – map of the way in which this totality can be thought to have constituted itself.

In this sense, the time and space of nature can not be treated as a simple fact, held at an "unbridgeable" distance from the process of thought and the development of spiritual phenomena. They are to be understood philosophically only in terms of a whole which exists and constitutes itself in all these forms. With reference primarily to thought, one may call this whole "the Notion". But, as we have seen, Hegel does not withdraw from the conclusion that one can no less refer primarily to nature and call the whole "Time" (die Zeit als Zeit).

As this chapter has been concerned with nature and the earlier phases of spirit, we have followed this latter terminology, adopting Hegel's treatment of time as a term of reference. The passage from nature to spirit and – in the latter realm – from intuition to Vorstellung and thought has thus been phrased as a question of the passage from the space and time of nature to the "proper" space and time of the subject. It is, we have seen, no simple unidirectional movement. Vorstellung was described as a synthesis in which the "mere inwardness" of the latter seeks verification in the former as much as the former is raised to the latter. In terms of the preceding chapter, it is the double movement of any attempt to pose a philosophical question. And Hegel's discussion of the remaining stages of Vorstellung, which we have now briefly to follow, will be determined by this repeated overcoming and reinstatement of the duality of signification and verification, "essence" and "appearance", "thought" and "experience".

[95] p. 10 above.

The Syntheses of Imagination

For the second of the three main stages of Vorstellung, Hegel chose the name "imagination" (Einbildungskraft). As with its predecessor, the name illustrates the process, which is the "inwardizing" of the "Bilder" in the last unsteady synthesis, a process which reveals itself here more explicitly as the power (Kraft) of the intellect. Hegel likewise finds illustration for his thought in various activities of imaginative thinking or phantasy. But perhaps the best reference of the term is that which draws our mind to Hegel's debt to Kant's doctrine of the synthesis of imagination.[96]

Hegel presents imagination in four stages, which he calls reproductive, associative, symbolizing, and sign-forming.[97] Without considering them in any detail, we may see them as stages of a varying relation between the "inner" meaning and its verification.

At the first level, opposition is merely implicit and Hegel speaks of a sheer "Willkür" and "Zufälligkeit" of images and thoughts. At the next stage, opposition has become explicit, yet the contingency of images is overcome, not by true verification, but rather by the external "Attraktionskraft" of the intellect. This appears historically in theories of the "Association of Ideas", according to which the meaning of any "idea" is had by designation of others which customarily accompany it.

It is in the third stage that verification pertains to "inner" and "outer" rather than to related elements of the same status. Hegel's use of the term "symbol" should not create a too lofty opinion of what is involved, for the illustrations he supplies are of a humble kind.[98] The ideas are "allgemeine Vorstellungen", exhibiting that which is common to particular images. In other words, they are abstract universals, empirical concepts, such as the redness of roses. He also includes as examples concrete universals in so far as they can be grasped at the level of Vorstellung; such as the species so far as it is a mere "empirischer Zusammenhang der mannigfaltigen Bestimmungen des Gegenstandes" rather than a concrete whole from which particulars develop.

The limitation of this stage has already been discussed: the synthesis of signification and verification remains external, because the thinker is not so internal to nature that he can grasp its distinctions as developing from within.[99] He studies merely from a standpoint that has emerged; his classification is "imposed". Hegel speaks of such concepts as being more concrete or

[96] Cf. pp. 135-7 below.
[97] Enc. § 455 Zusatz.
[98] Enc. § 456 Zusatz.
[99] p. 46 above.

less concrete.[100] We may perhaps correlate the abstractness of an empirical concept to the distance between it and the level of experience of its verification. Scientific "models of explanation" would serve as an illustration.

Verbal Language

The final stage of imagination is presented as the stage in which both sides of the opposition have developed in concreteness until the experience can internally verify the concept and this can find utterance in experience.[101] And in so far as this is effected, the intellect has come to "Selbstanschauung".[102] The advance over the previous stage is illustrated by Hegel as that from symbol to sign. A concept which is only partially verifiable may be likened to a symbol which retains much of its own being and is never fully taken over by its meaning. The sign, however, retains nothing of itself; it sacrifices itself to its sense.

It is at this stage that Hegel sets the word and the origin of verbal language. For it is in the spoken word that he sees the highest manifestation of the struggle of thought at the level of imagination. He had already indicated this at the end of his introduction to the section on "Psychology",[103] where, replying to those who consider the activity of will as distinct from, and superior to, that of intellect, he praised the activity which manifests itself in the word, "diese flüchtige, verschwindende, ganz ideelle Realization." And here again, he sees in the spoken word, which disappears in its very utterance, that sublation of an opposed particularity into an entire expression of meaning, which he tries to think in the sign as the final stage of imagination. For the spoken word is a "Dasein in der Zeit, ein Verschwinden des Daseins, indem er ist."[104]

This sacrificing of all particularity in the word which could stand against its meaning is, of course, itself somewhat imaginative. The word always persists against its meaning, and the following sections will reflect on this. It is, indeed, rather arbitrary that language should have been put at this precise point of the dialectic; for its role of expressing and yet opposing thought is applicable to any synthesis of Vorstellung.

Elsewhere Hegel uses the term "language" in ways that indicate its broader

[100] Enc. § 456.
[101] Cf. Enc. § 456 Zusatz: "Die Wahrheit der beiden Seiten ist die Einheit derselben. Diese Einheit, die Verbildlichung des Allgemeinen und die Verallgemeinerung des Bildes kommt näher zu stande, dass die allgemeine Vorstellung sich nicht zu einem neutralen, so zu sagen 'chemischen', Producte mit dem Bilde vereinigt, sondern sich als die substanziale Macht über das Bild betätigt . . . sich zu dessen Seele macht."
[102] Enc. § 457.
[103] § 444 Zusatz.
[104] Enc. § 459.

sense. It is more than a means of communication, for it is the most intimate self-expression, "das Element der Innigkeit", and no translation can capture the soul of language.[105] It is itself neither merely subjective nor merely objective, for it is the "Einheit und Mitte" of subject and object.[106] Nor may it be seen in a purely individual context, for every private thought is already, in its language, a communication with others and with the whole people that expresses itself in its language.[107]

The following chapter, which will try to find in Hegel's Logic a formulation for the duality of Vorstellung, must return to a deeper analysis of his doctrine of the predicament of thought in its efforts at self-expression in its language.

Dimensions of Time

In closing his consideration of imagination with the word which, as an existence in time, disappears in its utterance, Hegel returns to that question of the temporality of the subject, with which the section on Vorstellung began.[108] There may be grounds, therefore, for inserting here the suggestion that the subject, in his struggle to find and express his meaning, represents a certain "dimensionality" of time, no less than the past, present, and future of natural time.

The first stage is a mere identity of thought and its language. Meaning finds itself in its expression without struggle, because the identity is below opposition.

At the second stage, opposition has become explicit. Concepts seek verification in experience, and the latter seeks universalization in the former. But the identity remains an ideal, a mere future.

The third stage is that which realizes the presence of the identity. It is, however, no mere annihilation of the opposition, for this would be a simple return to the first stage. It is a true identity-in-opposition, a presence that has passed through the "seriousness, the suffering, the patience, and the labour" that constitute it. It is the concrete identity of abstract identity and its difference. For, as we have seen, each human situation is as much the contradiction of its spatial and temporal moments as their identity.[109] In practical terms, Hegel's constant rejection of an ineffable does not of itself exclude a deep sense of the "externality" of language within that final identity of thought which his philosophy must affirm.

---

[105] Nürnberg, pp. 310-11.

[106] JR, I, p. 213.

[107] p. 235.

[108] It may be remembered, too, that Hegel was re-thinking a system in which the imagination is the faculty that schematizes the pure categories in time.

[109] pp. 50-1 above.

e. Memory (Gedächtnis)

The final stage of Vorstellung, which marks thus the transition to thought, is called by Hegel "Gedächtnis". The name implies etymologically the holding-together of disparate elements in the unity of thought. In the earliest presentation of Hegel's philosophy of spirit, his lectures of 1803 at Jena, "Gedächtnis" and language are correlated to form the first of the three "potencies" by which the naive consciousness is raised to the culminating stage of "Volksgeist".[110] In this sense, we may say, it is only at this stage, where thought appears in its existence as language, that one can truly speak of consciousness and hence of a philosophy of spirit.[111] The transition from language to thought may, then, with some justice be considered the true point of transition from nature to spirit. This is mentioned because our concern later with the transition from logic to nature may give the impression that the other transition of the system has been neglected; whereas this and the following chapter are largely an effort to win a profounder meaning for it.

At the close of the stage of imagination, the word had appeared as a presence in which meaning and expression are one. It reveals itself no less, however, as a mere synthesis, an external "Verknüpfung der Vorstellung als eines Inneren mit der Anschauung als einem Äusserlichen".[112] Thought thus finds itself opposed to its word and passes through a dialectic of intuition *of* the word,[113] a parallel at this level to the original reflection of intuition. From this dialectic, Hegel derives a profounder unity of meaning and its expression in a "name", yet the identity again shows itself to be an external connexion: "Insofern der Zusammenhang der Namen in der Bedeutung liegt, ist die Verknüpfung derselben mit dem Sein als Namen noch eine Synthese und die Intelligenz in dieser ihrer Äusserlichkeit nicht einfach in sich zurückgekehrt."[114]

Thus it is that, at the point which should mark the highest stage before thought, two of the four paragraphs consecrated to "memory" deal with the persisting opposition to a true identity of meaning and language. So far, however, as memory be proposed as the synthesis of Vorstellung, this is to be expected. For the Hegelian synthesis is not merely the concrete whole of the two preceding phases: it is no less a relapse to an abstract immediacy that is the origin of the following triad. In terms of the category of "Werden", the

---

[110] JR, I, pp. 207-18.
[111] E.g., JR, I, p. 211: "Die Idee dieser Existenz des Bewusstseins ist das Gedächtnis, und seine Existenz selbst die Sprache."
[112] Enc. § 460.
[113] § 461.
[114] § 463.

archetype of every synthesis, this is – on the one hand – "eine haltungslose Unruhe. . . das Gleichgewicht, worein sich Entstehen und Vergehen setzen";[115] that is, it is the concrete equilibrium that respects as much the difference as the abstract identity of its moments. On the other hand, however, it is no less "das Verschwinden des Verschwindens selbst. . . [das] in ein ruhiges Resultat zusammensinkt. . . Die ruhige Einfachheit aber ist Sein." That is, the true identity-in-difference proves impossible to maintain and sinks to a mere abstract identity; the "unruhige für sich" of time is fixed in the "ruhige nebeneinander" of a further spatialization. Thought turns from its responsibility to the complacency of ready-made phrases.

f. Transition to Thought

Thus, the student of Hegel finds himself, it may be said, in a repeated state of disappointment. At every turn in the way he feels the end is in sight. He is coming to what is announced as a state of fulfilment from which he need, and can, go no further. But upon reaching it, he finds it is but another turn from which he must start again, as at the beginning.

So it is with a healthy scepticism that one reads, with Hegel, that he has now reached "das wahrhafte Allgemeine, welches die übergreifende Einheit seiner selbst über sein Anderes, das Sein, ist."[116] Now the intellect realizes "dass, was gedacht ist, ist; und dass, was ist, nur ist insofern es Gedanke ist." Thought is said to be at the level where it *is*, and no longer *has*, its meaning.[117]

Similarly, one will read, with a more moderate view of the claims proposed, Hegel's frequent rejection of any "beyond" to all words that try to express it. To repudiate all easy escape into an "ineffable", away from the burden and precision of expressed thought, is to suggest rather than deny a profound realization of that burden of the word, which opposes itself to thought in giving it expression. Thought must be expressed, but expressed thought is thought that is self-critical in its expression.

This chapter, in its confusing course, may have served to give some impression of an awareness of this burden of the word that may elsewhere seem to be lacking in Hegel. His conviction was of a final meaning that the philosopher may not simply project into an unattainable future. Yet this meaning is present only in the full course of its self-constitution. Part of this course we have tried to follow. It was no simple progression. For at every stage, meaning was seen to have two sources. It came from the designation of

---

[115] WL, I, p. 93.
[116] Enc. § 465.
[117] § 464.

particular experiences, and it came from a mere "inwardness", a totality inadequately verified in experience. The final identity that Hegel affirms is no abstraction that simply ignores the real differences. Nor is it a mere future, a distant goal that never bears on the responsibility of the present. It must be a true presence that yet contains its "other" within itself. The spatial metaphors here do no more than indicate the problem at hand. For its re-statement, at least in a fresh "Vorstellung", we shall turn in the following chapter to Hegel's Logic.

This chapter has been an attempt to understand, from a different age with different preoccupations, a part of Hegel's written thought. Both the thought and the understanding have been made possible, have existed, in the "Vorstellungen" of thinker and reader. Both have been limited by the "Grenzpunkt der Vorstellung".[118] This possibility and limit of thought, and of its renewal, is what constitutes the history of philosophy. Hegel's final contention would be that it is in a re-enacting, re-thinking of the history of philosophy that man can best hope to come to an understanding of what he truly means; and it is in the extensive and intensive expression of this affirmation that Hegel's system secures its own place in that history.

[118] Beweise, p. 91.

CHAPTER III

THE LOGIC OF ESSENCE

I. VORSTELLUNG AND ESSENCE

Hegel was fond of repeating, in his polemics against the advocates of "feeling" and "immediacy" in religion and philosophy, that human activity is such only in virtue of its thought. His own philosophy is, however, an extended statement of the dilemma at the heart of thought. We may perhaps say it is the dilemma that is expressed in the double sense of the genitive in the above phrase, "its thought". Human activity is the experience of thinking, which is no less the thinking of (about) experience.

That the two senses should have meaning only in a final identity may well be seen as the distinctive mark, and contribution, of Hegel's philosophy. It is, however, an identity which may be grasped only in passing through the full anguish of its many forms of diversity, indeed contradiction. Though all human activity must suffer under the embarrassment of the mutual inadequacy of experience and thought of experience, it is in philosophy, within the very thought of thought itself, that this embarrassment must be at its profoundest.

It is in terms of this dilemma that we wish to understand the paradox expressed in Hegel's tripartite system: that the pure thought of the Logic is at once the fulfilment of all experience and a "mere" thought opposed to its embodiment in the forms (Gestalten) of experience, which are represented by the second and third parts of the system, nature and spirit. As a particular point of entry to the problem, the identity-in-difference of thought and experience has been sought in what one may perhaps regard as the most intimate "otherness" of thought, its language. For thought comes to be only in a language which it forms or creates as its embodiment, but which nevertheless opposes it in the very achievement of this incarnation.

The preceding chapter followed Hegel's doctrine of the transition from Vorstellung to thought in the "Philosophy of Spirit". There it was seen that thought comes to a true recollection (Erinnerung) of itself only in so far as it repeatedly submits to its "other" in the syntheses of Vorstellung. As Hegel said more eloquently elsewhere, "the life of mind is not one that shuns death, and keeps clear of destruction; it endures death and in death maintains its being, for it only wins to its truth when it finds itself utterly torn asunder."[1]

The basically religious associations of such an attitude supplied Hegel with what was at least effective inspiration in his formative years and apt illustration in his maturity. It will be our task in the second part of this study to consider how he gave expression to his system as such in the medium of religious thought. But first it will be necessary, in this chapter, to examine the intimate "otherness" of thought in that work in which Hegel sought to reveal it in its purest and most acute form, the "Logic".

As it is the burden of this whole study to suggest, from various viewpoints, the relation between the thought of the Logic and that of other parts of Hegel's system, little can at present be said about the new "element" in which we shall find ourselves. It will suffice for the moment to say that whereas, in the Philosophy of Spirit, the contradiction that developed through the sections on Vorstellung was between sense and thought, in the Logic the attempt is made to follow the development of the same contradiction as interior to thought itself. We approached the dialectic of the Philosophy of Spirit at the point of self-transcending sense experience and tried to trace it toward those concrete experiences which mark the transition to philosophical thought. Hegel claims, in the Logic, to have overcome this standpoint and to have arrived at the timeless development of thought itself.

Yet "Aufhebung" is no less preservation than annihilation, and we have already had frequent occasion to suggest that the dialectic of consciousness does not simply vanish in the element of thought. The space and time in which consciousness finds and expresses its activity are a manifestation of an inner "spatio-temporal" movement of thought itself. The repeated reappearance of the "otherness" of thought, which we followed through the dialectic of intuition and Vorstellung, far from simply disappearing in the passage to Logic, returns there in a much acuter form. The timeless nature of philosophical thought lies, not in any simple vanishing of time, but rather in that very entering of thought into itself which is a recognition of itself as it is. It does not escape process but becomes process.[2]

Though this intimate duality of thought can be found in all parts of the Logic, it is intended here to examine it at that point where it becomes most explicit, in the second of the three "books" which form the Logic. The first

[1] Phän., pp. 29-30.
[2] Cf. pp. 47-8 above.

of these Hegel calls the "Logic of Being" (Sein). "Being" meant for Hegel, as for the German Idealists in general, merely objective being, that which presents itself without any sophistication of distinction between reality and appearance. As soon, however, as reflection enters, some such distinction becomes constitutive of knowledge, and reality is presented in dual categories typified by those of an appearance and an essential "behind" it. The full range of such dual categories is treated in the second book, which Hegel calls the "Logic of Essence" (Wesen). The third book, entitled "Logic of the Notion" (Begriff), is Hegel's attempt to think a true self-development: that is, it is a return to the unity of the first book without loss of the depth of experience gained in the second. It will be for the rest of this chapter to try to characterize more definitely the differences between these three books; for, unless they be appreciated, any understanding of the transitions of the system is likely to reduce the movement proper to the third book to that of the first with a loss of all that was achieved in the second.

In the preceding chapter, it was suggested that "consciousness" (Bewusstsein) forms a privileged point of entry into the dialectic of the Philosophy of Spirit, in that it is the point where man naturally "finds himself" before starting on the way that leads to a philosophical thought. As we shall see later, much the same suggestion may be made for "Essence" in regard to the Logic. It is in the second book that the reader finds the categories which express his "common sense" view of the world and which form the structure of the language in which he naturally thinks. Vorstellung, standing between the mere particularity of intuition and the true interiority of an achieved thought, represents the common human standpoint where meaning is always divided between a level of particularity "below" and one of sheer formalism "above". Similarly, the Logic of Essence may perhaps be seen as a human "place" between the yet implicit contradictions of "Being" and what must possibly always remain a still formal thinking of the "divine" standpoint of the Logic of the Notion.[3]

In its parallel to Vorstellung, in its correspondence to our "natural" language, and in its detailed presentation of the inner duality of thought through the double-categories, the Logic of Essence will be the principal source to which we must turn in this chapter to find our theme within the Logic. However, despite any "privileges" as point of entry, the way is no easy one. Hegel himself describes the thought of Essence as the most difficult branch of Logic.[4] For, in following the course of the dual categories, the

---

[3] Hegel, in his introductory division of the Logic, refers to the Logic of Essence as a "Sphäre der Vermittlung" between Being and the Notion: WL, I, p. 44.
[4] Enc. § 114.

thinker must adopt, not only the standpoint of each of the opposed moments, but also that of the true totality which expresses itself in both. This it
is which traces the development of Essence from the abstract opposition of
the coupled moments in the early phases toward the most concrete category
of "actuality", where each is fully expressed in its opposed member. So far as
this stage is reached, the thinker may make the transition to the Logic of the
Notion, and he will then realize that "the Idea is the dialectic which makes
understanding understand its finite nature."[5]

2. THE PLACE OF ESSENCE

It is one of the more evident signs of the finiteness of our thinking that
the intensive and the extensive treatment of any subject fall apart: it is only in
an achieved philosophical thinking that the one could be expected to develop
without being at the expense of the other.[6] To provide some of the advantages
of an extensive view of the Logic, the characteristics of thought at the level of
Essence will first be approached from a consideration of the place that the
Logic of Essence holds in the whole work (pages 71-91 following). Then a
somewhat more intensive treatment will be made of the opening chapter of
Essence, in which Hegel tries himself to summarize the nature of thinking at
this level (pages 91-116).

a. The Two Principles of Division in the Logic

The Logic, as we have seen, is divided by Hegel into three books (Bücher),
those of "Sein", "Wesen", and "Begriff" (cf. appendix of categories). He
also divides it into two volumes (Bände): the first, comprising the first two
books, is entitled the Objective Logic; the second, which is thus identical
with the third book, is called the Subjective Logic.[7]

The Three "Books"

Hegel's divisions are not always so clear to the reader as they presumably
were to the author. The second manner of dividing the Logic has been
variously explained. The first manner is, however, clear and fundamental. It
may be seen as a re-thinking of Kant's triple division in his *Kritik der reinen
Vernunft*. The categories proper to sense intuition, which Kant placed in the
Transcendental Aesthetic, viewed now "in themselves" and no longer as
forms of experience, become the categories of Being.[8] Similarly, the thought

[5] § 214.
[6] Cf. WL, II, p. 502.
[7] This latter division does not appear in the Encyclopaedia version.
[8] The comparison, particularly here, cannot of course descend to particulars: space and
time are not categories of the Logic.

of the Understanding (Verstand), which Kant treated in his *Analytic*, becomes for Hegel the Logic of Essence, and the re-appraisal of Kant's critique of Reason (Vernunft) in the *Transcendental Dialectic* becomes the basis for the achievement of the Logic in the Notion.

Indeed, it is through an assessment of Kant's doctrine of the transcendental unity of apperception that Hegel explains his "notion of the Notion" at the beginning of the third section of the Logic,[9] and comments on the relation of the three sections. Whereas for Kant, notions have validity only in relation to a manifold given by intuition, metaphysics demands that the reality of the Notion should finally be derived from the Notion itself.[10] Yet, Hegel states, it is vital to distinguish between the thinking of the Notion as it manifests itself in different sciences.[11] In Logic, the Notion is the culmination of a progress through Being and Essence; in Psychology, the progress is through Intuition and Vorstellung; in Phenomenology, through the various stages of Consciousness. The conclusion intended is that Kant remained, in his Transcendental Logic, at the level of a psychology. But so far as the Notion, that pure thinking which derives its meaning finally from within, may be seen as the culmination of various paths, the difference between the paths becomes perhaps less radical than it might otherwise seem. That is, the landmarks of that course through intuition and Vostellung to thought, which we followed in the preceding chapter may no less be expected on the path through Being and Essence to the Notion. The experience of consciousness has now become the experience of thought. Yet that fundamental "otherness' of thought in its quest for its meaning will not have been conjured away. Rather will it now appear in a more "original" form, showing itself as "das innere einfache Gerüste" of the stages of Subjective Spirit.[12]

Objective and Subjective Logic

Though the above triple division is the one on which attention is always fixed in studies of Hegel, it is not the original manner in which Hegel divided his Logic. That which he in fact gives first, and from which he derives the threefold ordering, is the division into Objective and Subjective Logic.[13] The two principles of division reflect, it is suggested, not merely arbitrary variations in classification, but a genuine fluctuation in Hegel's attitude toward his Logic.

---

[9] WL, II, pp. 220ff.
[10] p. 225.
[11] p. 223.
[12] WL, II, p. 224.
[13] I, pp. 41-7.

The Objective Logic seems to be so termed because it traces, at the level of the Logic, the path of the "Phenomenology" from a thinking that is "merely" objective ("about" experience) to a thought that is "truly" objective, in the sense that it is finally constitutive of experience. To say that one is now at the level of the Logic is, Hegel affirms, to know that the opposition of *consciousness* between "ein Subjektives" (Denken, Begriff) and "ein Objektives" (Sein, Realität) is overcome:[14] the thinker does not revert from this "element"[15] of logical thought to that of the oppositions of consciousness. Yet his thought is the self-criticism of those categories of thinking which make possible the element of consciousness. That is, within the element of pure thought itself, he must pass through all the forms of "externality" which are at the origin of the multiple oppositions of subject to object that appear in space and time.

We may say, then, that for Hegel, whereas "Phenomenology" is the self-criticism of the individual consciousness, "Objective Logic" is the self-criticism of the metaphysics that reflects the attitudes of consciousness. It is Hegel's criticism and reconstruction of the metaphysics of his predecessors: in a sense, his "history of philosophy". As he puts it himself, "Objective Logic takes the place of the former metaphysics, which was but a scientific construction of (über) the world, built of thoughts alone."[16] And, he adds, in so far as this metaphysics is an ontology, a study of "Ens" in general, Objective Logic must treat of "Sein" and "Wesen".

When he discusses the transition to the Notion, Hegel states that the Objective Logic constitutes "the genetic exposition of the Notion".[17] In its function as a "critique", it traces the growth of the true self-possession of thought as a gradual overcoming of a medium foreign to it. The same process can, however, be viewed, no longer as a critical reconstruction of former metaphysics but as a pure self-development, "on its own terms". This, as "the free, independent, self-determining subjective",[18] is called the Subjective Logic. The two logics thus present alternative views of what is basically the same. Or, as Hegel expresses it, the transition from one to the other reveals two "standpoints" or "sides" of the Notion.[19] From the first (Objective Logic), the Notion "proves" itself to be the "unconditioned ground" of Being and Essence (to which, he adds, belong – in another element – feeling, intuition, and Vorstellung). The second side (Subjective Logic) "shows how the Notion forms in and out of itself that reality which has vanished into it."

[14] WL, I, p. 43.
[15] Cf. pp. 74-5 below for comments on the term "element".
[16] WL, I, p. 46.
[17] WL, II, p. 213.
[18] I, p. 47.
[19] II, pp. 229-30.

In the first, the Notion is "ground" as term of the process; in the second, it is ground as origin. If one is to take Hegel's concept of the circularity of philosophy seriously (where the beginning must make itself result, but the result must equally make itself beginning), one would then have to say that each is a partial view of the whole.

In the following chapter, the question will be raised whether such a division into two "complementary" views receives any justification in Hegel's early ideas of a philosophical system. Even if some basis be found there, however, it must be admitted that Hegel's ideal of an achieved triple division soon predominated. The Objective Logic was split into its two parts, Being and Essence, and the Subjective Logic was presented as their "synthesis". With the publication of an abbreviated form of the Logic in the Encyclopaedia, all mention of Objective and Subjective Logic fell out. In this, Hegel's triadic formalism may have gained its most telling victory.

Externality within the Logic

If the considerations that are to follow in this chapter are to be given a provisional focus, this may be expressed as a question of the nature of that "externality" through which logical thought passes while yet remaining "within its element". Hegel frequently speaks of the "element", or "sphere", or "medium" in which a certain level of thought or experience comes to be.[20] The metaphor is expressive. Each living being has its proper element (air, water, habitat), in which it can live and from which it draws its sustenance. Each man has a certain atmosphere, in which he can truly feel at home and be, as one says, "in his element". One's profoundest knowledge of a person may come, not from a study of his particular actions, but from an understanding of the "element" which enables him to be what he is.

So, too, the advance of Hegel's dialectic may always be treated as a growth in understanding of the element in which particular oppositions and identities subsist. As we have seen, Hegel introduces the element proper to the Logic by contrasting it with the element of consciousness. The latter is a medium in which it is naturally assumed that the material of knowledge is a finished world apart from thinking, and that thinking comes empty to that world from outside.[21] The element of thought, however, is a "unity" which overcomes this form of externality: logical thought is not "thought about" but the self-determination of the content of thought, so that the Notion is

---

[20] E.g., cf. Phän., pp. 24-5, 33, 556, 562; WL, I, p. 53; Enc. § 14.
[21] WL, I, p. 24.

"the thing in itself as thought and thought as the thing in itself."[22] Thought no longer catches at things through examples and comparisons, but "comprehends them in and for themselves. . . raises to awareness what is immanent in them."[23]

Nevertheless, "within" the element of thought, and without ever reverting to the attitudes of consciousness, the Objective Logic (and particularly the section of Essence) passes through its own "externality"; indeed, Hegel describes Subjective Logic, in contrast to Objective, as that whose determinations are "no longer external".[24] Hegel is, nevertheless, nowhere very clear about the relation between the element of thought, the externality which remains within it, and the externality which reverts beyond it. However, the general problem with which this study is concerned – that of the paradox of a philosophical though which is the whole of reality (*includes* its other) and is yet only a part of reality (includes its *other*) – must be intimately connected with the question of an element of thought which has an "externality" within its own "interiority". The rest of this chapter will be concerned largely with stating this problem in terms of the Logic of Essence.

In conclusion of these introductory remarks, it may be noted that all attempts to "state" the problem so far have been carried by metaphors steeped in a space and time that are supposedly excluded from the "element of thought". Hegel's effort, so far as it is genuine, must thus be to penetrate the blunt spatiality of language (without renouncing it for an escape into the ineffable) towards an originality of thought that illuminates and explains the very obtuseness of the instrument.[25]

b. The Logic of Being

It has been suggested above[26] that, at least in some respects, Essence (Wesen) is a privileged point of entry to Hegel's Logic. For it is there that common sense finds the categories that constitute its thought and form its language. Yet Hegel "derives" Essence from Being (Sein),[27] so that this section must indicate the most general character of the Logic of Being, before we can make the "transition" to Essence in the following section.

[22] pp. 30-31.
[23] II, p. 491.
[24] WL, I, p. 47.
[25] The denial of any simple relation of "instrumentality" is, of course, fundamental to Hegel's thought. Yet the reappearance of externality within the element of thought might provisionally be seen as the repeated reappearance of a more subtle instrumentality "within" a basic grasp of the identiy of thinking and its expression.
[26] p. 70.
[27] Cf. pp. 69-70 above for preliminary comments on these terms.

Dialectic without Relations

The opening words of the Logic of Being indicate the difficulty of truly entering into its movement: "Das Sein ist das unbestimmte Unmittelbare; es ist frei von der Bestimmtheit gegen das Wesen, so wie noch von jeder, die es innerhalb seiner selbst erhalten kann."[28] Hence, he can not enter who comes with his common-sense world of thought and with an uncritical adherence to a language formed in that world. For this is a language of the categories of Essence: of relations, of things having properties, of causes producing effects. But the realm of Being is not merely "free" from such thought-forms; it is free from "determination against them". That is, at the beginning of the Logic, Hegel implies, the reader should not even be "aware" of the lack of these categories.

The "Phenomenology of Spirit" also begins with indeterminate immediacy, with immediate knowledge that is no less knowledge of the immediate.[29] But it is immediacy already set on the path of the forms of consciousness; and the reader is held for only two pages to the attempt of experiencing "pure this", before he finds himself in the more familiar surroundings of space and time and relations. The immediacy with which the Logic begins, however, has already been set on the path of pure thought. "Nur der Entschluss, den man auch für eine Willkür ansehen kann, nämlich dass man das *Denken als solches* betrachten wolle, ist vorhanden."[30] The attempt is a more rigorous one. It is to seek the ground of the experience of the immediacy of consciousness; to comprehend that in pure thought which makes possible the beginning of the Phenomenology and its initial development. It is the effort to understand the self-developing "innerliches Anschauen" which is the origin of the immediacy of a "sinnliche Anschauung oder Vorstellung" and of that designation (Monstrieren) in which meaning is sought.[31]

It may well be asked, if one does enter into the pure inwardness of this "essence-less" thought-intuition, how any development of the categories of Being is to arise. Hegel explicitly forbids the reader to consider as related (for relations belong to Essence) the categories which are in fact "expressed" as antithetical.[32] How, then, can any dialectical movement develop at this level; that is, without a transition to Essence?

---

[28] WL, I, p. 66.
[29] Phän., p. 79.
[30] WL, I, p. 54.
[31] II, p. 488.
[32] Cf. WL, I, p. 90. Hegel also corrects the language in which he excusably implies relations at levels prior to their appearance. For example, he points out that his speaking of "Etwas" as having qualities is inexact, for "having" is proper to Essence and not to Being: Enc. § 125.

The basis of Hegel's answer seems to be that the very indeterminacy of each category reveals itself as a certain determination: "eben die Unbestimmtheit ist das, was die Bestimmtheit desselben ausmacht."[33] Or again: "Dem Sein überhaupt tritt aber das bestimmte Sein als solches gegenüber, damit aber macht seine Unbestimmtheit selbst seine Qualität aus."[34]

It will, however, be suggested later that Hegel does in fact concede that each development "within" Being is in fact already a transition to Essence. Hence there is no reason here to try further to comprehend – much less to justify – this "primordial" dialectic. We shall, instead, try to understand something of this thought "prior" to Essence by its parallel to the "psychological" forms of thought examined in the previous chapter.

Intuition and Indifference

It has been seen that Hegel himself suggests a certain parallel between the series Being-Essence-Notion and the series Intuition-Vorstellung-Thought.[35] Accordingly, intuition is the stage of Subjective Spirit which corresponds to the Logic of Being.

In the preceding chapter, Vorstellung was characterized as the level of thinking at which the contradiction between mere formalism and mere particularity was at its most explicit. Intuition, though revealing its advance on the immediacy of sense with the first signs of this dilemma, had not yet developed to explicit opposition. It is the stage of thought in a still inadequate differentiation of its conflicting moments.

Lack of necessary differentiation is termed "indifference" by Hegel. And it is this character, above all, which Hegel assigns as typical of thought at the level of Being. "Das Sein ist die abstrakte Gleichgültigkeit".[36] This term, together with its equivalent "Indifferenz", is usually employed by Hegel to designate the isolation of any moment from that whole of which it is a part and in which it realizes its true "Differenz", or determination in relation to the other moments, The word "Indifferenz" is, however, also used by Hegel in Schelling's sense, to indicate the point of synthesis which reconciles opposing moments.[37]

It is clearly in the first, or pejorative, sense that Hegel speaks of the indifference of the Logic of Being. In comparison with Essence and the Notion, its dialectic is a mere "going-over" of one moment into what may be seen

---

[33] WL, I, p. 85.
[34] p. 66.
[35] WL, II, p. 223; Cf. p. 72 above.
[36] WL, I, p. 387.
[37] Cf. p. 134 below.

from a higher level as its opposite, but which at the level of Being must be "merely other". For the very experience of otherness and opposition demands a further "dimension" of thought, in which the original may be conserved as well as lost in its transition; but this dimension belongs to Essence.

Hegel distinguishes clearly between the transitions proper to Being, Essence, and the Notion. The mere "passing-over" of Being is referred to as "Übergehen" (in distinction to "Reflexion" for Essence, and "Entwicklung" for the Notion). It is a term which Hegel uses also outside the Logic where the dialectic implies an instability and lack of independence of its moments, a mere disappearance of one and appearance of another.[38]

Where the transition of thought is a mere "Übergehen", development is no more than interchangeability. Even where thought claims to have reached the "infinite", this turns out to be but the "finite". It is only in a *realization* of its indifference, of the impossibility of progress at that level, that a concrete totality may appear as a synthesis in which the abstract totality and its indifferent opposite are but moments. Yet this, it would seem, is already an advance from "Übergehen" to "Reflexion".

The Totality of Being

That there is more than sheer indifference at the level of Being is implied by the fact that Hegel does present this stage of the Logic as an ordered whole. Yet the self-realization of this totality is at its minimum. As neither true identity nor true opposition can be realized between any two categories at this level, no synthesis can fulfil its function as a totality. The ordering of indifferent moments must come from outside. In particular, the entire first book of the Logic can achieve its form as an ordered whole only by means of "construction" from outside it. Here especially, divisions have a merely provisional character and arbitrariness is at its greatest. Nor is it surprising that it is in the Logic of Being that Hegel makes his clearest statement of the fact that the Logic, no less than the Phenomenology, has a "für uns" as well as a "für sich".[39]

If it is, then, only from the level of Essence (with its categories of relation, whole and part, etc.) that the Logic of Being may rightly be seen as an ordered whole, it may perhaps be more just to regard each dialectical movement of Being as a place at which the transition may be made directly to the categories of Essence.[40] Such is at least a possible interpretation of Hegel's

---

[38] E.g., in regard to the early transitions of Nature: "Nur das Übergehen, Verschwinden ist die Realität und Substanz dieser Elemente" (JR, II, p. 68).

[39] WL, I, pp. 96-7.

[40] Where Hegel tries to show that the determinations of Being arise from its indeterminacy, he cites Parmenides and Spinoza; that is, he gives as examples the passage from

statement that "das Sein ist zuerst gegen Anderes überhaupt bestimmt. . . Es teilt sich gegen das Wesen ab, indem es weiterhin in einer Entwicklung seine Totalität nur als eine Sphäre des Begriffs erweist und ihr als Moment eine andere Sphäre gegenüberstellt."[41]

It would also help to explain why, in the first paragraph of the Logic of Being in the Encyclopaedia, Hegel stresses that the dialectic in Being is "ein Insichgehen des Seins, ein Vertiefen desselben in sich selbst", which abolishes the immediacy and brings out the totality of Being.[42] The dialectic of Being would then seem to be, from the beginning, a movement into a dimension (Vertiefen) other than that of Being itself. And this movement merely reaches the climax of its exposition when the indifference of Being is seen finally to be "Gleichgültigkeit gegen ihre eigene Gleichgültigkeit".[43] That is, the second dimension of experience is now manifested in what Hegel calls a "substratum", in relation to which further development at the level of Being is indifferent; for Being stands to its essence as a totality.

c. Transition to Essence

If the above attitude to the relation between Being and Essence be adopted, then the objection will be somewhat lessened, that Hegel – in making the "transition to Essence" – suddenly claims to "produce" what had been there all the time.[44] The categories of essence have certainly been there all the time, but a brief attempt to see and express thought without them does at least set them and their peculiarities in sharp relief when they are explicitly admitted to the course of the Logic. In this effort to "reflect" upon them, the thinker finds that the "self-evidence" of these categories and of the language in which he feels at home progressively vanishes.

Essence and Common Sense

Hegel, as has been mentioned, regarded Essence as the most difficult section of his Logic.[45] It is the one in which the thinker is most painfully conscious of the multiplicity of his standpoint and of the danger of simply neglecting part of its complexity to achieve a purely abstract reconciliation. For, if we

indeterminacy to the distinctions between opinion and truth, attributes and modes. Yet his seems to be already a passage to dual categories of Essence. (WL, I, p. 84).

[41] WL, I, p. 64.

[42] Enc. § 84.

[43] WL, I, p. 397.

[44] "Hegel has been led to [this new concept of Essence] by inadequacies in the various categories of Quality, Quantity and Measure, and the passage to it represents a leap of thought which Hegel's dialectical bridging fails to render mechanical and inevitable." (J. N. Findlay, *Hegel, a Re-Examination*, pp. 181-2).

[45] Enc. § 114.

have been justified in drawing a parallel between the stages of the Logic and those of Subjective Spirit,[46] then Essence will correspond to Vorstellung, and the dilemma of a thought split into mere particularity and formality must be retraced in the sharpened oppositions of the Logic.

What will here be sought especially is some further expression, within this "element", for that which appeared in the Philosophy of Spirit as the paradox of thought and language. Hegel claimed, in the introduction to his Logic, that no more is presupposed than the decision to enter into the nature of thought itself.[47] That he realized, however, what vast presuppositions are contained in this very decision is clear from his statements in the same introduction on the relation of Logic and Phenomenology: the full course of the latter is presupposed. Above all, the ability of thought to "enter into" itself implies a oneness with its own language which is by no means an unqualified assumption for those who have followed the course of Subjective Spirit.

The decision of thought to enter into itself is repeated at the opening of the second book of the Logic, with the statement that "das Wissen will das Wahre erkennen, was das Sein an und für sich ist."[48] Being, we may say, is the realm proper to the diplomatic uses of language: a different formula may satisfy consciences, but no true change is introduced in meaning. The resolution is now made, however, to penetrate this indifference and find what Being is in and for itself. Thought makes this decision, "mit der Voraussetzung, dass *hinter* diesem Sein noch etwas anderes ist als das Sein selbst, dass dieser Hintergrund die Wahrheit des Seins ausmacht." This grasp of a "beyond" within the self-presence of thought must introduce us to Hegel's complicated, but important, notion of "reflection" as the movement proper to Essence.

Transition as Reflection

We have seen that Hegel characterized dialectical transition at the level of Being as a mere "Übergehen in Anderes".[49] The true notion of an "other" could, however, never be attained at that level; for it was a thinking without any depth of retention in its "going-over", a form more akin to substitution than to genuine movement. With neither explicit contradiction nor identity possible, the impression was that of "merely roving from one determination to another."[50]

---

[46] Cf. p. 72 above.
[47] WL, I, p. 54.
[48] II, p. 3.
[49] Enc. § 84.
[50] § 112 Zusatz.

Essence, however, is "the negation of the sphere of Being as such".[51] It turns from the mere "externality" or "surface" of Being to that which is "within" or "behind" it. This constitutes an immanent self-mediation,[52] a return to itself from a true otherness.[53] Its determinations have independence only in their unity with each other.[54] And the term Hegel chooses to suggest this movement in "Reflexion".

The metaphor comes from his earliest theological meditations and he read into its many possible meanings a great deal of the subtlety of his thought. We shall try here to indicate its meaning sufficiently to portray the general movement of Essence, and shall return in the second part of the chapter to a somewhat closer analysis of Hegel's exposition of the types of reflection. For the notion is fundamental to his grasp of the complex standpoint of human thinking and to his attempt to express a concrete totality. In the second part of this study, it will be asked what this implies in regard to the transitions of the system, so far as their moment of "reflection" is, in its "Aufhebung", not merely superseded but conserved.

The term "reflection" is commonly used, Hegel points out, when a ray of light strikes a mirror and is thrown back from it.[55] There are two aspects of this phenomenon: the immediate fact and its derived phase. Similarly, the term is frequently used in regard to thinking when, uncontented with an immediate fact, we reflect upon it and understand it as mediated, as derived from something more ultimate (cause, essence, etc.). Thus, to the common understanding, at whose level of thought our language has been formed, reflection implies two movements, an objective and a subjective, which common sense holds to be independent. Something which exists in itself causes manifestations through which a thinker may happen upon it: this is thus a movement, "in reality", from immediacy to the mediation of reflection. Secondly, and independently, these manifestations are the cause in a thinker of a subjective thought which moves from them to the thing as their essence: this is then likewise a movement from immediacy to the mediation of reflection, but it is of an opposite direction and is "in thought".[56]

It was the whole task of the Phenomenology to transcend this level of thinking. But as it is Hegel's express intent to reconstruct in the Logic of Essence "the common-sense thinking of metaphysics and the sciences in

[51] WL, II, pp. 7-8.
[52] Enc. § 112.
[53] WL, II, p. 4.
[54] p. 5.
[55] Enc. § 112 Zusatz.
[56] "Der Verstand hält *seine* Reflexion. . . für eine äusserliche Reflexion": Enc. § 214.

general",[57] it reappears there, though "in the element of thought".

Hence Hegel is at pains, at the beginning of this treatment of Essence in both versions of the Logic, to affirm that the true sense of reflection is not to be held to "external reflection". Reflection is indeed a passage from an immediate to a mediate, but not as a mere activity of knowledge external to Being, an activity that is consequently a movement from a determinate reality to an indeterminate essence that is a mere product of thought.[58] This negative form of abstraction falls outside Essence and leaves it as a result apart from its premises,[59] as an immediate scarcely different from the stage it claims to transcend. It is, too, a reflection that is subjective in the sense of private and arbitrary, and it is in such abstract thinking that the false originality of "eigene Reflexionen und Einfälle" finds itself at home.[60]

The transcendence of this purely external form of reflection demands, however, a more subtle interpretation of the metaphor of reflected light. This has been viewed so far only in the sense of Plato's cave, where the reality is shadowed or reflected into an observer distinct from both reality and reflection; and the impression has perhaps been left that the reality would better be seen "in itself" apart from its reflections. But Hegel will understand it in a sense where these material relations fall short: "Das Wesen ist das Sein als Scheinen in sich selbst."[61] It is not a movement external to Being but the movement of Being itself into a dimension where it is one with itself in its separation from itself and reflection into itself from that separation; every attempt to turn from the cave and see reality "in itself" would be to lose the greater reality of original-in-reflection and revert to the level of Being.

And here for the first time in the Logic appears the related metaphor of "Erinnerung",[62] with all the associations of complex standpoint that we tried to follow in the last chapter. "Inner reflection", then, is not simply a reality passing into manifestation; nor is it simply a manifestation which, in its immediacy, leads to and expresses an essence. It is that entry of Being into itself which divides itself into both movements or standpoints and yet retains its oneness in this division. And only when (and if) this totality can be thought without falling back into the "comparison" of external reflection, can relapse to the level of Being be avoided and the initial determination be satisfied of knowing what Being is in and for itself.[63]

---

[57] Enc. § 114.
[58] WL, II, pp. 3-4.
[59] Enc. § 112.
[60] WL, I, p. 20.
[61] Enc. § 112; WL, II, p. 12.
[62] WL, II, p. 3.
[63] Cf. Phän., p. 178: "Sein und Selbstbewusstsein sind dasselbe, nicht in der Verglei-

Double Sense of Reflection

The double sense of reflection (external and inner), along with a similar duplicity in the terms "Bestimmung" and "für sich", is to be found as early as the fragments on which Hegel's writings on "The Positivity of the Christian Religion" and "The Spirit of Christianity" were based. In his early opposition to positivity (immediacy) in religious thought, he used the term reflection primarily in the external sense; in his condemnation, for example, of the strife over the properties of God as coming from use of the "Reflexionsbegriffe von Verschiedenheit".[64]

However, as his thought matured, the second sense of reflection appeared increasingly alongside, or rather as a profounder thinking of, the first. Thus of Abraham he wrote that "Trennung von seinem Vaterland trieb ihn zur Reflexion, aber nicht zur Reflexion in sich selbst."[65] That is, the reflection to which Abraham was driven was that which is a *mere* separation from a life of simple union with nature (immediacy, "an sich"), to a life of isolation and rejection, of theoretical knowledge *about* an opposed reality, where reflection supplies merely a mirror-image separated from its reality. It is the state of "für sich" in the pejorative sense, as isolated from – and opposed to – the concrete synthesis of the "an und für sich". But the reflection which remains yet possible is a return of the "an sich" from its alienation, to that concrete unity for which Hegel sometimes uses "für sich" in its good sense, as a reflection of the thing into itself to a new depth of experience in a living unity with the world. The subject has left the stage of shallow immediacy, has passed into and retained the dimension of experience which Abraham discovered; but it has no less returned to itself in this dimension, such that its essence and its manifestation have risen to adequate reflection, each in the other, thereby retaining the depth of difference and achieving the fulfilment of identity. No longer is it determined in its relation to an alien other: it determines itself in and through its otherness, "es bestimmt sich", be-voices or utters itself.

By the time of his move to Jena, Hegel was explicit about the two senses of the term reflection. The "good" reflection is no subjective thought or "proof" but is an identity of this subjective movement with the self-realization of the object itself.[66] Opposed to this, "die schlechte Reflexion ist die Furcht, sich in die Sache zu vertiefen, immer über sie hinaus und in sich zurückzukehren."[67]

chung, sondern an und für sich."

[64] Nohl, p. 227; cf. also Hegel's condemnation of Jacobi's "subjektive Reflexionsphilosophie" in *Glauben und Wissen*.
[65] Nohl, p. 370.
[66] E.g., cf. JL, p. 187.
[67] Dokumente, p. 366.

The "good" reflection is thus neither merely external nor merely internal: it is a synthesis that retains the value of each. And this follows necessarily from the purpose of the Logic of Essence, which is inseparably (a) a re-thinking of, and hence truth *to*, the exterior thinking of Verstand, and (b) its criticism and reconstruction, and thus the transcending truth *of* it.

Language and the Double Categories of Essence

It is this double movement of reflection – from a mere outer to an inner, and from a mere inner to an outer – which accounts for the peculiarity of the dialectic of Essence, in relation to that of the Logic of Being and the Logic of the Notion. Whereas in the first and third book of the Logic, the moments of each triad are simple, in the second book each moment is split into a dual category. For example, the triad Hegel calls "essential relation" has as its thesis, "whole and parts"; as its antithesis, "force and manifestation"; as its synthesis, "outer and inner".

For here, in the explicit self-criticism of thought, the duality which we traced in the last chapter between thought and sense has now become apparent "within" thought itself, as an "externality within its element". The effort of thought to reflect into itself shows that each stage of thought is itself a duality of inner and outer, universal and particular, essential and unessential. Its meaning comes from each of the two "aspects", as opposed to the other, yet is always more than this opposition.

The origin of this duality is apparent even at the earliest stages of the Logic of Being, in so far as these carry already the germs of a transition to Essence. Hegel was perfectly aware that, on the one hand, since Being is immediate, it is "ein nur gemeintes, und man kann von ihm nicht sagen, was es ist;"[68] and that, on the other hand, the transition within Being, in which its very indeterminacy becomes its determinateness, is not free from an expression which transcends it.[69] The most rudimentary transition, from Being to Nothing, is an ineffable outside thought unless it is in some manner expressed; and however it be expressed, the expression transcends the level of Being.[70] But this is no less true at any other stage of the Logic. Indeed, the fact that the expression of the "content" of thought is not at the same level as the content itself may be seen as the origin of what Kroner calls "der

---

[68] WL, II, p. 241.

[69] pp. 249-50.

[70] E.g., cf. Hyppolite, *Genèse*, p. 568: "Comment dire d'ailleurs de cet être – purement positif – qu'il est en soi, ce qui introduit une sorte de rapport avec soi-même, de recul sur soi, qui relève de la catégorie de l'essence (identité, différence etc.) et qui ne s'applique pas à l'immédiateté affirmée de ce premier moment?"

phänomenologische Anteil des dialektischen Fortschreitens" in the Logic;[71] to this question we must return in the second part of this study.

Thus, the Logic of Being, so far as not yet transcended in Essence, is a "limiting case" in which thought and its expression are not as yet opposed. Thought makes its "Übergang" without opposing itself to itself as a mere thought to its expression. But as soon as the transition to Essence is admitted, this "interior externality" appears; language is shown, no longer as a mere sense-factor "outside" thought, but as an externality at the heart of thought.

As thought develops into, and through, its dual categories, a further paradox becomes apparent. Not only is each moment of thought split into "essential" and "unessential", but the meaning of these terms alternates at each stage: what was "essential" becomes "unessential" and vice-versa. It is, one may say, the survival of "indifference" at the level of Essence. Hegel's explanation varies at each stage, but the general movement may be suggested by the initial appearance of an expression at variance with its thought. As we have seen, as soon as any part of the Logic of Being is expressed, the expression says more than that which was immediately "gemeint". Yet one's expression is always less than one's true meaning, for the very opposition which it engenders falls short of the unity that must belong to one's full meaning.

That is, even though it is one of Hegel's fundamental tenets that thought is only in its expression, that it can never retreat into an ineffable simply beyond its language, nevertheless he finds an alternating duality at the heart of this identity. On the one hand, the expression of thought always says "more" than the "mere" thought in its particularity; here expression is the formal, essential moment, in relation to which thought is unessential, yet without which expression would be nothing. On the other hand, thought is always "more" than its expression; here the latter stands in the relation of unessential, with all the particularity of language, to an essential which is yet "hidden" and would be nothing without its manifestation.

In this fashion, the Logic of Essence is a complicated, but profoundly experienced, reconstruction of that "otherness" which the thinker finds at the heart of his thought, however much he try to purify it. It may be seen as the parallel, in the Logic, to the movement traced in the last chapter, in which every effort to unify the mere "designation" and mere "signification" of Vorstellung in a true concrete turned out to be but another external synthesis, revealing a renewed duality. There, the movement of "Erinnerung" was found to be no less a return to externality from a false interiority than an

[71] *Von Kant bis Hegel*, II, p. 425; cf. p. 37 above.

attempt to pass from an outer space and time to the true spatio-temporality of the subject. Here, the movement of "Reflexion" is also a complex synthesis, of which external and internal reflection are but moments: thought, even within its own element, must pass into a state of "isolation and rejection", to a multiplicity of standpoints, in the act by which it returns to itself.

That thought does finally and adequately return to itself, that these dualities are all "aufgehoben", is evidently Hegel's claim. To try to interpret the transitions of the system merely in terms of the model of reflection would clearly be false. Yet the traditional interpretation, in its emphasis on Hegel's final unity, tends to reduce the complex notion of "transition" to a simple harmony that is not easily distinguished from the "Übergehen" proper to the first book of the Logic. It will be for the second part of this study to suggest some of the depths which may lie in Hegel's thought of a philosophical system if his claim be taken seriously that "Aufhebung" preserves as well as annihilates: that is, if the deep experience of a multiplicity of standpoints at the heart of thought itself be not simply suppressed in the triumph of a final unity.

d. Development to Actuality

The last section tried to understand the character of the Logic of Essence which distinguishes it from the rest of the Logic: that reversing duality of essence and manifestation, inner and outer, formalism and particularity, in which the true unity of philosophical meaning comes to itself.[72] The development of thought is no longer a simple "passing-over" from one determination to another. Each of the "definitions" in which thought grasps itself is a pair of correlatives, neither of which is "schlechthin in sich reflektiert."[73]

At this level of thinking, one may, Hegel claims, pass once more through all the terms of the Logic of Being, seeing each now appear in a "reflected form",[74] as both self-identical and self-differing. No such attempt is, in fact, made to relate each of the categories of Essence to a "corresponding" category of Being. It might indeed seem a happier attitude to regard any category of Being as constituting an immediate point of access to the full development of the categories of Essence: each would manifest itself as

---

[72] There are, as Hegel points out, no such things as philosophical *opinions*. It is precisely that "inner moment" of final meaning in opinions which is philosophy – or which it is the task of philosophy to bring to itself from the many forms of its self-alienation. Cf. Gesch. Phil, XVII, p. 40.

[73] Enc. § 112.

[74] § 114.

essential and unessential, thing and properties, matter and form, whole and parts, inner and outer, possibility and actuality.

It would, however, go considerably beyond our purposes to consider the categories of Essence in detail. This section will merely suggest what bearing their development has on two topics fundamental to any treatment of the system: Hegel's notion of totality, and the question of the verification of thought-categories in the world of space and time.

The Growth of a Totality

Hegel's philosophy is rightly seen, in relation to contemporary concerns, as a philosophy of totality. Yet his own concept of totality differs according to the place in the system "from" which it is thought.

We have already seen that, in terms of the Logic, the level of Being can scarcely form any basis for thought of a totality. It is first in the Logic of Essence that the conditions are present for an ordered whole. Here we are no longer in the sphere of relationless categories. Each is an explicit contradiction between two moments, which form and divide a totality into A and not-A. In proportion as the basis of contradiction, the category "A not-A", is trivial and abstract, so is the totality which it reveals and which makes it possible.[75] As the dialectic of Essence proceeds to increasingly concrete categories, therefore, so is depth and experience added to this first grasp of the whole.

The progress of the coupled categories from abstract to concrete passes through stages that Hegel terms "Schein, Erscheinung, Wirklichkeit (Offenbarung)".[76] At the lowest level, reflection is at its most external and the coupled category is scarcely more determinate than Being. The essential moment in it is the mere beyond of all determinate predicates, the "caput mortuum" of abstraction.[77] It would, however, be a misinterpretation of Hegel's thought to suppose that because the essential is at its greatest abstraction, the unessential must be most concrete, and that growth in the concreteness of the former corresponds to diminution in that of the latter. The development toward actuality is a mutual growth of the opposed moments, where each has no being apart from the other; each is only in its reflection in the other. The clearest example is the mutual development of thought and

[75] Or we may say that the contradiction of moments is achieved only at the expense of limiting the universality or "field of discourse". Mure offers an interesting approach to this question in his discussion of the possibility of a dialectic whose opposed phases achieve universality, contradiction, and contrariety. (*Study*, pp. 351-3; *Introduction*, pp. 123-4.)

[76] "Das Wesen scheint zuerst in sich selbst oder ist Reflexion; zweitens erscheint es; drittens offenbart es sich." (WL, II, p. 6).

[77] Enc. § 112.

language. Thought can become more profound only so far as its language is refined, but its language is refined only so far as thought becomes more profound.[78]

Thus, we may distinguish in the progress of Essence a double sense of the totality. The abstract totality is the formal, essential moment, which exists in opposition to the particular and unessential. The concrete totality, however, is the true unity of philosophical meaning which finds itself only in and through this duality. It is the concrete identity of abstract identity and abstract difference. Always present in the dual categories, it becomes increasingly "actual" as the opposed moments progress to fuller expression in each other, until the stage of "Wirklichkeit" is reached, where "the utterance of the actual is the actual itself."[79] The abstract totality has risen to full expression as the concrete totality, and the transition is made from the halting dual movement of Essence to the Logic of the Notion.

Verification and Recognition

In this movement of the dual categories of Essence toward a totality which is no simple abolition of their difference but an "utterance" of each in the other, a parallel may be seen to the movement of Vorstellung that was followed in the last chapter. For thought at the level of Vorstellung was split into a formal totality, devoid of concrete experience, and a mere particularity which complemented rather than fulfilled it. The movement toward the concrete totality of thought was likewise defined by Hegel as an effort at adequate expression, in which the merely signified totality sought "verification" in the particularity of experience; and this was in turn deepened (erinnert) so far as the synthesis was achieved, but reverted to opposition so far as the union remained external.[80]

Thus, the attitude toward "verification" which Hegel presented there, and which is similarly implied in the Logic of Essence, is no mere application of an already established thought to the realm of experience outside it. Both thought and experience, essential and unessential, are changed in the verification.

This is an attitude that must be of importance in any interpretation of the system as such. For the form of the system seems to imply that the logical categories develop to fullness on their own, and then begin to appear through the long range of forms of experience in nature and spirit. Hence it is a common interpretation of Hegel,[81] and one which finds support in some of

[78] A parallel development which does not deny that they are likewise opposed, and that each is both more and less than the other (as explained above, p. 85).

[79] Enc. § 142.

[80] Cf. pp. 59-60 above.

[81] A more sophisticated example will be examined on pp. 121-3 below.

his statements, to suppose that the philosopher fulfils his task in *first* thinking the categories of logical thought and *then* (much in the attitude of an uninvolved spectator) *searching* for them as they are verified in nature, individual experience, and history.[82] So Hegel seems to imply when he states that since the Absolute Idea, the summation of all the categories of the Logic, contains all determinations, "das Geschäft der Philosophie ist, die Idee in ihren verschiedenen Gestaltungen zu erkennen."[83] And he continues, "in diesem suchenden Erkennen ist die Methode gleichfalls als Werkzeug gestellt."[84]

These metaphors of an uninvolved recognition and of philosophy as an instrument, apart from their denial by the whole tone of Hegel's philosophy, are clearly contradicted by the attitude toward "verification" which has been suggested above. Thought is not simply "applied" to experience as a fixed rule. Certainly, he who has made the effort to follow the movement of pure thought in the Logic will realize that it is not first at the end that the question of passage to verifications in experience arises. It comes at every step of the Logic, as thought seeks its development in a language which it forms, yet no less forms as opposed to itself.

The second part of this study must ask if Hegel's system, in any of its expressions, does allow of an interpretation that would take into account the dialectic of formal thought and particular experience, which we have followed in this and the preceding chapter. Interpretation and criticism may here come particularly close. Yet so far as the Logic be an instrument that is applied to experience or a plan that a spectator recognizes in experience, then its totality must remain abstract and but one side of that profounder experience which Hegel described as "das unendliche Urteil, dessen Seiten jede die selbständige Totalität sind, und eben dadurch, dass jede sich dazu vollendet, in die andere eben so sehr übergegangen ist."[85]

e. Transition to the Notion

When Hegel wrote in the Phenomenology that the heart of his notion of philosophy depended on grasping and expressing the ultimate truth, not as substance, but as subject as well,[86] it was Spinoza that he had especially in mind as representing the stage to be transcended. So in the Logic it is the

---

[82] A simplicity that becomes more pronounced where the dialectic of "Geist" has been reinterpreted as a dialectic of "matter".

[83] WL, II, p. 484.

[84] p. 487.

[85] Enc. § 215.

[86] Phän., p. 19.

thought of Spinoza that dominates the stage of "Wirklichkeit", in which the Objective Logic culminates: the stage which Hegel considers his own thought, to be developed anew in the Subjective Logic, must surpass. Spinoza's metaphysics, Hegel holds, represents the final point of reflection that remains external.[87] For all its grandeur, it does no more than take up determinations that are given and predicate them of the Absolute, rather than deriving them from the Absolute with the immanent necessity of thought. Spinoza's totality remains, in the end, merely formal and abstract.

The transcendence of the standpoint of substance, however, demands no radical new departure. It demands simply that substance be realized for what it is in the development of thought. "Die einzige und wahrhafte Widerlegung des Spinozismus. . . ist die *Enthüllung* der Substanz, und diese ist die Genesis des Begriffs."[88] Thus, if Hegel tried to help the understanding of the transition from Being to Essence by posing the spatial metaphor of a new dimension, of a "Substratum" and a "Vertiefung", no new dimension is proposed here for the transition from Essence to the Notion. So far as the true nature of Essence is realized, so far as reflection develops its true sense, the thinker is *ipso facto* in the Logic of the Notion. For the Notion is precisely that totality which appears in the full mutual manifestation of the coupled moments of Essence.[89]

Thus there may be some justification for the suggestion, made at the beginning of this chapter, that the Logic of Essence constitutes a privileged point of entry into the thought of the whole Logic.[90] From that dual thinking which is our thought as we find it, Being appears as a "limiting case" in the one direction, transcended the moment its thought is expressed, yet remaining constantly to reduce the movement of reflection to an external comparison. And the Notion appears as a "limiting case" in the other direction, an ideal that is no mere "Sollen" but is the most intimate presence of thought to itself in its reflection, so far as that reflection is achieved.

Consideration of the movement of thought in the Logic of the Notion will be postponed until the final chapter.[91] For it is in terms of this movement that Hegel discusses the transitions of his system at the close of the Encyclopaedia. It is, indeed, this third book of the Logic which the traditional interpretation of Hegel has taken as its model. And rightly so, since Hegel's philosophy of totality here finds its most characteristic expression. For the dialectical process is no longer the mere succession of "Übergehen", nor the

---

[87] WL, II, pp. 164 ff.
[88] p. 218.
[89] WL, II, p. 218.
[90] Cf. p. 70 above.
[91] Cf. pp. 197-203 below.

dual movement of "Reflexion": it is described as "Entwicklung", a pure development of thought producing itself out of itself and leaving no un-sublated stage behind in its progress.[92]

Whether Hegel consistently presented his system as such a final harmony, apparently devoid of any suggestion of partial philosophical standpoints, must be considered in the second part of this study.

Here it may simply be emphasized that the harmonious self-development of the Logic of the Notion becomes a mere "play" unless the attempt be made to understand it as a true "Aufhebung" of all the seriousness, toil and patience of Essence.[93] "Spirit" is not merely "*der* Begriff"; it is also "*eine* Vorstellung".[94] If thinking remains empirical so far as it understands facts with a logic proper only to a lower level of human thought, no less does it remain empirical so far as a hard-won logic forgets the stages of thinking and experiencing through which it has passed.

Indeed, the difficulty of remembering one's origins in passing from the second to the third book of the Logic may persuade the student that Hegel's original division into an Objective and Subjective Logic was preferable. For there a greater scope would be afforded for viewing the two logics as comple-mentary approaches to the grasp of the whole. The first, in its gradual and painful re-thinking of traditional metaphysics toward an understanding of the true objectivity of thought would always remain unsatisfactory unless complemented by the "view from above" afforded by the Subjective Logic. Yet this, as the effortless self-constitution of the totality, would ne less re-main an abstract, formal whole unless complemented by the multiple stand-point of the Objective Logic.

To stress this suggestion too much is clearly to pass from interpretation to criticism of Hegel. The following chapters will ask, however, what support such an attitude receives in Hegel's early writings and whether, in the con-fident harmony of his mature system, any suspicion remains that the "refuta-tion of Spinoza" is always to be achieved anew.

3. ESSENCE AS REFLECTION INTO ITSELF

The first part of this study is an attempt to find an approach to the paradox of Hegel's system – whereby logical thought is both the whole of philosophy and but a part of it, opposed to its "other" in nature and spirit – by an under-

---

[92] E.g., cf. WL, II, p. 502.
[93] Cf. pp. 13-14 above.
[94] Cf. p. 17 above.

standing of his doctrine of language as the "other" of thought which is yet sublated in thought.

The second chapter sought this doctrine in Hegel's treatment of language as a stage of Vorstellung. This chapter is an attempt to find an expression within Hegel's Logic for the movement that manifests itself in the syntheses of Vorstellung. For reasons which should by now be apparent, the search has been directed primarily to the Logic of Essence.

The first half of this chapter tried, by a general view of the whole Logic, to characterize Essence in terms of its place between the Logic of Being and of the Notion. More particularly, it examined the transition proper to Essence, "Reflexion", as a dual movement with a depth beyond the simple succession of "Übergehen", yet a self-development short of the perfect harmony of "Entwicklung".

In conclusion, it was suggested that, even though the transitions of Hegel's system must finally be presented in terms of "Entwicklung", this must – if justice be done to Hegel's whole thought – preserve the full depth of thought-experience contained in "Reflexion". It will be the purpose of the following chapters to focus attention on these "strata" of Hegel's system; for, if they are ignored, "Entwicklung" tends to slip to the simplicity – if not banality – of "Übergehen".

Meanwhile, it will be for the rest of this chapter to examine the movement of Essence, no longer in contrast to that of Being and of the Notion, but at that point where Hegel explicitly describes it. This is in the opening triad of the Logic of Essence. No commentary is to be attempted, but various pertinent themes will be selected.

The opening triad of Essence bears different names in Hegel's two versions of his definitive Logic (i.e. in the "Wissenschaft der Logik" and in the Encyclopaedia). For it was not merely in his addition of "Anmerkungen" that Hegel recognized the need for supplementing the internal development of his Logic with illustrations drawn from other "elements" of thought and experience. The need for, and impossibility of, adequate illustration showed itself in his choice of words and particularly in his selection of titles for the categories. His was an intense effort to draw thought from the shades of common meaning in words, but it remained inevitable that the words chosen would suggest a merely objective or merely subjective interpretation of his categories rather than the complex process of thought they demand. The choice of titles was always to a large extent arbitrary, and it is understandable that notable differences should occur between the two versions. These are, however, most evident in the opening triad of the Logic of Essence. Hence the appendix shows both versions.

The Logic of Essence is divided into three sections. In both versions, the second is called "appearance" (Erscheinung). It is Essence "als heraustretend in das Dasein", and contains the majority of the dual categories. The third section is called "actuality" (Wirklichkeit). Though it has a considerable development of its own, it marks the conclusion of the process of Essence, in which the dual categories have grown to adequate "utterance" in each other.[95]

The first section is, in each version, Hegel's own reflection on the process of "Reflexion". In the Encyclopaedia, it is called "Wesen als Grund der Existenz". In the longer Logic, it is called "das Wesen der Reflexion in ihm selbst". It is primarily to this version that we shall refer for the comments that compose the rest of this chapter.

a. Essential and Unessential: "Schein"

The Logic of Being comes to its conclusion, we have seen,[96] when the "indifference of its own indifference" becomes evident. At the level at which reality is grasped simply "in itself", one face merely succeeding another, no further advance can be made. It is then that a further dimension of thought-experience is realized, and the Logic delves "behind" the face of Being with the will to recognize what Being is "in and for itself".[97] It is the realm of "reflected" categories, where each thought "is" only in its self-opposition and return.

The new dimension is, however, not so easily grasped. Thought is able merely progressively to rid itself of the direct, un-reflected attitudes of Being. The opening triad of Essence, which Hegel entitles "Schein", outlines the manner and complexity of this progress. Hegel compares it explicitly to the opening triad of the whole Logic, the dialectic of Being, Nothing, and Becoming.[98] There he had stressed that the synthesis, Becoming, is the "first concrete thought", of which Being and Nothing are but "empty abstractions";[99] we may say that they are abstract attempts to avoid the concrete movement of Essence and return to the easier standpoint of Being. "Sie beide bestehen in weiter nichts als darin, dass das Wesen zuerst als ein unmittelbares genommen wird."[100]

---

[95] Cf. p. 88 above.
[96] p. 79 above.
[97] WL, II, p. 3. Cf. p. 80 above.
[98] WL, II, p. 12.
[99] Cf. Enc. § 88 Zusatz.
[100] WL, II, p. 12.

The Presupposition of Being

The thesis of this first triad bears the title of the most general duality of the second book of the Logic, "Essential and Unessential". In this, Hegel suggests that the very advance from Being to reflected thought exposes the thinker at once to a more subtle influence of the immediacy of Being. For Essence is only "the first negation of Being". Thought, in its first grasp of itself as an essential that is only in its reflection from an unessential, and as an unessential that is likewise the "shadow" of the essential, falls to regarding its essential and unessential moments as two levels, each with the mere "an sich" of Being. It lapses to the more simple interpretation of Plato's cave.[101] "Der Unterschied vom Wesentlichen und Unwesentlichen hat das Wesen in die sphäre des *Daseins* zurückfallen lassen, indem das Wesen, wie es zunächst ist, als unmittelbares Seiendes, und damit nur als *Anderes* bestimmt ist gegen das Sein."[102]

Thus, at this first stage Hegel emphasizes the dependence of Essence on Being. It "begins with Being".[103] It "presupposes" Being as its origin. In what may be the most apt illustration, thought "comes" from language as an "Erinnerung" of the incipient meaning of language. Thought becomes the essential, to which language is the unessential. Yet their profound relationship of mutual reflection is not at once realized. Thought appears as a level of Being "underlying" its words yet of fundamentally the same structure.[104] Thought presupposes and "finds" its language.[105]

Hegel himself supplies here two illustrations of his meaning. The first is the understanding of God which is limited to this first, naive level of Essence. For the thought of God "als ein höchstes Wesen" reduces him to one among many beings which are thereby "wesenlos".[106] Similarly, the persistence of Being in the transition to an essential is shown in the Cosmological proof, in which "aus dem zufälligen Sein der Welt, über welches sich darin erhoben wird, wird noch das Sein mit hinaufgebracht."[107]

The second illustration is a reference from the Logic to the "temporality" of the transition from language to thought. Hegel suggests that as "Wesen"

---

[101] Cf. p. 82 above.

[102] WL, II, p. 8.

[103] p. 5.

[104] One may note the bearing on certain atomistic theories of meaning.

[105] Cf. also Hegel's discussion of universals at the level of "Verstand"; there they stand in such a relation to their particulars that they are themselves reduced to the character of particulars (e.g., Enc. § 80 and Zusatz).

[106] Enc. § 112 Zusatz.

[107] WL, I, p. 86. Cf. RN, p. 44: "Reflexion ist Festhalten, Stehenlassen der unterschiedenen Bestimmungen."

would seem to come from the past participle of "Sein",[108] our language retains a true sense of the passage from Being to Essence. The past is often denoted by the word "have", which implies reflection-into-self;[109] the reality is conserved in the very denial of its immediacy.[110] Yet the limitation of "having" is no less pertinent. It implies also a retention of the immediacy of Being, which prevents full reflection-into-self.[111] "Have" stands between the "is" of sheer identity in Being and the "is" of fully reflected identity in the Notion. At the first stage, thought is one with its expression only as below distinction. With utterance, opposition appears and one "has a meaning". Hegel's dialectic of Essence must remain formal unless it be seen as an acute attempt to transcend this survival of Being, this profoundly spatial separation of thought and expression, and to pass from "having" a meaning to "being" one's meaning.[112]

The Positing of Being

The antithesis of the first triad of Essence is called "Show" (Schein). It forms the complementary abstraction of that concrete reflection which is sought. For, as Hegel describes the transition, if both terms of the duality are reduced to the level of Being, the difference (as a difference of Essence) collapses. To lose opposition by mere equivalence of the terms is effectively to lose it (as an opposition of Essence) by the annihilation of one term in favour of the total predominance of the other.

That is, if the previous stage was characterized by an externality which treated the essential moment as merely at the level of Being, this stage seeks a false interiority in which the essential becomes all-important and the unessential is reduced from a true correlative to a mere "show". Show has its existence precisely in its non-existence.[113] Hegel illustrates this abstraction of Essence by those forms of thought, whether philosophical or common, which effectively deny Being before a false essence. He mentions scepticism, subjective idealism, and all thinking which sets its meaning finally in an ineffable simply beyond every experience.

Thus, the unessential moment loses the independence it had as "origin" of the essential. Now it is simply "posited" (gesetzt) by the essential. "Show is

[108] WL, II, p. 3.
[109] Enc. § 125.
[110] § 112 Zusatz.
[111] For Kroner, the limitation of Essence is that the coupled terms statically reflect each other without strictly "going over". Totality remains a "relation between". Hence, with the transition to the Notion, "die Reflexion reflektiert sich in sich und hebt eben dadurch ihre Gegensätzlichkeit gegen das Sein auf." (*Von Kant bis Hegel*, II, p. 448).
[112] Cf. p. 66 above.
[113] WL, II, p. 9.

the self-positing of Essence."[114] If the previous stage was illustrated by thought finding its origin in a language that is "already there", this stage is shown in the view that thought simply creates its language as a perfect self-embodiment. Both, however, are correlatively false abstractions of the true experience of the struggle of thought to come to itself in its expression.

Similarly, both the presupposing (Voraussetzung) of Being and the positing (Setzung) of Being are abstractions of the synthesis of this first triad of Essence, which Hegel makes the act of reflection itself. As we shall see in the next section, this concrete act is described as that of "Setzung als Voraus-gesetzt". The complete Logic of Essence is an attempt progressively to think this enigmatic totality which is at once a self-positing and self-presupposing. Its stages are a repeated breaking-down into a merely inner (positing) reflection and a merely external (presupposing) reflection. We shall now follow Hegel as he tries to trace some of the characters of these two forms of reflection.

b. Positing Reflection

The thought that we are trying to follow at this point is unfortunately well exemplified in the very difficulty of "following" it. With each section or sentence of the Logic, two courses present themselves and each shows itself as a strategy to avoid thought rather than enter into it. The first is the way of illustration; but every illustration is an escape from the "element of thought". The second is the way of mere repetition; this is not merely futile but offers no assurance that more is achieved than a self-deceiving and purely formal play on words. Hegel's attempt to surpass the level of thinking at which language was formed can not be re-thought and re-expressed without going outside his original expression, and this "outside" will always be tainted with "illustration".

It is in the consciousness of this dilemma that the problem of meaning and language has been offered in these pages as the most plausible compromise: it is that illustration which perhaps comes closest to the self-alienation of "pure" thought which is the true topic.

Where the example is proposed, it is intended that language be taken in the widest sense. It is not to be limited to what is vocalized or written, but is that most general and most intimate articulation in which an "unthematic" meaning can find itself. In this sense, it is the topic that dominates the "Phenomenology of Spirit", and even in a somewhat more restricted sense of language, the question is prominent there. It is language which brings

---

[114] p. 7.

forth the truth of "Meinung".[115] Conversely, it is the task of thought to transcend the propositional form of language and bring out the dialectic inherent in it, without departing from systematic statement to the ineffable of intuition.[116] Yet though meaning can be present only so far as it achieves systematic expression, Hegel states explicitly in this work that language expresses at once too much and too little.[117] It falls alternately into the extreme of "Schein", where opposition is apparently abolished, and the extreme where both moments are reduced to the independence of Being, so that language gains a "meaning of its own" and hides rather than expresses its true meaning.[118]

Positing and Presupposing

The paradox of language which is the *other* of thought, and yet no less the other *of* thought, may also be expressed by saying that thought becomes "concrete" only by opposing itself as a "mere" essential moment to its expression as a "mere" unessential moment. Or, in terms of Hegel's celebrated paradox of identity, one's true meaning is always the identity of a meaning simply identified with its language and a meaning still opposed to its language.

If the true identity or totality is to be described as a self-reflection from self-opposition, then its concrete nature must recognize, not merely the moment of return-to-self, but also the return *from* a persisting alienation. In his explanation of "positing reflection", Hegel relates his doctrine of reflection to the actions of positing and presupposing which have appeared as basic to the initial triad of Essence.[119]

For in so far as thought does "return" to itself in the dual categories of Essence, it reduces the unessential moment, its self-alienation, to a mere "Gesetztsein".[120] Or, as Hegel expresses it in introducing the Logic of Essence in the Encyclopaedia: "Das Wesen, als das durch die Negativität seiner selbst sich mit sich vermittelnde Sein, ist die Beziehung auf sich selbst, nur indem sie Beziehung auf Anderes ist, das aber unmittelbar nicht als

---

[115] Cf. Phän., pp. 88-9: "Das Sprechen, welches die göttliche Natur hat, die Meinung unmittelbar zu verkehren."

[116] Phän., pp. 52-3, 542-3.

[117] "Man kann darum ebensosehr sagen, dass diese Äusserungen das Innere zu sehr, als dass sie es zu wenig ausdrücken." (Phän., p. 229).

Related themes are to be found in Hegel's discussions of the expression of the artist in his work. For example, cf. Phän., p. 429, where the return of the artist's self to himself is described as both above and beneath the work itself.

[118] Cf. the comments on Hegel's doctrine of symbol, sign, and word (pp. 62-4) above.

[119] Cf. pp. 95-6 above.

[120] WL, II, p. 15.

Seiendes, sondern als ein Gesetztes und Vermitteltes ist."[121] In terms of the
preceding chapter, as the semi-articulate levels of intuition and Vorstellung
rise to the stage of "having a meaning", this meaning at first reduces the
particularity of its origin to a mere expression over which it has full control;
the meaning "posits" itself in creating its language. Language (Being) is no
longer an origin, but exists only as a creature of the meaning (Essence) which
rose from it.[122]

However, Hegel points out, this is but an abstraction of the full experience.
It emphasizes the identity in opposition to the exclusion of the opposition in
identity. The moment of "return" is possible only in what is "already", in
some sense, constituted as distance, as a beginning which retains its reality
and allows the "to" and "from" of return. "Die Reflexion in sich ist wesentlich das Voraussetzen dessen, aus dem sie die Rückkehr ist."[123] Thus it is no
less true that the reflection of Being into itself as Essence is realization that
the Essence is derivative, that its whole reality comes from the original
Being and postulates the reality of that origin. In terms of meaning and
language, this experience hardly needs further illustration. Thought finds its
origin in expressions not of its making, and its growth, far from being a
separation from its origins, is a painful affirmation that they constitute its
very texture. Meaning presupposes, is derivative from, language.

If we have been right in following Mure's suggestion that Hegel's difficult
dialectic of Essence may well be understood from the paradox of positing
and presupposing in thought and language, then it is in these pages that Hegel
tries to convey an element that must be fundamental to any understanding
of the "transition" from pure thought to its "other" in his system. For it is
in the phrase "setzen als vorausgesetzt" that Hegel tries to express what may
be regarded as the original phenomenon of thought. Thought is one with itself, at each of its levels, only in "finding" itself as derivative from that which
is derivative from it. "Das Denken setzt sich voraus, stellt sich vor". And it
is in this "voraus", the externality within the element of the Logic, that the
originality of the space and time of nature may well be sought.

The transition proper to "Reflexion" is thus a concrete whole of positing
and presupposing. Each stage that is short of the whole is a partial grasp of it
"in so far" as it is a positing *or* a presupposing.

Die Bewegung wendet sich als Fortgehen unmittelbar in ihr selbst um und ist nur
so Selbstbewegung, – Bewegung, die aus sich kommt, insofern die setzende

---

[121] Enc. § 112.
[122] "Statt von dieser Unmittelbarkeit anfangen zu können, ist diese vielmehr erst als die
Rückkehr oder die Reflexion selbst." (WL, II, p. 15.)
[123] WL, II, p. 16.

Reflexion voraussetzende, aber als voraussetzende Reflexion schlechthin setzende ist.[124]

Hence, before continuing to Hegel's description of the externality of reflection, it may be well to pause at his doctrine of the "insofern".

The "In So Far"

The metaphysical concept of totality which stands under heavy criticism may be described as a complacent assurance of a final, meaningful, and contradiction-free "whole" of knowledge and experience, such that the metaphysician, proceeding "from" the whole, may bring all its parts harmoniously together, provided he applies properly a method of "distinctions" which will grasp all apparent contradictions as "respects" of a higher unity.

It is by no means the purpose of this study to ask whether metaphysics can hope to avoid what is just in this criticism. Nor is it the theme of this work that Hegel avoids it. No thinker has developed so extensive and intensive a philosophy of totality. It is our intention merely to try to understand more fully some of the complexities of his notion of totality, as it is verified in the paradoxical structure of the "final" triad of his system.

Here, in continuing our examination of Hegel's doctrine of transition as "reflection", it may be of value to emphasize his explicit rejection of any metaphysical method that proceeds by a method of "distinguishing into respects". This rejection is to be found clearly stated in the second chapter of the "Phenomenology", in which the naive consciousness is led through a self-criticism of its attitude to perception. To avoid the contradictions of a thing that is a unity in the sheer multiplicity of its properties, consciousness introduces the idea of an "insofern". This allows it to withdraw from the object and resolve the antinomy by putting unity alternatively in the object and in the subject, such that the multiplicity of "aspects" falls respectively in the other.[125] Eventually, however, the final qualifying "in-so-far" drops away, and it is realized that the object is "in einer und derselben Rücksicht das Gegenteil seiner selbst".[126] The "in-so-far" is revealed as a mere "sophistry" to set universality and particularity "alongside one another", rather than to attempt the experience of their concrete identity.[127]

The same "sophistry" is at work throughout the following chapter, in which Hegel presents a self-criticism of understanding (Verstand) in its attempts to maintain a contradiction-free universe by its distinctions of

[124] WL, II, p. 16.
[125] Phän., pp. 93-7.
[126] p. 99.
[127] p. 100.

inner and outer, essence and manifestation. It is the "logic" of the dialectic of these two chapters which Hegel tries to think in his Logic of Essence. The particular categories appear in the second part, "appearance", but it is in the earlier pages on the nature of reflection itself that Hegel makes his clearest rejection of any claim to a final unity based on the distinctions of an "insofern". For instance, in his comments on the category of variety (Verschiedenheit), he writes:

> Das *Zugleich* der beiden Prädikate wird zwar durch das *Insofern* auseinander gehalten: dass zwei Dinge *insofern* sie gleich, *insofern* nicht ungleich, oder nach einer *Seite* und *Rücksicht* gleich, nach der andern *Seite* und *Rücksicht* aber ungleich sind. Damit wird die Einheit der Gleichheit und Ungleichheit aus dem Dinge entfernt, und was seine eigene und die Reflexion der Gleichheit und Ungleichheit an sich wäre, als eine dem Dinge äusserliche Reflexion festgehalten.[128]

But this, as in all the other manifestations of Reflection in Essence, is to "forget":

> ...dass damit der Widerspruch nicht aufgelöst, sondern nur anderswohin, in die subjektive oder äussere Reflexion überhaupt geschoben wird.

Thus the "remembering" of Reflection, the "Erinnerung" with which Hegel associated it at its appearance in the Logic,[129] is a realization of the experience of thought that the contradiction is in "one unity",[130] in an "identical relation".[131]

The final interpretation of such texts – whether they imply an "ultimate" contradiction for the system as a whole – is one of the most disputed questions among commentators of Hegel. We shall have to return to the problem later in this chapter, in the section on contradiction.

For the present, one fundamental qualification need be made. Even if a thinking "by different respects" means a retreat from "the thing itself", it is a retreat that is an essential part of the advance of the dialectic. All that has been considered in this section forms part of "positing reflection", so that the unity of positing and presupposing remains abstractly on the side of the former. Before this can attain the synthesis of its triad, "determining reflection", it must pass through the antithesis of "external reflection". This latter is precisely that externality within thought which is the incapacity to think the unity of positing and presupposing. Yet the thinker can no more "leap over" these many attempts of thought at the final harmony of an "insofern" than the philosopher can understand the thought of his day without

---

[128] WL, II, p. 40.
[129] p. 3.
[130] p. 40.
[131] p. 42.

passing through the history of all the "final syntheses" of his predecessors.

It is, indeed, as has been suggested before,[132] the history of all preceding metaphysics which Hegel is trying to think throughout the course of the Logic of Essence. And it is not until the transition to the Notion is made that the true unity of positing and presupposing can be achieved. "Der Begriff ist es allein, der als sich setzend die Voraussetzung macht, wie sich in der Kausalität überhaupt und näher in der Wechselwirkung ergeben hat."[133]

c. External Reflection

Hegel's expression at this point is more than usually difficult, as one might expect of an attempt to think, in the terms of "pure" thought, the basis of the very inability to realize the pure thought of reflection.

This inability, so far as it constitutes the antithetical abstraction of the synthesis of positing and presupposing, is not a simple separation of the two moments: it is a movement by which reflection "setzt sich als das Negative ihrer voraus. Sie ist in dieser Bestimmung verdoppelt, das eine Mal als das Vorausgesetzte oder die Reflexion in sich, die das Unmittelbare ist. Das andere Mal ist sie die als negativ sich auf sich beziehende Reflexion; sie bezieht sich auf sich als auf jenes ihr Nichtsein."[134] This would seem best to be illustrated in what has already been described as the objective and subjective movements of reflection.[135] Common sense would say that an object is essence-and-manifestation apart from our thinking it. That is, we presuppose its own self-mediation. But no less is this mediation a movement of our own thought from the object as manifestation. The subjective movement is held to be independent of the objective, yet, "the determinations that are derived are counted as its proper being."[136]

The Origin of Vorstellung

This remains, however, an illustration in so far as it regards a subject-object relation proper to Phenomenology rather than to Logic. What Hegel seems here to be trying to think is the externality of thought within its own element that is the origin of all the stratagems of the "Insofern" in the Phenomenology:

Das formelle Denken macht sich die Identität zum Gesetze, lässt den wider-

---

[132] p. 73 above.
[133] Enc. § 159. Cf §§ 153-5 for the references.
[134] WL, II, p. 17.
[135] p. 81 above.
[136] WL, II, p. 19.

sprechenden Inhalt, den es vor sich hat, in die Sphäre der Vorstellung, in Raum und Zeit herabfallen, worin das Widersprechende im Neben- und Nacheinander aussereinander gehalten wird und so ohne die gegenseitige Berührung vor das Bewusstsein tritt.[137]

That is, the "origin" of the space and time which constitute the element of Vorstellung as opposed to that of thought is to be found in a thinking of identity that averts the concrete contradiction of positing as presupposing. Hence, every stage of the Logic of Essence, which thinks the totality under a coupled category yet remains at that stage by regarding each moment of the category as simply self-identical, is thereby a manner of passing out into the space and time of illustration and Vorstellung. And conversely, we may say that each attitude of experience is, through its form of Vorstellung, a limitation of thought to one of the pseudo-totalities of Essence. Thus, rather than regard Vorstellung as a stage simply below thought, it would perhaps be truer to see it as the "Beispiel" of the Notion which is formed by each level of thought in its attempt to understand the whole in terms of itself. Again, what is sought is a more subtle understanding of the relation between the pure categories of Logic and the "schematized" forms of nature and spirit; the complexities of positing and external reflection may at least modify the common image.

Hegel's doctrine that limits are known only so far as they are transcended means that common sense can rise to a true knowledge of the limits of thinking Essence as a subjective and objective movement only so far as it can attain that reflection which is one in both standpoints. This, as we have seen, is the whole course of the Logic of Essence up to the stage of "Wirklichkeit". Or, as Hegel expresses it at this point, it is the way of realizing that reflection does not merely presuppose an external movement as an immediate that is the start of its own movement. "Das Unmittelbare ist auf diese Weise nicht nur an sich, das hiesse für uns oder in der äussern Reflexion, dasselbe, was die Reflexion ist, sondern es ist gesetzt, dass es dasselbe ist."[138] And so far as this is realized, determining reflection is reached and Essence is manifested as it is in and for itself.

Though as Historical

These words, with their reference to an overcoming of the "phänomenologischer Anteil" of the Logic, the separation between the "für uns" and the "für sich", may raise the question of the relation that the externality under consideration has, not merely to categories of thought, but to historical

[137] WL, II, p. 496.
[138] WL, II, p. 18.

systems of thought. This question recalls the problem posed by Hyppolite of the transition to absolute knowledge which "is in history but is not a historical fact".[139] It is implied by Hegel, when in the introduction to the Encyclopaedia, he discusses the relation between the history of philosophy and the system of philosophy:

Dieselbe Entwicklung des Denkens, welche in der Geschichte der Philosophie dargestellt wird, wird in der Philosophie selbst dargestellt, aber befreit von jener geschichtlichen Äusserlichkeit, rein im Elemente des Denkens.[140]

The question may then be posed: what is the "externality" which makes the historicity of that development of thought which, freed from it, is "philosophy itself"? That Hegel does not here mean by externality the particular circumstances in which philosophical thinking has been "embodied" is affirmed in his Lectures on the History of Philosophy.[141] There he rejects from his consideration all that can be reduced to "outward history" and to "opinions"; he asks rather how the inner content of the thinking of absolute truth can have a history.

His reply contains a reference to principles of his system, but falls short of any attempt to think them out afresh in the light of this question. He begins by explaining the notion of "Entwickling" in systematic thought: we are in a position to grasp more of its subtlety than is there expounded, by seeing it as the fulfilment of "Übergehen" and "Reflexion". Each stage in this development, he stresses, is not "für sich" merely as a stage to the whole: each is for itself "das Ganze" and contains "die Totalität der Idee".[142] In accord with what we have said about experience of the totality at the levels of Essence,[143] the whole that is thought is that which is made possible by the concreteness of the category or "principle" attained.[144] It constitutes an "explanation of the world" from this principle, and may be called a philosophical system.[145] It derives its meaning from its "place", which is a manner of posing the questions made possible by the categories it has reached. Hegel often commended Greek scepticism for the depth of its doubting, but maintained that it failed so far as it insinuated uncriticized presuppositions upon which its criticism might be based.[146] What the philosophical question gains

---

[139] Cf. p. 5 above.
[140] Enc. § 14.
[141] Gesch. Phil., XVII, p. 35.
[142] Gesch. Phil., XVII, pp. 63-4.
[143] pp. 87-8 above.
[144] Such that the function of philosophical criticism is not merely to discuss particular points but finally "das Prinzip zu erkennen". (Gesch. Phil., XIX, p. 686).
[145] XVII, p. 67.
[146] E.g., cf. Enc. § 24 Zusatz.

is the ability further to question, rather than "mit den Worten herumzu-schlagen". So it is that we can not expect to find the questions of our age in the philosophy of an earlier one, for questioning is a reflection of a stage in the development of thought.[147] Hence it is fundamentally that the individual is the offspring of his world, and a philosophy can no more escape out of its age than an individual out of his skin.[148]

These considerations, however, while emphasizing Hegel's claim to a correspondence between the stages in the history of philosophy and the categorial levels in philosophy itself, have not strictly touched the original question why philosophy should have, not merely an "Entwicklung", but a "Geschichte". Hegel, in fact, consciously avoids the question with the remark that it encroaches on the metaphysics of time.[149] The remark, it may be suggested, was possibly more apt than any answer he might have attempted, for his own historical position did not admit of sufficiently profound questions on the metaphysics of time. But the comments with which he follows this remark are of some interest for our attempt to understand his doctrine of the externality of reflection, and they may serve to close this section:

Das In-der-Zeit-Sein ist ein Moment nicht nur des einzelnen Bewusstseins über-haupt, das als solches wesentlich endlich ist, sondern auch der Entwicklung der philosophischen Idee im Elemente des Denkens ... Die Idee als konkret, als Ein-heit unterschiedener ... tritt in ihr selbst ins Dasein und in die Äusserlichkeit im Elemente des Denkens; und so erscheint im Denken die reine Philosophie als eine in der Zeit fortschreitende Existenz.[150]

These words[151] may perhaps modify the impression left by the quotation given above from the Encyclopaedia (§ 14) that the "Äusserlichkeit" which constitutes the historicity of thought is *outside* the "element of thought". The system of philosophy would here appear to be distinguished from the history of philosophy only in that its development is "*rein* im Elemente des Denkens". Thus, the time "in" which historical stages are is that which constitutes thinking as not "pure", not "befreit". And since freedom is for Hegel the transition from Essence to Notion,[152] we are left with the conclusion that our considerations throughout this chapter, so far as they have tried to understand something of the "eccentric" movement of reflection be-

---

[147] Gesch. Phil., XVII, p. 75: "Solche Fragen setzen gewisse Bildung des Gedankens voraus."

[148] XVII, pp. 75-6; cf. Recht, p. 16.

[149] Gesch. Phil., XVII p. 61.

[150] p. 62.

[151] which occur in Hegel's own manuscript for the introduction to his lectures at Berlin: cf. Hoffmeister's critical edition of the Introduction, p. 37.

[152] E.g., cf. Enc. § 159: "Der Übergang von der Notwendigkeit zur Freiheit oder vom Wirklichen in den Begriff. . ."

fore the transition of Essence to the Notion, have no less been an approach
to Hegel's concept of time than were the thoughts of the last chapter on the
transition from Vorstellung to Denken.[153]

d. Contradiction

With the category of determining reflection, Hegel closes the first of the
three sections consecrated to the "essence of reflection" in the "Wissenschaft der Logik". The second deals with the "Wesenheiten oder Reflexionsbestimmungen" and the third with "ground" (cf. appendix of categories).
These sections are among the richest in the Logic, but the purposes of this
chapter have already been served adequately by the general survey of the
Logic of Essence and the more detailed examination of reflection "in itself".
As a further preparation for the problems of the system triad, however, it
may be well to close with a few remarks on the most important of the
"essentialities", contradiction, and on Hegel's notion of "ground".

The Principle of Contradiction

The "Reflexionsbestimmungen", or most universal determinations in which
reflection utters itself, are its identity, its difference, and their synthesis in
contradiction, where "der Gegensatz reflektiert sich in sich selbst und geht in
seinen Grund zurück."[154] The notion that the final expression of reflection is
in contradiction has been implicit at every stage of our considerations in this
chapter. Nor is the recognition of a fundamental contradiction peculiar to
Hegel: it is present, in some form, in any metaphysics that seeks to rise above
empirical thinking and achieve a concrete thought. It must in all such
attempts sooner or later be uncovered or forever hidden by manipulation of
the evasions and distinctions of diplomatic language.[155] As suggested briefly
in the preface,[156] Hegel may be seen as choosing to face it at the beginning
and make it the ground principle of his thought. Formally stated, this may
have the appearance of the greatest ruse of all. On the other hand, one
might regard it as just that a philosopher should lay bare the contradiction
of his system at the beginning, rather than leave it to appear at the end with
the aura of a "philosophical mystery". Hegel's "ruse", however, may be
that of presenting his paradox, not merely as a principle of explanation,

---

[153] As suggested above (p. 73), there is a sense in which it may be said that Hegel's Objective Logic is his true "history of philosophy".

[154] WL, II, p. 23.

[155] "Die Wendungen und Einfälle der Reflexion, die Auswege und Absprünge, womit
sie sich ihren Widerspruch gegen sich selbst verdeckt." (WL, I, pp. 79-80).

[156] p. XII above.

but as the principle of adequate intelligibility: to this criticism we shall return in the following section.

What Hegel seeks to express formally in the section of his Logic on "contradiction" may be seen as that which is at the origin of all development in his thinking and experiencing.[157] Development may be pure growth without loss,[158] but it is no less "ein harter, unendlicher Kampf gegen sich selbst".[159] The "deeper" spirit goes, the more violent the opposition,[160] for true reconciliation can be reached only in the extreme of contradiction.[161] "Denn der Mensch ist dies: den Widerspruch des Vielen nicht nur in sich zu tragen, sondern zu ertragen und darin sich selbst gleich und treu zu bleiben."[162]

That the realization of contradiction (in some sense, at least) is fundamental to Hegel's thought is denied by no commentator. Yet possibly no problem in the interpretation of Hegel has received so much attention as the question whether he truly denied the principle of contradiction. It is not intended here to take any "position" in regard to the vast literature involved. Nor is it intended, however, to imply that the question is a false one. It will be sufficient, and of pertinence to our theme, to suggest what the question itself implies.

The most detailed explicit discussion of the problem is that of F. Grégoire.[163] No evaluation of his own position could be attempted without a consideration of the various possible answers he analyzes (i.e. senses in which Hegel held that everything is contradictory). Yet some indication of his position may be gained briefly from those pages[164] in which he discusses the study of Hegel's Logic by E. Coreth.[165] Based largely on an examination of the texts of the "Wesenheiten",[166] this latter study defended the opinion that Hegel's category of contradiction represents, not merely the constant threat of logical contradiction from the standpoint of "Verstand", but a true logical contradiction even for "Vernunft". Grégoire's criticism may briefly be stated in saying that if the movement of the dialectic in Verstand is to be

---

[157] E.g., cf. Gesch. Phil., XVII, p. 54: "Der innere Widerspruch des Konkreten ist selbst das Treibende zur Entwicklung."

[158] WL, II, p. 502.

[159] Phil. Gesch., p. 90.

[160] Gesch. Phil., XIX, p. 684: "Je tiefer der Geist in sich gegangen, desto stärker der Gegensatz.

[161] XIX, p. 684: "Dei wahrhafte Versöhnung des Gegensatzes ist die Einsicht, dass dieser Gegensatz auf seine absolute Spitze getrieben, sich selbst auflöst."

[162] Ästhetik, p. 255.

[163] Etudes Hégéliennes, pp. 51-159: a developed version of an article, "Hegel et l'universelle contradiction", Revue Philosophique de Louvain 44 (1946), pp. 36-73.

[164] pp. 114-8.

[165] Das dialektische Sein in Hegels Logik, Wien, 1952.

[166] and prominently those mentioned above, page 100.

explained as an attempt constantly to escape threatening contradiction, then unless Vernunft itself be a stage of reconciliation that finally overcomes contradiction, the finality of the process is nullified and we are left with an ultimate unintelligibility. "Se développer pour dépasser la contradiction en vue même d'y retomber plus profondément, voilà certes une conception bien étrange."[167] And he adds in a footnote that no escape is afforded to those who deny that Hegel's dialectic "doit aboutir à un stade final", for logical contradiction would still characterize the movement of transcendence itself: that is, the finality of the final stage is simply transposed to the present in its transition.

The Final Stage of Thought

The embarrassment of any commentator on Hegel is, or should be, at its highest at this point. Into the question, as so posed, can be read the whole problem of Hegel's metaphysics. Yet it is here especially that the burden of language is felt, and the warning of Hegel remembered, that speculative truth can not be expressed in propositional form: "The form of the proposition or judgment is unsuited to express the concrete and speculative – and the true is such; the judgment is, through its form, one-sided and in this sense false."[168]

The dispute whether Hegel denied the principle of contradiction or not is clearly one of those, common in the history of philosophy, where a lifetime devoted to the study of the texts has led, and always will lead, the commentators to take opposing positions. In such a situation, one is perhaps entitled, rather than giving his assent to one "side" or the other, to ask what the dispute itself may suggest about the philosopher under discussion.

Should one, in this case, be allowed to assume that there is solid textual support for the opinion that Hegel regarded contradiction as an ultimate of philosophical thought, and no less solid support for his final resolution of all contradictions in a last identity, what is then suggested – in this purely *a priori* fashion – about his thought? If mere inconsistency be excluded (for Hegel certainly regarded the problem as central), then one would have to conclude that he regarded the question itself – though fundamental and hence true – as yielding to no final affirmative or negative answer. This is not to imply any lack of respect for the repeated attempts that have been made to come to grips with the question and to state it more precisely, least of all for the two works cited. That is a necessary task for any full discussion of the problem – which this is not. Yet it may be that, for Hegel himself, the

[167] *Etudes Hégéliennes*, p. 116.
[168] Enc. § 31; cf. Phän., p. 52.

very question of the persistence or cessation of contradiction must have been susceptible of no propositional reply. It is, as Grégoire clearly indicates, a question of the "stade final" of thought.

That is, it may be that the deliberate ambiguity of Hegel's notion of "Aufhebung" would prevent him from affirming that contradiction ultimately ceases or remains. For the final stage of thought must be, for him, the "identity of identity and non-identity". This means that the dichotomy of identity and non-identity, as we think and experience it, is not final. The true identity is equally the origin of both terms, itself neither a simple identity nor a mere difference.

To say that the synthesis of each triad is an identity of two "moments", which avoids their threatened contradiction, is true but a one-sided attitude. For the synthesis is more than the identity of two "simple" moments: each is complex. The "thesis" is a mere, immediate self-identity which needs to be diversified. The "antithesis" is a mere self-difference which needs to be resolved. Hence, the "synthesis" is the reconciliation of self-identity and self-difference, without any retreat into the abstract identity of the "in so far." When this is expressed in the form of pure categories, Hegel terms this synthesis "contradiction".

Hence, to affirm that the synthesis is an identity which avoids "contradiction" is one-sided; it is equally a non-identity which avoids mere identity. In terms of the opening triad of the Logic, Becoming avoids what "would be" a contradiction of Being and Nothing: but it equally avoids what "would be" an incapacitating identity.

As Grégoire expresses it: "Plus subtilement, l'union d'identité et de non-identité que constitue la relation essentielle est elle-même paradoxale et cet aspect explique lui aussi que la relation essentielle se nomme contradiction."[169] He seems, however, to maintain that if the final identity, the system itself, were – in this way – to remain "paradoxical", this would constitute a final unintelligibility: hence Hegel can not have meant this.[170]

It is in this final conclusion, rather than in any of his textual analysis, that this study respectfully suggests some disagreement with Prof. Grégoire. The disagreement is perhaps largely verbal, but the following notes may suggest what is intended:

1. It is readily conceded that Hegel would never have called the final stage "unintelligible". For him it is the supreme intelligibility of "Vernunft", the speculative identity in terms of which all else becomes intelligible.

2. Hegel nevertheless regarded it as unintelligible when viewed *from* any

[169] *Etudes Hégéliennes*, p. 88, note.
[170] pp. 115, 121, 122-3.

lower stage of thought or experience. He relates speculative truth to mysticism in two senses: it attains that which is finally real and true, and it remains a mystery when regarded from stages short of it.[171]

3. The final identity is, however, no "intellectual intuition" of the sort which Hegel rejected so vehemently in Schelling, but a *result* achieved only by passing through all these subordinate stages. And this passage indicates no less the historical origin of Hegel's own thought from his early non-philosophical interests. A brief study of this development of the notion of speculative identity from the "non-positive faith" of Hegel's youthful writings will be made in the following chapter.[172]

4. It follows that:

a. The final identity pretends to "explain" all lower stages.
b. It is no dogmatic intuition but is grasped only in passing through these stages: that is, it is in turn "explained" by the stages of its genesis.
c. Nevertheless, it is not intelligible "from" any of these stages.

5. Thus, Hegel's notion of the supreme intelligibility of the final speculative identity can be:

neither the intelligibility of an autonomous "self-luminous" *beginning*, from which all else is rendered intelligible,
nor the intelligibility of a *result*, illuminated from the stages of its genesis,
but it must be the intelligibility proper to that which fulfils the three conditions under note 4 above.

6. From this point, the question of "final contradiction" becomes one of terminology. This study maintains simply that language is not violated by the statement that the final identity of Hegel's system may be interpreted (and not merely criticized) as "paradoxical".

7. So far, however, as interpretation verges on criticism, much more than a mere question of terminology is involved. The suggestion proposed in the preface may be repeated. Most thinkers advance cautiously from that which they know toward that which they do not know. Hegel's stroke of imagination was to set at the very centre of his thought precisely that paradox by the means of which all else – he claimed – could be "explained" and the "ineffable" thus banished. This study has so far been a protracted effort to see how this identity of identity and non-identity is *verified* in our most intimate awareness of thought stuggling for self-presence in its language. If the student of Hegel could satisfy himself at this and at all other stages of human experience that the speculative identity explains the stages and the stages

---

[171] Enc. § 82 Zusatz.
[172] Cf. especially pp. 127-8 below.

explain the speculative identity, then he would have fully grasped Hegel's notion of "intelligibility".

As a critic, however, he may well ask if he has then reached the "self-luminous" possession of intelligibility itself. He has been given a profound and immensely fruitful form of "explanation". Yet it may be that the peculiar mark of human thinking – that, above all, which gives it its "finite" nature and separates man by an ultimate facticity from "Aufhebung" to "absolute knowledge" – is that explanation can not simply be identified with intelligibility. The very process of explanation from a principle to an "explained" leaves explanation bound to its origins, exposes it to legitimate philosophical questioning, and ensures that it remain a stage in a continuing history.

8. Hegel seems thus to have identified intelligibility with a comprehensive dual process of explanation from beginning to result and from result to beginning. The duality entitles the interpreter to speak of Hegel's thought as paradoxical precisely in its intelligibility. The duality likewise entitles the critic to suggest that human explanation has not in Hegel overcome its sheer facticity.

It is this duality which dominates Hegel's treatment of the final section describing the "essence of reflection": namely the category of "ground", to which we must now turn.

e. Ground

We have seen that Hegel speaks of the overcoming of the duality of Essence, the genesis of the Notion, as "die Enthüllung der Substanz".[173] The presence of the absolute is a process suggested by the metaphor of a gradual uncovering. Truth is "die Enthüllung dessen, was der Geist an und für sich ist."[174] Yet this metaphor is inadequate so far as it implies a process of a single direction, which is false to all that Hegel has tried to think under the term "reflection".

It is, instead, with reference to a term we have not yet examined that Hegel frequently tries to express the thought of spirit:

Indem der Begriff sich als die Wahrheit des Seins und Wesens erwiesen hat, welche beide in ihn als in ihren Grund zurückgegangen sind, so hat er umgekehrt sich aus dem Sein als aus seinem Grunde entwickelt.[175]

---

[173] WL, II, p. 218; cf. p. 90 above.
[174] RA, p. 69.
[175] Enc. § 159.

Self-Grounding of the Totality

The category of "ground" is exposed by Hegel as the final "determination of reflection" in the Encyclopaedia. In his longer Logic, it appears as the synthesis to which the "Reflexionsbestimmungen" themselves are the antithesis (cf. appendix of categories). The difference is of no great importance, for in either event "ground" is revealed as that "into" which the dual categories of Essence return (i.e. the culmination of Objective Logic) and as that "from" which the Notion arises (i.e. origin of Subjective Logic).

Its place among the determinations of reflection is justified by its traditional formulation as the principle of ground (or sufficient reason), which stands with the principles of identity and contradiction as an expression of that which moves thought from the immediacy of Being to the dualities of reflection. Hegel makes it clear that he understands the thought of the ground, or sufficient reason, of things as more than a search for their efficient cause; the concept also embraces all that Aristotle included under formal, material, and final cause – indeed the latter will reveal itself as fundamental in the Logic of the Notion.[176] So, in Hegel's time, metaphysics was described as a "Untersuchung über die Gründe der Welt."[177]

Thus, Hegel's concept of ground must be suggestive of what he sought in his own metaphysics. In relation to what was said in the previous section about Hegel's attitude to the "final stage" of thought, it is of interest that he here emphasizes that, if the ground or reason of things be regarded as the identity of identity and difference, this final synthesis is not to be seen as an "abstract identity".[178] That is, it is never to be reduced to the formal identity or totality which is but one of the coupled moments in which it progressively reveals itself as the concrete totality. "Der Grund ist nicht nur die Einheit, sondern ebensowohl auch der Unterschied der Identität und des Unterschiedes".

Within the dialectic of ground itself, the process of Essence is shown in the deep-seated duality that informs all our attempts at "explaining". Ground shows itself in the coupled moments of "formal ground" and "real ground".

On the one hand, an explanation may be complete, but remain a ground that is a merely formal re-statement of its consequent. Hegel gives as examples the tautologies of natural science, such as the explanation of movements of bodies by appeal to a "force" which makes them move in this way.[179]

---

[176] WL, II, p. 66.
[177] Haering, II, p. 83.
[178] Enc. § 121 Zusatz.
[179] WL, II, p. 79.

This, he states, merely expresses in the language of reflection the fact of immediate being. It formulates our true desire for mediate knowledge but arrives at no difference of content; further, it is radically misleading if it induces the belief that the formal ground (force, aether, molecules) exists in the same way as does the consequent.[180]

On the other hand, explanation may avoid tautology, but only at the expense of an externality and incompleteness which remove it equally far, in the other direction, from satisfying the demands of a "sufficient reason". Here, Hegel returns to one of his favourite polemics, against mere argumentation, or "raisonnement", as the method of philosophy. "The search for and indication of grounds – in which 'raisonnement' consists – is an endless meandering, which attains no final determination; there are good grounds for anything – and for its opposite."[181] Plato called it sophistry, and opposed to it the contemplation of the Idea, in which the thing is revealed in and for itself, or in its Notion.

These two attempts at explanation may typify the coupled categories of Essence. The one remains merely formal and essential, the other particular and unessential. What is truly sought is that which Hegel calls the "complete ground", an explanation that is at once universal and particular. Yet this can be conceived on the model neither of the universality of the former, nor of the particularity of the latter. It can, indeed, be nothing but that concrete totality toward which the whole movement of the Logic of Essence has tended. "Der Grund ist das Wesen als Totalität gesetzt."[182]

That is, the difficulties connected with philosophical explanation (in all its many forms, such as the traditional problem of cause and effect) are insoluble so long as – on the one hand – ground and consequent are looked upon as simply different. They must finally be seen as two aspects of the same process. The ground-relation can truly be thought only as self-grounding, and this ultimately only as a self-grounding of the totality. On the other hand, any attempt to understand from a totality which is simply assumed, rather than itself being the result of the whole process in all its differences, is a lapse to the abstract totality of formal ground.

One sees then that the dual process of Essence is shown, in its culmination in the dilemma of ground, to be basically the same as the two-directional movement of the Logic of the Notion (from beginning to result, and result to beginning). This dual movement Hegel also explains, on a number of

---

[180] WL, II, pp. 81-2.
[181] p. 88. Cf. Gesch. Phil., XVIII, p. 24: "Gründe sind eine wächserne Nase; für Alles gibt es gute Gründe."
[182] Enc. § 121.

occasions, in relation to the term "ground". At the start of his Logic, he writes:

Man muss zugeben ... dass das Vorwärtsgehen ein Rückgang in den Grund, zu dem Ursprünglichen und Wahrhaften ist, von dem das, womit der Anfang gemacht wurde, abhängt und in der Tat hervorgebracht wird.[183]

This is repeated in his discussion of the category of contradiction,[184] and again at the beginning of the Logic of the Notion:

Ob nun wohl der Begriff nicht nur als eine subjektive Voraussetzung, sondern als absolute Grundlage anzusehen ist, so kann er dies doch nicht sein, als insofern er sich zur Grundlage *gemacht* hat.[185]

One might say that philosophy is a progressive realizing of the experience of thought, but that every step in the progress, that it may be a true step, is a presupposition of the experience. And the dialectic of positing and presupposing, which we tried to follow in the Logic of Essence, receives its most fitting illustration in the final chapter of Hegel's complete Logic, where, under the speculative proposition that the beginning is the result, he passes in review the method by which thought moves from its ground and returns to its ground.[186]

In the second part of this study, where we shall see how the Notion develops as the complete system, it will be well to remember that this development can proceed only by pressupposing its result and presupposing a movement in the reverse direction. The "circularity" of the system is, if this be remembered, but a different expression for the process of Essence. In Essence we saw how the true totality can appear only in the dual categories of the merely formal and the merely particular. In the system we shall see how the true totality can appear only through the mutual positing and pressupposing by which we start with the result (as abstract) and proceed towards its self-particularization, and at the same time start with particulars and proceed toward the result. It is in this paradox that the deepest sense of the transitions of the system (and their kinship to "Reflexion") is to be found.[187]

[183] WL, I, p. 55.
[184] II, pp. 52-3.
[185] WL, II, p. 213.
[186] especially pp. 502-4.
[187] The following chapter will, in sketching the historical origins of Hegel's system, suggest the relation of this paradox of circularity to Schelling's system of two sciences as "partial totalities": where the "ideal" posits and presupposes the "real", and the real posits and presupposes the ideal (cf. pp. 134-5 below).

The Nature and Element of Spirit

As "ground" is finally the self-grounding of the totality, then this complicated chapter may well conclude with the naive question: If philosophy is a search for the ground of things, then what, according to Hegel, are we looking for? His dismissal of "formal ground" will not permit us to reply with a merely equivalent expression. Perhaps most commentators would reply that the question itself, which is the question of philosophy, manifests the first, most abstract, definitions of "Geist", and that the progress of philosophy is toward the fully concrete self-definition of spirit. What we are thus looking for is the full nature of spirit, which is itself the entire process of philosophical questioning.

Hyppolite, at the close of his essay on Hegel's Logic, suggests what may be a somewhat different answer. His question is rather what Hegel is looking for in his "most obscure dialectical synthesis of all", the passage from history to absolute knowledge.[188] History is creative of itself as Logos; not, however, of a Logos that is simply the nature or essence of history, for "le Logos n'est pas une essence, il est l'élément où l'être et le sens se réfléchissent l'un dans l'autre."[189] What we are looking for, then, is not finally the "nature" of spirit; it is the "element" of spirit.

This answer is left shrouded in its metaphor, but it is possible that our concern with the question of the "element" of thought may have offered some basis for an understanding. So also may the question of universal contradiction, for this is a question whether thought, in mounting its stages, is finally looking for its nature in terms of those stages, or whether its goal is in the end unintelligible in these terms. It is the question whether the "stade final" can be regarded as a *stage*, reached or aimed at[190] by a continued reflection of the philosophical question on the categories in which it is posed; or whether that which is reached or sought is fundamentally "non-categorial".

The truth and originality of the question of universal contradiction lies thus in its re-thinking of that question which Hegel posed through the deliberate ambiguity of the word "Aufhebung",[191] and which he renewed with each synthesis of his dialectic:

Sein und Wesen sind die Momente des Werdens [des Begriffs]; er aber ist ihre

[188] *Logique et Existence*, p. 246.

[189] *Logique et Existence*, p. 246; cf. p. 6 above.

[190] For, as Grégoire rightly points out, the difference in regard to this problem is not fundamental.

[191] Cf. Mure's views on "sublation", pp. 10-11 above; this whole study may, in a sense, be seen as a protracted development of this attitude, which seems to be at once a criticism and an interpretation of Hegel.

Grundlage und Wahrheit als die Identität, in welcher sie untergegangen und enthalten sind. Sie sind in ihm, weil er ihr Resultat ist, enthalten, aber nicht mehr als
Sein und als Wesen; diese Bestimmung haben sie nur, insofern sie noch nicht in
diese ihre Einheit zurückgegangen sind.[192]

Language makes it easy to say that Essence *is* contained in the Notion, but
not *as* Essence. Language makes it easy to explain reality on the model of
this paradox of "spirit". One may then say that all has thus been rendered
intelligible in this manifestation of the nature of spirit. Or one may say that
spirit can so manifest its nature only "within" the intelligibility of its
"element". The first statement stresses the identity of the final stage and
subordinate stages; the second stresses the difference. The true "speculative
identity" of the two, however, escapes language; and it is this which makes it
so difficult to draw a just line between criticism and sympathetic interpretation of Hegel.

Transition

In 1810 Hegel wrote for his young pupils of the Mittelklasse at Nuremberg:
"Indem wir das Denken des Denkens denken, verschafft sich damit der
Geist seine Kraft."[193] In the next six years he completed his monumental
attempt to think pure thought in the Logic. After this, however, for the remaining fifteen years of his life, his studies were concerned with "recognizing"
the forms of pure thought in those worlds of history, culture, and religion
which fall naturally into the element of Vorstellung. Apart from a revision of
the first book of the Logic, the thought of thought in its purity received no
more attention from him. Most would say that he regarded it as complete
and admitting of no original re-thinking. Some might say that the completion
was rather a sign of his consciousness of historical position. From his place
in the history of philosophy he could come to no more original thought. His
function was rather to think more fully the position of his time, to penetrate
its culture with *its* thought and *recognize* its need. "Man muss das Bedürfnis
des denkenden Geistes unserer Zeit kennen oder vielmehr dies Bedürfnis
haben."[194]

For the historicity to which each is bound as to his own skin is that intimate externality within the element of thought. The "Denken des Denkens"
remains bound to a "Denken der Vorstellung". It is only in this externality
that spirit can recognize what it means, can be "sich gegenwärtig".[195]

[192] WL, II, p. 213.
[193] Propäd., p. 113.
[194] Gesch. Phil., XVIII, p. 179.
[195] Cf. pp. 24-5 above.

If, then, Hegel demands this complementary movement for the presence of meaning, we shall be true to his own attempts at understanding by continuing our thought of the Logic and system in the closest "Beispiel" of thought that experience offers us. "Nichts wird gewusst, was nicht in der Erfahrung ist, oder wie dasselbe auch ausgedrückt wird, was nicht als gefühlte Wahrheit, als innerlich geoffenbartes Ewiges, als geglaubtes Heiliges vorhanden ist."[196]

[196] Phän., p. 558.

PART II

LOGIC AND SYSTEM

CHAPTER IV

DEVELOPMENT TOWARD SYSTEM

I. THE PROBLEM RE-STATED

The revival of interest in Hegel which this century has witnessed, in Germany and later in France, has many explanations. One is certainly to be found in the publication, in 1907, of the essays Hegel wrote in his youth, up to his departure for Jena in 1801.[1] These essays, together with the "Phenomenology of Spirit" which Hegel himself published in 1807, reveal an intense interest in concrete experience, its development and contradictions, and a relative freedom from traditional philosophical formulations. Those who had seen in Hegel nothing but an arid logician and ruthless systematizer now found in him an inspiration for their own concern about a return "to the thing itself".

Some would today hold that Hegel's "Encyclopaedia" remains of purely antiquarian interest and that his value for the future lies entirely in the descriptions and "real" dialectic of his early writings. Certainly, much that the Encyclopaedia contains will concern none but the historian. Yet it may be that any study of Hegel's "pre-logical" writings must raise, if pursued far enough, the basic question with which the system, as such, grapples. No study of the "Phenomenology" can finally avoid the question what is meant by "das absolute Wissen", how it "appears", and what is the relation between the standpoints that are "für sich" and "für uns".

These are all questions of the "transition" from Phenomenology to Logic. The introduction to this study tried to suggest that this involves no less, as a mutual presupposition, the complementary transition from Logic to Phenomenology, the problem of which is at the heart of Hegel's much disputed transition from "Idea" to "Nature". In other words, the question of the transitions of the Encyclopaedia is not to be avoided. A contemporary

---

[1] Published by Herman Nohl, under the title, *Hegels theologische Jugendschriften.* The bias of Nohl's selection, his omission of other than theological writings, is today generally recognized (e.g., cf. Lukacs, pp. 30, 34).

statement of this question was sought in the studies of Hyppolite, Litt, and Mure.

The controversies that raged in the last century over the meaning of Hegel's system took their stand on Hegel's own explicit discussion of the system and its transitions.[2] This seemingly correct approach has been rejected in this study. Such passages are few and reflect Hegel's formalism rather than his thought. Their metaphorical language provides a convenient cover for basic ambiguities. Hyppolite, in discussing the interrelation of Logic and Phenomenology, admits that Hegel himself poses and resolves these problems "assez symboliquement".[3] Thus, the test for any interpretation must be, not so much whether it accords with these texts, as whether it can find verification at points within the system where Hegel has expressed himself more extensively and more incisively in the "element of thought": finally, that is, in the Logic, which Hegel always regarded as the ultimate criterion of interpretation.

The first part of this study has been concerned, then, simply with one such point of approach. The relation between thought and the "other" of thought, which is fundamental to an understanding of the system, has been traced in Hegel's doctrine of Vorstellung as the language which thought both presupposes that produces. Of this, and of the ground that was sought for it in the second book of the Logic, a summary will be given at the beginning of the next chapter.

It is, however, in terms of the third book of the Logic that Hegel developed the final form of his system. The problem that must now be faced is, therefore, how the attitude of the first part may be verified in this form. It is, at heart, the question which has been indicated, but by no means solved, how the second book of the Logic is "aufgehoben" in the third.

In a letter written to Schelling in 1800, Hegel said that he now felt himself driven to express the ideals of his youth in a philosophical system.[4] The understanding of his system from its historical origins is, as stated in the preface, not the method or claim of this study. Yet to ignore this approach completely would be to miss the wealth that Hegel's early writings have made available for any interpretation of his thought. Hence, this chapter will

---

[2] Examples may be found in the essays that compose McTaggart's *Studies in the Hegelian Dialectic* (1896).

[3] *Genése*, p. 575. Cf. also p. 578: "Le Savoir absolu, comme moment de l'histoire du monde, réconciliant ce moment temporel avec une vérité en soi intemporelle, nous est présenté sous une forme trop vague pour ne pas ouvrir la voie à des interprétations diverses, sans que nous puissions indiquer exactement celle qui constitue l'héritage authentique de l'hégélianisme."

[4] *Briefe*, I, p. 59.

summarize those aspects of Hegel's early ideals and first efforts at system which bear most closely upon the theme of this study.

Chapter V will then ask more directly what verification may be found for the attitudes of the first part in the form of the system. As the introduction explained, and tried to justify,[5] this verification will be sought in the expression Hegel gave to his system in his lectures on the philosophy of religion, his proximate and most detailed "illustration" for the system he elsewhere so little explained. That chapter will also form a continuity with the present one, in that the lectures mark Hegel's return, at the end of his life, to the religious questions of his early essays.

The third chapter of this part will try to draw together some of the themes of the whole study. It must serve as a conclusion. Yet the "circularity" of Hegel's thought, and no less its ambiguity, prevent both Hegel and his commentators from drawing any final conclusion.

2. DUALISM AND SYSTEM

The first part of this study has, with its application to the problem of thought and language and to the movement of the coupled categories of the Logic of Essence, been concerned with a Hegelian expression for certain of the fundamental dualities of experience. The term "duality" comes readily to mind, but is far from excluding its own ambiguities. Before extending the problem to the system itself, it may be of interest, and may help to clarify the interpretation sought, if reference be made to a recent, yet already "classical", interpretation of Hegel's system as a "dualism".

Interpretation of Iljin

This is the work of Iljin, which, though it first appeared in Russian in 1918, became generally known only after its German translation in 1946. A large and exceptionally well-documented study, it seeks to understand the many sides of Hegel's thought in terms of a development, through which he is held to have passed, from a radical monism to a final dualism. Dates are not supplied – it would clearly be impossible so to precise the theory – but it is implied that Hegel passed through three periods, each marked by the predominance of one of three themes that run through his work.

The first theme is a "panlogism", or "panepistemism" as Iljin prefers to call it, the romantic religious dream which inspired Hegel's most audacious

___
[5] pp. 19-20 above.

efforts at a philosophical system.[6] Had he been able to carry it through, one would have had to conclude that there is only one science, that of Logic.[7] For all others do no more than apply to the manifestation of their special realms the pure thought of the Notion.

The second theme is the immediate consequence of the obvious failure of the first when it found itself "helpless before the rebel chaos of the world".[8] The reaction was an "acosmism", which simply denied the reality of the world "outside" the Notion.[9] It is under the influence of this theme that texts containing such phrases as "Täuschung" and "List" come into prominence.

However, this theme was clearly as much a renunciation of philosophical effort as the first was a utopian appeal to it. Hegel was forced to adopt, as his mature philosophical position, a dualism of thought and intractable reality, though he would not gladly admit it and continued to express himself frequently in terms of his earlier themes.[10] For him, the "Poem des göttlichen Weltganges" had become the "Tragödie der göttlichen Leiden",[11] and of this it was not easy to speak.[12]

Nevertheless, Iljin gathers the evidence of an "ausgesprochenen dualistischen Charakter"[13] in Hegel's thought, which he summarizes in the thesis, reminiscent of that which Litt sought in Hegel's system,[14] "dass der Weg Gottes sich entzweit und dass sein Gang sich zugleich und parallel auf zwei Linien bewegt: in der Wissenschaft und in der Welt."[15] The result is that Hegel's thought came, in the end, close to the unfulfilled process of Fichte's philosophy, which he had once combatted so strongly,[16] and his panlogism became effectively, a "pan-teleologism": "Ihr letztes Wort ist nicht Begriff, sondern Organismus."[17]

Evaluation

How is this interpretation to be judged? In trying to disengage various themes in Hegel's thought and expression, Iljin has clearly gone beyond the custom-

---

[6] *Die Philosophie Hegels*, p. 196.
[7] p. 216.
[8] p. 240.
[9] p. 250.
[10] p. 278.
[11] p. 349.
[12] p. 379.
[13] p. 256.
[14] Cf. p. 9 above.
[15] *Die Philosophie Hegels*, p. 277.
[16] p. 360.
[17] p. 368.

ary interpretations, which seek to simplify to one persistent theme a thought that was always of many strata. Yet it may be asked whether this work, for all its erudition, does not over-simplify. The result may be that the "final dualism", rather than touching the depth of the "divine tragedy", or even of Hegel's own intellectual struggle, remains almost a banality unworthy of the serious metaphysical effort that led to it.

For Iljin's interpretation seems to imply the view, rejected in the last chapter,[18] that Hegel regarded his task as that of thinking the categories of logical thought and then merely searching for their verifications in nature and in the various forms of human experience. He met with resistance and accepted a dualism that had no positive content of its own but meant simply a tactful lowering of his early ideals.

It was the burden of much of the first part of this study to try to go beyond this view of verification as a simple observation by an uninvolved spectator. So far as this has been achieved, it is hoped that it will make possible an acceptance of Iljin's main thesis of a certain dualism in Hegel's system. Yet this is the dualism which comes from a re-appreciation of the thought epitomized in the Logic of Essence. It is a dualism with a positive content, rather than a mere failure. And it is a "final" dualism only in the sense – however it be understood – that Essence is "final" when "aufgehoben" in the Notion: that is, conserved as well as surpassed in the final identity.

Iljin speaks of Hegel's drama as that of a philosopher, "der die empirische Welt ablehnt und dennoch anerkennen muss."[19] Yet how much greater is the drama of a philosopher who realizes this predicament and makes of it the inner principle of his thought? Thought is no more simply "applied" to experience than meaning simply "clothes" itself in language. It is in the position rather of the essential moment of a category of Essence, which finds no simple expression in the unessential moment, but both develop – in an "Ablehnung" and "Anerkennung" – toward an adequate verification, each in the other, but which is not simply "modelled" on either.

So far, then, as it is possible to turn Hegel's own categories to the predicament that Iljin portrays at such length, it may be possible to accord him the "dualism" and "zweigleisiges Denken" without going so directly against Hegel's fundamental conception as to reduce his philosophy to a teleology, of which logic is but a species. Hegel's basic insight could then be held to have remained, that experience and the thought of experience are finally one – yet they realize their true identity only in the repeated rejection of all over-simple "verification".

[18] pp. 88-9 above.
[19] *Die Philosophie Hegels*, p. 359.

3. THE "JUGENDSCHRIFTEN" AND ORIGINS OF THE SYSTEM

a. Tübingen, Berne, Frankfurt

As has been seen from a letter to Schelling,[20] it was first in 1800 that Hegel turned to the task of formulating his thought as a system. He was then thirty years old, and forty-seven when his system finally appeared in the form of the "Encyclopaedia". Schelling himself had produced his first complete system before the age of twenty-six.

Hegel finished his studies at Tübingen in 1793. The seven years that passed before he joined Schelling at Jena were spent as a private tutor, first in Berne and then in Frankfurt. The essays he wrote in this period, without thought of publication, give little direct reference to what would then have been regarded as the problems of philosophy. They reveal, instead, a deep interest and wide reading in all realms of the culture of his day, particularly religion and history, a scrupulous concern for the ways in which the profounder regions of experience escape the customary forms of expression, and a painful effort nevertheless to bring them to more adequate formulation. It was from this long maturation that his system was able later to appear, almost unheralded and little explained.

First Attitude to Positivity

If any theme is to put into the compass of a few pages the intensive and complicated essays of this period, it may be the notion of "positivity". This is to be understood in its varying relation to the two profoundest influences of Hegel's youth. The first of these was the passion he shared with his friend Hölderlin for Greek thought and literature. Of modern philosophers, there is perhaps none so thoroughly steeped in the culture of Greece as Hegel. There he found the ideal of a religion of imagination and enthusiasm, humane and beautiful, through which the individual is brought into an immediate harmony with nature, with his people and his destiny.[21] The second influence was that of Kantian ethics. Hegel read Kant's *Kritik der praktischen Vernunft* (1788) and *Die Religion innerhalb der Grenzen der blossen Vernunft* (1793) when they appeared; and alongside Hegel's ideal of a "Volksreligion", drawn from Greece, may be found that of a "Vernunftreligion", in which all religious aspirations and forms should spring from the funda-

---

[20] p. 120 above.

[21] The ideal is first found in a school essay at Stuttgart (Dokumente, pp. 43-8), and runs through the writings collected by Nohl (e.g., pp. 23, 47, 376).

mental law of reason itself. This found its fullest expression in his "Life of Jesus", the portrait of a teacher of a purely moral religion.[22]

In relation to both the natural religion of Greece and the rational religion of Kant, Christianity showed the character of "positivity"; and the essays of Tübingen and Berne are devoted largely to expressing and explaining this characteristic, which Hegel found so distasteful.[23] Rather than deriving from man's concrete life or his reason, the doctrines, laws and institutions of Christianity are imposed on him from without.[24] Christianity thus, in the sheer particularity of its "givenness", withdraws man from his true spontaneity and harmony with life.[25] Correspondingly, the language of its dogma is abstract, it claims an absolute truth divorced from the experience of centuries, and submits itself to no norm of verification.[26]

Second Attitude to Positivity

In 1796 Hegel went to Frankfurt, and with this move comes a sudden and profound change from essays typical of the Age of Reason to writings that show a spirit imbued with the aims of Romanticism, the desire to pass beyond the conventional lines drawn between the divine and the human, the ideal and the real, the actor and the spectator.

The change is shown in a re-assessment of the positivity of the Christian religion. Firstly, without losing any of his enthusiasm for Greece, Hegel came to realize more fully the lack of that dimension of experience explored by the "unhappy consciousness" of the Christian. Secondly, without lessening his appreciation of the interiority of experience at which the Kantian revolution was finally directed, Hegel now wrote increasingly of the limits Kant himself imposed on the statement of his problem. In one fragment, Hegel explicitly identifies Kantian philosophy and positive religion.[27] For both show the same radical incapacity to reconcile the particularity of experience and its universal doctrine, law or thought. Even if Kant made this universal immanent to reason, he left it basically opposed to man's individuality.[28] Against the sheer "is", Kant set a merely formal "ought".

It thus became clear to Hegel that positivity could no longer simply be

[22] Nohl, pp. 75-136.
[23] To the question why and how the pure religion of Jesus thus became "distorted", Hegel devoted the longest of his essays of this period. Nohl has entitled it "Die Positivität der christlichen Religion" (pp. 152-231).
[24] E.g., pp. 212, 233.
[25] E.g., pp. 60-69, 215.
[26] E.g., pp. 43-4, 360, 40: "d.h. durch die christliche Religion könne man gut werden, wenn man schon vorher gut ist."
[27] p. 385.
[28] E.g., pp. 388, 390, 394.

rejected as opposed to the universality of reason, and his further development may be seen as an unceasing effort to find and express a reconciliation
of this basic duality, in such a way as to do justice to both extremes. This
was the ground for his philosophical thought, for his system, and for the
varied interpretations he and his commentators were to find in that system.

Hegel now re-wrote the preface to his longest essay on the "Positivity of
the Christian Religion".[29] He repudiated the claim of "analytic reason" to
separate what is natural and what positive.[30] Human nature is no mere concept which can be opposed to its accidentals; it must particularize itself in
these, and the manner of particularization that is true or false (which he now
called "positive") will vary from age to age.

Reconciliation

The "principle of reconciliation" which Hegel first proposed was love. It
forms the subject of a fragment of several pages[31] and of a long essay in
which Hegel tried to express his new-found appreciation of the "Spirit of
Christianity".[32] What is there developed at length is an attitude to experience
which composes the one-sidedness of the Greek and Kantian principles.
The "undeveloped unity" of the former becomes a "unity of identity and
division".[33] And the enforced unity of the Kantian imperatives is replaced by
a free conformity, in which there are "unendliche Unterschiede und unendliche Vereinigungen".[34]

In a related fragment, Hegel contributes a phrase which might well have
served him for a self-criticism in his later efforts to extend this vision to a
full system. "Begreifen ist beherrschen."[35] It is a criticism that he repeated
often in his portraits of what he considered to be the spirit of the Jewish
patriarchs: a hostility to reality whereby contradictions are mastered in an
identity that remains simply thought.[36] Christianity overcame this with the
doctrine of love: "Nur in der Liebe allein ist man eins mit dem Objekt, es
beherrscht nicht, und wird nicht beherrscht."[37] That is, Hegel's efforts at

---

[29] Nohl, pp. 139-51.

[30] E.g., p. 141: "Die lebendige Natur [des Menschen] ist ewig ein anderes als der Begriff derselben, und damit wird dasjenige, was für den Begriff blosse Modifikation, reine
Zufälligkeit, ein Überflüssiges war, zum Notwendigen, zum Lebendigen, vielleicht zum
einzig Natürlichen und Schönen. Damit erhält nun der anfangs aufgestellte Massstab für
die Positivität der Religion ein ganz anderes Aussehen."

[31] pp. 378-82.

[32] pp. 243-342.

[33] p. 379.

[34] p. 380.

[35] p. 376.

[36] E.g., pp. 244-7.

[37] p. 376.

this period (and hence his system, so far as it truly springs from them) must be understood as an attempt to avoid that very imposition of notions on reality, to which he may later himself have succumbed. True understanding can come, as in love, only in submitting oneself to an appreciation of that which is no less a separation that an identity. "Der Geliebte ist uns nicht entgegengesetzt, er ist eins mit unserem Wesen; wir sehen nur uns in ihm – und dann ist er doch wieder nicht wir – ein Wunder, das wir nicht zu fassen vermögen."[38]

In this perspective, what was Hegel's attitude to positivity? The term remains, and retains its pejorative sense. But it no longer refers to the "given" element of experience; that there must be. It designates now any mode of uniting universal and particular by a domination that does not respect their difference: "Wenn unvereinbares vereinigt wird, da ist Positivität."[39] The change of perspective from Berne is radical.

"Glauben und Sein"

Only two fragments of the Frankfurt period suggest explicitly that Hegel then saw these analyses of experience as specifically philosophical themes. The first has been entitled "Glauben und Sein".[40] Here, Hegel identifies what he had previously treated as antinomies of moral and religious experience with the reconciliation of particular subject and universal predicate in any judgment as such.[41] He is thus able to say simply: "Vereinigung und Sein sind gleichbedeutend." But how do we achieve this fundamental reconciliation and attain being? Hegel excludes two methods as false. One is the way of "positive faith", which merely presupposes the reconciliation as achieved.[42] The other is the way of rational proof, which simply destroys the "independence" of the reconciled terms and hence the true nature of the antinomy.[43] One is left, therefore, with reconciliation by a "faith" that is not "positive". How this is to be understood is not developed. But the essay as a whole would, it seems, best be interpreted as a re-affirmation of that attitude to experience which neither simply presupposes nor imposes a "meaning" but which submits itself to the identity that is no less an opposition. How this "faith" was to become "Vernunft" and how the "attitude" was to become a dialectical movement, all this was for the years at Jena and Nuremberg to expose.

[38] p. 377.
[39] p. 377.
[40] pp. 382-5.
[41] p. 383.
[42] p. 384.
[43] pp. 382-3.

"Systemfragment"

The other fragment that suggests a philosophical theme is the so-called
"Systemfragment von 1800",[44] dated four months before Hegel left for Jena.
Only a few pages remain from what must have been an essay as long as "The
Spirit of Christianity". It seems likely this was another study of religious
experience, and no attempt at a system. Yet what remains serves as a fitting
conclusion to the vital preparatory years at Frankfurt, for it shows clearly the
germs of the Logic and yet raises explicitly a key question for the interpretation of the system.

Hegel treats here of the principle of reconciliation as life. As with love, he
concludes that what is effected is no mere unity, but that one is obliged to
say, "Das Leben sei die Verbindung der Verbindung und der Nicht-Ver-
bindung."[45] He then remarks that (so far as one is thus speaking of a true
totality) every statement one makes calls forth its opposite. He adds, however, that this process does not go on without rest, for the final "union of
synthesis and antithesis" has a "reality beyond all reflection". That is, he
concludes, "die Philosophie muss mit der Religion aufhören."

It is perfectly true, as commentators have pointed out,[46] that this placing
of religion above philosophy for the final synthesis is not as striking as it
may seem. For by "philosophy" Hegel here meant the thought of "Verstand",
and "religion" stood for the rational "Vernunft" that he had not yet elabo-
rated. Yet it may be that, even so, the text touches upon a vital point. For in
the movement of Vernunft which was to be developed, each particular
synthesis would be achieved only by passing beyond it to a further triad, in
which it would be but a thesis. Yet what of the final triad? If this is to be
regarded as "closed", then this "standpoint" must have a "reality beyond"
any stage of that reason which has led up to it.[47] Whether Hegel's mature
expression leaves any room for such an interpretation is a question that
must be posed in the following chapter.[48]

---

[44] Nohl, pp. 345-51.

[45] p. 348.

[46] Cf. Haering, I, pp. 542-3; Asveld, p. 204.

[47] That is, the whole problem of "Aufhebung" is posed already. Hegel admits that the
"final stage" is a mystery from stages short of it (cf. pp. 108-9 above). Yet contact with these
stages (and hence rejection of dogmatic intuition) is obtained with the assurance that the
stages are "preserved" when "aufgehoben" into the final identity.

[48] In discussing Hegel's early thought of life as "the union of union and non-union",
Hyppolite suggests the origins of such a notion in the Romanticism of the time, and adds:
"L'originalité de Hegel n'est pas tant dans l'image mystique que dans la traduction *con-
ceptuelle* qu'il en donne." (*Etudes sur Marx et Hegel*, p. 17). It may be asked, however,
whether a "conceptual translation" of a "mystic image" can do more than modify a principle of explanation: i.e. whether it can free itself from its origins and produce an internal
intelligibility (cf. pp. 108-110 above).

b. Publications at Jena

Transition to Philosophy

If Hegel's move to Frankfurt had brought a remarkable change in the character of his essays, his move to Jena at the beginning of 1801 showed a no less sudden flowering of the philosophical themes which had been implicit in those essays. Here, for the first time, he wrote for publication. His first two years produced his habilitation thesis ("De Orbitis Planetarum"), various writings on moral and political philosophy,[49] and a series of articles which announced his attitude to philosophy and to his philosophical contemporaries. It is these articles which will form the subject of this section.

Hegel came to Jena as a disciple of Schelling. He qualified for his appointment as lecturer with a thesis in which he subscribed to Schelling's philosophy of nature. His first book was, at least ostensibly, a defense of Schelling's system in opposition to Fichte's: "Über die Differenz des Fichteschen und Schellingschen Systems" (July, 1801). With Schelling he edited the "Kritisches Journal der Philosophie", in which their articles were published anonymously.

Yet the origins of Hegel's own philosophy lay in his own meditations on the contradictions and reconciliation of experience, and his first publications reveal more explicitly how these themes stand at the heart of his notion of system than do any of his later writings. To this subject he devoted the first part of the "Differenzschrift" and the first three articles he wrote for the "Kritisches Journal".[50] These views will be outlined first. Then the same question will be considered so far as light is thrown on it by the position Hegel took toward Fichte and Schelling in the book devoted to them, and toward Kant in his fourth article, "Glauben und Wissen". Reference to the lectures Hegel was giving at the same time, which trace the details of his own developing system, will be reserved for the next section.

Philosophy as System

Hegel did not come to a philosophical system as a self-evident form of expression. He was obliged to justify the notion of system, for himself and for others. Hence he devotes a third of his book on Fichte and Schelling to a discussion of the "Bedürfnis der Philosophie" and of the fulfilment that

---

[49] "Die Verfassung Deutschlands", "System der Sittlichkeit", "Über die wissenschaftlichen Behandlungsarten des Naturrechts".

[50] To which are related a few shorter articles published by Hegel in the "Erlanger Literaturzeitung"; these have been reprinted by Lasson in his volume of *Hegel: Erste Druckschriften* (1928) pp. 131-42, 159-60, 212-19.

systematic thought must accord to this, the profoundest of human needs.[51] It is, indeed, this need for philosophy which is its presupposition, and its only one.[52] When expression is given to it, however, there appear to be two "presuppositions", such that "die Aufgabe der Philosophie besteht darin, diese Voraussetzungen zu vereinen."[53] The first is the absolute itself, which is already present to us. The second is the "Herausgetretensein des Bewusstseins aus der Totalität", its division into being and not-being, thought and being, finite and infinite. It is to be noticed that the primary task of philosophy, and hence of a system, is not to reconcile these "particular" dualities. It is to effect a reconciliation between the basic identity of the absolute, as it is abstractly present to us, and the fundamental dualities of our "own" finite experience. This Hegel now states in a formula that is familiar from Frankfurt:

So gut die Identität geltend gemacht wird, so gut muss die Trennung geltend gemacht werden ... Das Absolute selbst ist aber darum die Identität der Identität und der Nichtidentität.[54]

Hence it is the task of a philosophical system to raise to the realm of thought that attitude of "equilibrium" before the antinomies of experience, which Hegel had expressed in religious terms at Frankfurt. Its aim is to avoid the "positivity" of any reconciliation that is achieved from the side of abstract identity by "dominating" a merely finite duality; for this is to leave the terms of the antinomy simply "nebeneinander"[55] and make of the true identity a mere indefinite regress.[56]

Hegel stresses again that while we may say that the task of philosophy is "festgewordene Gegensätze aufzuheben", this does not mean simply to overcome the oppositions:

Denn die notwendige Enzweiung ist Ein Faktor des Lebens, das ewig entgegensetzend sich bildet: und die Totalität ist, in der höchsten Lebendigkeit, nur durch Wiederherstellung aus der höchsten Trennung möglich.[57]

[51] E.g., Differenz, p. 37: "Wenn man von einem System sagen kann, dass es Glück gemacht habe, so hat sich ein allgemeineres Bedürfnis der Philosophie, das sich für sich selbst nicht zur Philosophie zu gebären vermag, (denn damit hätte es sich durch das Schaffen eines Systems befriedigt) – mit einer instinktartigen Hinneigung zu demselben gewendet. Und der Schein der passiven Aufnahme rührt daher, dass im Innern das vorhanden ist, was das System ausspricht, welches nunmehr jeder in seiner wissenschaftlichen oder lebendigen Sphäre geltend macht."

(p. 40) "Der lebendige Geist, der in einer Philosophie wohnt, verlangt, um sich zu enthüllen, durch einen verwandten Geist geboren zu werden."

[52] p. 48.

[53] p. 49.

[54] p. 124.

[55] Differenz, p. 69; cf. also GW, pp. 285-6.

[56] Differenz, pp. 44-5.

[57] p. 46.

Thus, it may be noticed that the philosophical grasp of totality is attained in the true reconciliation (and hence respecting) of that basic duality between merely abstract identity and simply finite dualities. The concept of totality which is rightly to be criticized is that of the merely abstract identity: that is, but one of the extremes of the true totality.

This true totality is thus, for Hegel, the aim of philosophy, and the attitude of "equilibrium" by which it is sought must find expression in a system, of which any part – taken in abstraction from the whole – will represent a divergence toward one of the extremes. Hence, any philosophy which avoids expression as system is an "eternal flight" from those self-limitations through which the true totality is progressively manifested.[58] However, Hegel adds, in a sentence that may well be offered for his self-criticism:

Es ist möglich, dass eine echte Spekulation sich in ihrem System nicht vollkommen ausspricht, oder dass die Philosophie des Systems und das System selbst nicht zusammenfallen.[59]

Scepticism, Common Sense, and Philosophy

These attitudes toward philosophy are reflected in Hegel's first three contributions to the "Kritisches Journal". In the longest of the three, he develops for the first time the theme, later to become central to his view of "Phenomenology", of that asceticism by which the naive consciousness makes its way toward true philosophical knowledge.[60] That which passes in modern times for "scepticism" (that is, positivism) is merely a concealed dogmatism that fails to question the unconscious presuppositions of its own position. The true scepticism, Hegel maintains, is a repeated turning into the source of experience, from which its antinomies appear.

What, however, is the nature of this "turning-in"? Hegel comes closest to suggesting his attitude in regard to the fundamental identity-in-opposition of thought and being.[61] On the one hand, philosophy may not merely presuppose this identity; on the other hand, this may not be "proved" (erklären, ergründen). The task of philosophy is rather to bring it to manifestation (aussprechen, erkennen, zum Bewusstsein bringen). The relation to Hegel's Frankfurt essay on "Glauben und Sein" may be noted.[62]

A further article on the relation of "common sense" to philosophy[63] sur-

[58] Differenz, pp. 71-2.
[59] p. 72.
[60] "Das Verhältnis des Skeptizismus zur Philosophie", pp. 215-75.
[61] Skept., p. 258.
[62] p. 127 above.
[63] "Wie der gemeine Menschenverstand die Philosophie nehme", pp. 193-212.

vives to fame as Hegel's reply to Herr Krug's challenge to deduce his pen.[64]
The reply is more an exhibition of Hegel's propensity for sarcasm than a
satisfactory account of his notion of philosophical deduction. But the essentials of such an account are implied. No singular thing can be "deduced"
from a universal concept. If Herr Krug wishes to reduce his human nature to
the level of life of a dog or a rose, and thus "grasp" their being as it is in its
pure singularity, he is welcome.[65] But philosophical understanding, far from
simply starting with a universal and passing to a singular, is a progressive
appreciation of that totality which manifests itself only in the radical duality
of universal and singular.

It is, however, in the first article he contributed to the "Kritisches Journal"
that Hegel discusses most explicitly his notion of philosophical system.[66]
Together with "parallel" passages of his book on Fichte and Schelling, this
article is the first indication of the relation Hegel was to see between philosophical system and history of philosophy – a conception which, as much as
any, marks the position Hegel was himself to occupy in that history. He
begins by considering the condition of possibility of philosophical criticism
as such. This, he maintains, is "meaningful" only in the affirmation of a
fundamental unity of philosophy in its history.[67] This history can not, then,
be seen merely as a succession of particular affirmations about reality, one
simply opposed to the other. It must finally form a system, such that particular philosophies are each a grasp of the whole from the standpoint of one of
its parts – hence both a distortion and a presence of the whole.[68] The function of a contemporary philosopher is therefore not merely to oppose one
more view to those of his "adversaries" but to seek an understanding of
the true totality that reveals itself in these partial views, to aim at "individuality" rather than "subjectivity"[69] or "particularity".[70]

With this ideal before him, Hegel was to lecture on the history of philosophy for the first time in 1805, and the attitude of "incorporation" rather
than of "refutation" was to find its most exalted expression in the spiritual
autobiography of the "Phenomenology". The system of philosophy which
followed was his final claim to have found a "principle of reconciliation"
which was at once the presupposition and completion of the philosophy of
his predecessors. That this principle remained but a principle, bound to the

[64] p. 199.
[65] p. 201.
[66] "Über das Wesen der philosophischen Kritik überhaupt", pp. 173-89.
[67] p. 175.
[68] Cf. also Differenz, pp. 39-44.
[69] PK, p. 177.
[70] Differenz, pp. 41-2.

"subjective originality" of its time, can not now be doubted; but whatever his actual "Darstellung", it is important to keep in mind Hegel's view of philosophical system as that expression of thought which makes possible a "lebendige Originalität",[71] and opens the thinker to "eine Wegbereitung für den Einzug wahrer Philosophie".[72]

Attitude to Fichte and Schelling ("Differenzschrift")

In an obscure sentence which closed the last essay at Frankfurt, Hegel implied that it would be better to remain without reconciliation than to accept any which were "unedel und niederträchtig".[73] The reference may be to the systems of Fichte and Schelling and to the critical attitude he was already forming toward both: for his final judgment, and that which came to the open in the preface to his "Phenomenology", was that neither achieved a "noble" reconciliation.

In the book he published in 1801, Hegel still defends the position of Schelling against Fichte. But the criterion of his judgment is that attitude of philosophical "equilibrium", against which Schelling would be found later to be as defective as Fichte. Its application to Fichte is stated concisely by Hegel as the thesis he is to establish: the reconciliation achieved by Fichte remains "eine subjective Identität des Subjekts und Objekts".[74] That is, it remains a "positive" union, achieved from the side of abstract identity.

Into the details of Hegel's long account of Fichte's system there would be no reason for entering here. Hegel regarded this system as "the completion of the Kantian philosophy".[75] Hence he reveals in his criticism of it no basic conception of system that was not already contained in the attitudes toward Kant that he developed at Frankfurt. Fichte gave to Kant's philosophy a "speculative unity", but the unity remained simply other than the dualities which opposed it: it is therefore subjective and "gewaltsam".[76] Though this runs throughout his system, it is clearly expressed in the structure of the three principles of the Ego, expounded at the beginning of the *Wissenschaftslehre* of 1794. The first two remain simply opposed, and there is no true synthesis possible for the third.[77] That which is imposed must render the subjective term absolute and negate the objective.[78] For all the nobility of

---

[71] Differenz, p. 44; PK, p. 179.
[72] PK, p. 188.
[73] Nohl, p. 351.
[74] Differenz, p. 76.
[75] Gesch. Phil., XIX, p. 611.
[76] Differenz, p. 73.
[77] pp. 82-4.
[78] p. 87.

Fichte's doctrine of liberty, he never truly transcends the outlook of the Old Testament patriarchs, and his final word must remain "domination".[79]

Hegel's conception of system may, however, receive some further illumination from a brief account of the way in which he exposes Schelling's system of 1800 as successfully avoiding the one-sided synthesis of Fichte. As he intended a favourable interpretation, his presentation could be expected to incline toward his own ideal.

Hegel's exposition minimizes the priority of Nature over Ego that Schelling actually maintained, and he emphasizes all indications of their complementarity. For in the "Indifferenzpunkt" of Schelling he found an apt expression for the ideal of true reconciliation, and hence of systematic "equilibrium", which he held. In this, the subjective identity of Fichte is complemented by an objective identity, such that the absolute is fully expressed only in both one-sided unions taken together.[80]

There results a system of two complementary sciences. The "System der Intelligenz" (Transcendental Philosophy) treats objects merely as in consciousness. But this assimilation of nature to consciousness is complemented by a "System der Natur" (Philosophy of Nature), which treats intelligence simply as rising from nature.[81] The two sciences are not, however, to be set in any causal relation, nor is one in any way reduced to the other. The point of view that must be adopted is a unique one which sees the two sciences as truly distinct and yet as necessary manifestations of the same absolute.[82] "Das Absolute... muss sich in einer Zweiheit der Form setzen. Denn Erscheinen und Sich-Entzweien ist Eins."[83] Each science is itself a totality, but one that is "relative", for it reveals itself as tending beyond itself to this unique standpoint, the "Indifferenzpunkt", from which the duality is grasped as such.[84] This "tendency", however, never in practice gets beyond a certain disequilibrium, which, according to the preponderance of sense or thought, constitutes the realms of art, religion, and speculation.[85] Yet even the latter remains a relative totality, subjective, formal, and opposed to nature.[86] The true totality is to be attained only in an intuition beyond thought: "absolute, weder subjektive, noch objektive Identität, reine transcendentale Anschauung".[87]

---

[79] p. 110.
[80] pp. 122-3.
[81] p. 128.
[82] p. 130.
[83] p. 135.
[84] pp. 140-1.
[85] p. 142.
[86] p. 143.
[87] p. 144.

Hegel was not long to rest content with the mystical "night" of this intuition,[88] and his efforts at Jena were to be directed largely toward understanding the ways in which the true totality is no less revealed than hidden in the dialectical relationship of "partial totalities".[89] Two questions, however, must remain.

Firstly, even when he replaced the transcendental intuition with "absolute knowledge", did Hegel not perhaps retain, in respect of its final "indifference", some sense of its being radically other than all those stages of knowledge which lead up to it?[90]

Secondly, in what way was the above form of the "two sciences" preserved when "aufgehoben" into the triadic form of Hegel's own system? It might be an apt criticism of Hegel to say that his success at evolving a dialectical movement was at the expense of the ideals of system he expressed in this book: that he was himself to pass from a strict equilibrium of opposites to the very primacy of the subjective he had criticized in Fichte. Yet is it not possible that these ideals of "philosophical equilibrium" may always have guided the vision that sought expression in a triadic system? The suggestion would then be that this system may have clothed, somewhat unhappily, a thought that had not strayed so far from his early exposition of Schelling: of a system which reveals the absolute only in the complementarity of two "parallel" sciences, each a relative totality that both presupposes and interprets the other.

It will be for the following chapter to apply this suggestion at one point of Hegel's mature expression.

Attitude to Kant ("Glauben und Wissen")

The longest of Hegel's contributions to the "Kritisches Journal"[91] marks for him a return to the interest of his earliest meditations, "the old opposition between philosophy and positive religion".[92] Now, however, Hegel sees the scene of the conflict as transferred; it has been set within philosophy itself. Merely positive faith has returned in the guise of a subjective thought whose presence to itself is no more than an indefinite future. For the pre-critical dogmatism of the object has been substituted a dogmatism of the subject.[93]

In this sense, Hegel analyses the philosophies of Kant, Jacobi, and Fichte. For the theme of the present study, nothing basically new is to be derived.

---

[88] "Das Absolute ist die Nacht, und das Licht jünger als sie. . ." (p. 49).
[89] For his mature criticism of Schelling, in this respect, cf. Gesch. Phil., XIX, pp. 662-3.
[90] Cf. p. 128 above.
[91] "Glauben und Wissen", pp. 279-433.
[92] p. 279.
[93] p. 431.

But a short reference will be made to the comments on Kant. For at Frankfurt, Hegel had known only the Kant of the moral and religious writings. In this article, however, he takes a position to the *Kritik der reinen Vernunft*.[94]

Hegel's criticism here is constructive. The subjective one-sidedness of Kant's philosophy, he maintains, is to be found precisely in its greatest achievement: in the doctrine of the *a priori* synthesis, and particularly in that of the productive imagination.[95] This, "the most interesting point of the Kantian system",[96] is not simply a middle-term introduced between subject and world. It is "das, welches das Erste und Ursprüngliche ist, und aus welchem das subjektive Ich sowohl als die objektive Welt erst zur notwendig zweiteiligen Erscheinung und Produkt sich trennen."[97] It is in this originality, productive of its opposites,[98] that Hegel finds the proper field of philosophy and the way to develop to thought the strivings of his years at Berne and Frankfurt. The productive imagination is, for him, "a true speculative idea",[99] "nothing but reason itself".[100] This "zweiseitige Identität"[101] would grasp the positive side of the antinomies of understanding.[102] It would, in fact (though Hegel does not explicitly suggest it), be the point of Kant's system which Hegel would develop to overcome the "transcendental intuition" of Schelling.

All this, however, was interpretation. Hegel points out that Kant himself failed to appreciate the way of approach that he opened. Instead of thinking from "within" the identity-in-opposition of the imagination, he treated it as a unity that Hegel describes as formal, mechanical, psychological.[103] The imagination becomes a faculty, the property of the subject, and hence imposes unity on that which is foreign to it.[104]

Again, this exposition stresses Hegel's view of the "impartial", yet truly "involved", situation of the philosopher. There is certainly a sense in which, as in the common estimate, Kant remains the philosopher of duality, Hegel of identity. Yet it must be seen that Hegel's fundamental criticism of Kant was that his merely "external" dualism prevented him from penetrating the most intimate "Doppelseitigkeit" of experience.

[94] and also the third "Critique".
[95] GW, p. 297.
[96] p. 315.
[97] p. 301
[98] p. 297
[99] p. 299.
[100] p. 301.
[101] pp. 299, 301.
[102] p. 313.
[103] pp. 303, 305.
[104] p. 322.

Further, part of the interest of Hegel's exposition here may lie in the emphasis it places on his own doctrine of imagination. For, as we have seen in Chapter II, it is at this point that Hegel sets the origin of language. Hence the approach to Hegel, adopted by this study, through the complicated dialectic of thought and language, may find some justification in Hegel's own designation of the "two-sided identity" of imagination as the ground that is "first and original" for the development of a system of philosophy.

c. The Jena "Systems"

Their Content

Apart from what has been mentioned in the previous section, Hegel published nothing until the "Phenomenology", the manuscript of which he finished in October 1806, four months before he left Jena.

Yet he lectured during his years at Jena over the "whole science of philosophy": that is, logic, metaphysics, philosophy of nature, and philosophy of spirit. The "Phenomenology", with its profound and extensive analyses, was written at immense speed, hence clearly from material already at hand. And in 1808, Hegel was to produce without effort a complete "Philosophische Enzyklopädie" for his pupils at Nuremberg.[105]

What was the written source for these lectures and compositions? Three manuscripts survive. They are certainly more than lecture notes. As early as 1802, Hegel announced the appearance of a book, which his lectures would follow. Whether any of the manuscripts that remain was intended, as such, for publication is not certain. But it is safe to say that they represent a stage close to the intended form of publication.

The first manuscript is to be dated 1802.[106] It contains a logic, a metaphysic, and a philosophy of nature up to the section on "physics". It is thus clearly incomplete, and the material which would have concluded the philosophy of nature and added a philosophy of spirit may be presumed from the later manuscripts and from Hegel's writings on moral philosophy at that time.

In relation to Hegel's later development, the most striking character of this first "system" is the separation of logic and metaphysics. The division is, however, by no means clear. The logic contains the following sections: quality, quantity and infinity; the relations of substance, causality and reciprocity; notion, judgment and syllogism; and finally a section, entitled

---

[105] Propäd., pp. 168-227.

[106] published in 1915 by Ehrenberg and Link, as *Hegels Erstes System*; Lasson produced a better edition, in 1923, under the title, *Jenenser Logik, Metaphysik und Naturphilosophie*.

"Proportion", on the analytic and synthetic methods of knowledge. The metaphysic begins with the principles of identity, excluded middle, and sufficient reason; then comes a metaphysic of "objectivity", treating of the soul, the world, and the supreme being; finally, a metaphysic of "subjectivity" comprises the theoretical ego, the practical ego, and absolute spirit. Thus, the mingling of themes traditionally proper to logic and metaphysics is apparent.

In the presentation of absolute spirit as the conclusion of the metaphysics, there is, however, a clear continuity with Hegel's later system. This is the point where the form of knowing becomes finally one with its content. "Diese Idee des Ansich realisiert sich in der Metaphysik, indem das Erkennen sein eigener Inhalt wird."[107] Spirit nevertheless shows itself to be "only" thought: "Der Geist, wie er aufgezeigt worden ist, ist darum nur Idee."[108] It passes by an "Abfall" to nature, the "other" through which it must make its way to return to itself.[109] Thus, the question of "transitions" is raised even in the earliest formulation Hegel gave to his thought as a whole.

If the first manuscript lacked a philosophy of spirit and much of the philosophy of nature, the second and third contain no logic (or metaphysic)[110] They cover only the matter Hegel presented in his lectures on "Realphilosophie", that is, the philosophies of nature and of spirit.[111] Yet this was regarded by him as part of a full "system". The manuscript dated 1803/4 has the numbers II and III against the philosophies of nature and spirit respectively, and there is an explicit reference to a "first part": "Der erste Teil der Philosophie konstruierte den Geist als Idee. . . Diese Idee fiel in der Philosophie der Natur absolut auseinander."[112]

The manuscript dated 1805/6 contains a developed form of this philosophy of nature and spirit. Haering suggests that the relative clarity of its script may indicate that it was intended for publication.

The Principles of Division

There is, then, justification for seeing in these three manuscripts together the first expression Hegel gave to his system. Further into their content, however, this study can not go. This is a task renounced in a book which makes

---

[107] JL, p. 175.

[108] p. 185.

[109] p. 186.

[110] published in 1931-2 by Hoffmeister as *Jenenser Realphilosophie* I & II.

[111] Hegel used the term "Realphilosophie" himself in 1805, and effectively retains it in the preface to the first edition of his Logic: ". . . die beiden realen Wissenschaften der Philosophie, die Philosophie der Natur und die Philosophie des Geistes." (WL, I, p. 7).

[112] JR, I, p. 195.

no claim to a purely historical approach to the intentions underlying the form of Hegel's system. It is probably on these writings of Hegel, set in their full situation, that such an approach would have to concentrate. And it is an almost completely unexplored land; the only one to have ventured far beyond its frontiers is Haering.[113]

For the different approach that has here been adopted, and for the purposes of this chapter, it will be sufficient to summarize the conclusions to which Haering himself comes on what Hegel meant by the form he gave to this early system. Haering stresses that the system is to be understood in continuity with the effort, shown in the Frankfurt essays and Jena publications, to establish how each particular experience or thought, in its very claim to absoluteness, reveals at once its own partiality and the true totality against which this is seen.[114] The first system is therefore best approached through an analysis of the various principles of organization (or division) which Hegel applied in his attempt to achieve this aim. The principles Haering finds are three:

1. A division by mere *grades of generality*. This, the principle predominant in traditional philosophy, organizes its matter in steps that pass from the most particular to that which is the most universal and the ground of all. It remains, however, a classification without internal "movement" from one step to the other.

2. A *dialectical* division. Under this heading is included the various ways in which such a movement is achieved. There is no completely uniform pattern, but all try to show how each step, in its very isolation, reveals its insufficiency in relation to another step, whether contradictory or simply "other". The identity-in-opposition of the two manifests the truer totality of which they are moments. But this shows its own partiality, and the process is repeated.

3. A strict division of the whole in terms of a *Spiritual Monism* ("Geistes-monismus"). This is the dialectical division applied to the whole system as "achieved". That is, the standpoint of the true totality (Spirit) is attained, from which it is seen to be perfectly verified in its two proximate moments (Logic and Nature). Even to state this principle is to raise profound questions of its interpretation, but it may be identified with the theme of "Panepiste-mism" discussed by Iljin.[115]

Haering's task thus becomes that of applying these three principles to the manuscript of 1802, seeking their relative predominance, first in the system

[113] in volume II of *Hegel, sein Wollen und sein Werk*.
[114] p. 61.
[115] Cf. pp. 121-2 above.

as a whole, secondly within its various parts. Only the first will here be summarized.

He begins by affirming that the longer one studies this system, the more clear it becomes that, if one treats of the three parts as logic, metaphysic, and Realphilosophie, the basic principle of organization remains one by grades of generality.[116] The attempts to establish a dialectical relation between the parts are genuine but remain ambiguous. This ambiguity rests fundamentally with the metaphysics, which takes its place in a scale of generality at once with the Realphilosophie and with the Logic.[117] The later identification of logic and metaphysics[118] would set this ambiguity at the heart of the new science of "logic", which would have both the reality of a self-sufficient metaphysics and the ideality of a mere thought that requires completion by nature and spirit.

However, it is an ambiguity of which Hegel was aware, even in the Frankfurt period, in the form of that paradox by which nature is both an opposition to spirit and the developing process of spirit.[119] His system may justly be seen as covering (and expressing) various approaches to this paradox. Yet the question of assigning to him any single "final" interpretation remains "ein ungelöstes und. . . unlösbares Problem der Hegelinterpretation".[120]

Thus, if one is to say that the tripartite division of the first system expresses basically a progress by grades of generality, one must nevertheless allow for a progress along two lines, ambiguously parallel:

Man kann freilich versuchen – und Hegel selbst macht ebenfalls solche Andeutungen – beides so zu vereinigen, dass man sagt: Hegel gehe zunächst von isolierten Begriffe aus und zeige (und zwar von den formalen wie den gegenständlichen, den Begriffen des Seins wie des Denkens) in Logik und Metaphysik zunächst, wie diese, rein begrifflich, immer mehr und weiter über sich hinaus bis zum Begriff des wahren Absoluten treiben. Und dann beginne erst auch am realen Sein dieselbe Entwicklung. . . durch alle Einzelphänomene der Realphilosophie.[121]

What, then is to be said of the presence in this system of the third principle of division, the Spiritual Monism? That Hegel regarded a perfect triple self-division, on the analogy of the Trinity, as the ideal of a philosophical system is indicated by a fragment, from the early Jena period, which has been entitled "Vom göttlichen Dreieck".[122] The need for force in completing the

[116] Haering, II, p. 67.
[117] pp. 255-6.
[118] As long as Hegel remained at Jena, he would keep them, at least ostensibly, separated.
[119] pp. 130-44.
[120] p. 146.
[121] p. 144.
[122] Dokumente, pp. 304-6.

analogy, at least in regard to the Second and Third Persons with Nature and Spirit, is evident.[123] Yet the ideal of this final "model of reconciliation" never left Hegel. In the first system, it is to be found at certain isolated points, notably in the transition to Nature.[124] But for the true movement of the system, and for almost all of its parts, this principle of division comes into no account at all.[125]

The second principle, however, that of particular dialectical ascents toward a concrete totality, remains the ideal which Hegel proposed to himself most effectively in this first attempt to give a living organization to the vast matter at hand.[126] There are some parts which verify it well, others in which it is clearly artificial, others in which it is absent and the first principle stands alone. But the application of a dialectical principle to the system as a whole remains fundamentally ambiguous.

In conclusion, Haering stresses that this conflict of principles survived throughout the subsequent development of Hegel's system.[127] His initial intuition remained, that particulars could be understood only in the true totality and that the truth of this totality was revealed only in the abstractness of the particulars. His system represents a complex and many-sided attempt to develop the meaning of the guiding intuition. In particular, Haering maintains, the principle of a final "Geistesmonismus", under which the Logic is the thought of absolute spirit "before creation", never attained supremacy over the other principles.[128] He holds that Hegel himself never radically denied the viewpoint expressed in his first system, "wonach die Logik nur die allgemeinsten Bestimmungen alles Seins darstellen soll, die erst zusammen mit dem konkreten Gehalt der Realphilosophie (wie freilich auch umgekehrt) etwas, d.h. mehr als blosse Abstraktionen, sind."[129]

Conclusions

The preceding section has presented the verdicts of another, but of the only one who has published a detailed examination of the Jena system.[130] Their bearing on the interpretation sought in the present study may be summarized as follows:

[123] Haering, II, pp. 134-5.
[124] JL, pp. 185-7; JR, I, p. 195.
[125] Haering, II, p. 147.
[126] p. 95.
[127] pp. 151-3.
[128] p. 147.
[129] p. 83.
[130] Studies of particular aspects of Hegel's work at Jena have been made by Hoffmeister, Lukacs, and J. Schwarz.

Firstly, it may be emphasized that Hegel's system is prior to his "Phenomenology of Spirit". Six years before the publication of this book, Hegel had
worked out a detailed proof that he took seriously his own principle, that
philosophy must exist as system. The view, not uncommon, that Hegel's
system represents a distortion which first appeared after the Phenomenology,
is certainly an oversimplification.

Secondly, such light as has been thrown on this period, so critical for the
formation of Hegel's system, tends to justify the approach taken by this
study. Hegel was himself struggling to find his own meaning, and it would
seem rash to affirm that any single interpretation of the system, to the exclusion of all others, was his, even at the end of his career. Hence the function
of a commentator may be rather to reveal, and even "develop", one such
philosophical "attitude" that Hegel expressed in his system. This interpretation must take the final form of the system as a guide, but seek its origin in a
less equivocal domain.

Thirdly, the findings of Haering show in Hegel's earliest efforts at system a
dualism more basic than that which Iljin holds to be only a late result of
failure. And if the comments of this chapter on Hegel's Frankfurt essays and
Jena publications are not far wrong, such a "dualism" may be a truer expression of Hegel's early notion of philosophy than the unqualified monism
in terms of which his later triadic form is usually interpreted. His philosophy
was certainly the pursuit (and attainment) of a "final unity". But this unity
would be falsified, made subjective, formal, positive, so far as it involve any
standpoint simply beyond the terms to be reconciled: that is, so far as the
true "beginning" cease also to be a true "result". Hence, any "Geistes-
monismus" which would unambiguously adopt the standpoint of the final
totality, "at the expense of" lower stages, and imperiously expect perfect
"verification" at these levels, would remain a "subjective identity" or abstract totality, a domination from the side of the logic. The true "point of indifference" is at the heart of the duality. And nowhere is there a more intimate duality than that between experience and the logic of experience. If
Hegel's first system served at all to bring this, among its many other themes,
to expression, then it may be a worthy development from Schelling's transcendental intuition toward the thought that is an "externality" within its
own "element".

d. Origin of the Phenomenology

The system of 1805/6, if intended for print, was never produced as such. Instead, the intensive efforts of the Jena period finally yielded their fruit in the
book that many regard as the antithesis of Hegel's "systematic" philosoph-

izing. The "Phenomenology of Spirit" is, and must remain, an enigma of Hegel's development, set as it is between the prosaic paragraphs of the Jena system and those of the Nuremberg and Heidelberg Encyclopaedias. It is well, however, to see in what the enigma consists, and that will be the sole purpose of this postscript to the chapter on Hegel's early writings.

Starting in 1802, periodic references appeared to the book Hegel intended to publish. All indicated that it would follow the plan revealed by the Jena manuscripts and Hegel's lectures: that is, it would start with the Logic and conclude with the Realphilosophie. It seems to have been as late as 1806 that Hegel changed his form of exposition. The reason was probably pedagogical, and may have had its source in the difficulties students found with his lectures. The new plan was to start, not with the Logic, but with that point of the philosophy of spirit which represents the stage at which the beginner is most likely to be, the attitude of naive consciousness:[131] that is, the point at which the "Phenomenology" actually begins.

The course Hegel then intended his book to pursue has been explained by Haering,[132] and his theory is now generally accepted.[133] It was a course subsequently followed in the first lessons Hegel gave at Nuremberg to the Mittelklasse, in 1808/9.[134] It had been outlined in 1793 at Berne,[135] and was before Hegel as he composed the "Phenomenology", in the form of a note inserted in the second Jena manuscript.[136] In this latter form, there would be a passage direct from the stages of Intuition, Imagination, and Memory to the beginning of the Logic. In the form which Haering proposes, the "Phenomenology" would have developed through the stages of "Bewusstsein" (A) and "Selbstbewusstsein" (B) to "Vernunft" (C), and there, at the point now entitled "Logical and Psychological Laws",[137] would have passed directly to the beginning of the Logic. It seems, indeed, that it was Hegel's original intention to include the Logic in the same volume with the Phenomenology.

However, when Hegel reached this point of transition, there occurred the second, and more mysterious, change of intention. Instead of expounding the development of the pure thought of absolute spirit through its categories, he proceeded to convert the mere "introduction" of his system into a complete

---

[131] Cf. p. 44 above.

[132] Originally in his contribution to the Third Hegel Congress, Rome 1933; cf. also *Hegel, sein Wollen. . .*, II, pp. 479-81.

[133] Cf. Hoffmeister's introduction to his edition of the "Phenomenology" and Hyppolite, *Genèse*, pp. 55-9.

[134] Nürnberg, pp. 11-50. Here, § 34 is still in the "Phenomenology" and, without interruption, § 35 marks the beginning of the "Logic".

[135] Dokumente, pp. 197-217.

[136] JR, I, p. 207.

[137] Phän., pp. 221 ff.

philosophy of spirit, reaching absolute spirit only after exposing the full portrait-gallery of "Gestalten" of subjective and objective spirit.

Many are the explanations, based on Hegel's circumstances at the time, which have been proposed for this change.[138] It may be of value, however, to suggest, not so much what "explains" the change, as what the change itself indicates.

Firstly, it indicates a point in Hegel's system where, contrary to the usual metaphor of a circle, he was able to choose between divergent paths. This point is the one to which the commentary of Chapter II was devoted, the stage of "imagination" and "memory" where language passes into thought, where the "psychological" order is raised to the "logical" – though not without remainder.

Secondly, the change indicates that the choice of either path necessitates a transfer "later" to the other. Hegel chose to follow the "Gestalten der Welt", the path of the Realphilosophie. But this choice was at the expense of the other, and the final attainment of "das absolute Wissen" meant a transition to the way of the Logic:[139] that is, a return to the path that had been rejected in making the choice. Yet suppose the path of the Logic had originally been chosen. This choice would have been at the expense of the first, and it would no less have revealed the limits inherent in every choice. The full realization of these limits would mark its transition to the path of the Realphilosophie:

Das Wissen kennt nicht nur sich, sondern auch das Negative seiner selbst, oder seine Grenze. Seine Grenze wissen heisst, sich aufzuopfern wissen. Diese Aufopferung ist die Entäusserung, in welcher der Geist sein Werden zum Geiste, in der Form des freien zufälligen Geschehens darstellt . . .[140]

Thus, the enigma of the Phenomenology, set between the Jena system and the Nuremberg Logic, is the enigma of the system itself. And this is only partly represented by a circle, which carries no suggestion of choice. Hegel might have found apter metaphors for his system if, instead of succumbing to misguided religious reflections which would make of the doctrine of the Trinity a model of philosophical explanation, he had stayed closer to the terminology of Schelling. For, in his varying plans for the "Phenomenology", Hegel illustrated well the predicament of human thought and experience, rent between two "relative totalities" or "parallel ways".

However, there was for Hegel, unlike Schelling, no simple intuition in which reconciliation could be found. He was faced with the labour, and the

---

[138] E.g., Haering, II, p. 482.
[139] Phän., p. 562.
[140] Phän., p. 563.

dilemma, of thought. He might choose the path of thought in its "purity" or the "real" dialectic of the spatio-temporal forms of thought. Yet each would reveal itself as "abstract" and as presupposing the other. He might, as he did, follow one and complement it "later" with the other. But philosophy will not allow of a "later". The true reconciliation is no mere future, which faith sees as the final convergence of disparate lines. Nor is it the simple presence of attainment. It shows itself, for Hegel, only in the most intimate opposition that human thought realizes in itself. And it is this "divided-identity", or "incomplete-completion", that Hegel tried to symbolize by speaking of his system as a circle.

CHAPTER V

THE SYSTEM IN THE ELEMENT OF VORSTELLUNG

I. RECAPITULATION

If much of this study has been concerned with the difficulty of posing a philosophical question, in that the question is itself made possible only by that depth of thought which – in a sense – constitutes its answer, then it can hardly be expected that the question which the study as a whole is trying to pose can have been clearly formulated from the beginning. The whole first part was perhaps not so much an instrument for solution as a means of invention.

The adequate expression of any philosophical question would suppose a place of questioning which overcomes that multiplicity of partial formulations and alternative expressions to which the questioner finds himself condemned. It is a condemnation of which Hegel is traditionally represented as being happily unaware. Yet if the interpretation given in the introduction was not totally awry, it is this human predicament which each of the three authors there quoted hoped, in his way, to discover in that metaphysical insight of Hegel which underlies the forbidding formalism, and "final identity", of his system.

It was in this sense that the attempt at expressing the problem was turned to the question of the transitions of the system. For it is in his central, but scarcely expounded, transitions from phenomenology to absolute knowledge and, complementarily, from Idea to Nature that Hegel's thought of the all-comprising identity-in-difference of human and absolute experience is focussed. The problem was formulated more precisely as that of the place of the Logic in the System. Granted that the Logic can be held neither as a simply autonomous beginning nor as a conclusion that sublates all the foregoing without remainder, how can one think the movement of logical thought as a mutual development with non-logical experience? What was sought was expressed as a "zweigleisiges Denken", or as a process of "imperfect sublation", or as an understanding of the paradox that the Logic can pass out of itself while remaining itself, constitute the whole of the system and yet only a part of it. All such formulations were, however, interpreted as an attempt to realize more fully that the totality or final identity of Hegel's system – far from being a simply dogmatic beginning – comes progressively to light only in the duality of human thinking: namely in the complementarity of a merely finite experience and a formal "talking about" an absolute experience of which it is still largely innocent.

One further interpretation, that of Iljin, was briefly discussed in the preceding chapter. According to this, awareness of the condemnation of human thought to such a duality must be seen as the final word that Hegel had to offer. But it was a whispered word, drowned for must students by the triumphant optimism of Hegel's early conviction of the unopposed presence of the Logos in the world and by the pessimistic tones of a certain "acosmism" which resulted from the first failures.

It was agreed with Iljin that various strata may be found in Hegel's thought, despite its confident air of conclusive uniformity. It was agreed, further, that his system might be described as a "dualism" in the sense that the dualities of human experience come to a profound expression in it. Yet it was objected that to speak of this dualism merely as a failure of Hegel's original monism, and as "final" in the sense of simply overcoming identity, is to sacrifice the basic character of Hegel's philosophy and to blunt the absolute metaphysical will that inspired him no less at the end than in the beginning. His was the unceasing affirmation of the identity of experience and the thought of experience, the unwavering conviction that the task of philosophy is to pass through the fullness of experience and reveal it as the experience of thought. It is only "within" this final identity that Hegel's dualism may be understood and presented.

Yet the very spatiality of the word "within" suggests what is of value in Iljin's attempt. If it be a distortion of Hegel's thought to suggest that duality overcomes identity, it is no less a distortion to follow Hegel with the image of an identity that simply "dominates" duality or with spatial metaphors, to the criticism of which Hegel devoted much of his Logic. If duality or difference is understood only "from" identity, it is no less true that identity is understood only "from" difference. The paradox which Hegel himself so clearly identified in his method, and which we discussed in the section on "ground", must weigh upon any commentator.

The concern of the four authors may thus be seen as a search for an original approach to Hegel's thought and experience of human duality in absolute identity. Any such approach – if it avoid the banality of mere repetition – must be an "illustration" and must adopt a certain distance from

Hegel. Its merit will come with the extent to which it nevertheless gives access to the self-alienation of pure thought, which was Hegel's ultimate topic.

For whatever merits it may have shown, the approach adopted in the first half of this book studied the problem of a philosophical language: the attempt of human thought to realize its final presence to itself in and through the identity-in-difference of meaning and expression. As a commentary on Hegel, this became an examination of his doctrine of the transition from Vorstellung to thought.

The first chapter tried to open the problem by a development of Hegel's analysis of the double movement involved in the question of meaning. Vorstellung was seen as the point of transition of all forms of "lower" experience into thought; its inadequacy appeared as a spatio-temporal multiplicity of externally related elements, in opposition to the pure self-possession of a thought that should find and express its meaning in itself. Yet it was seen that the thought to which transition was made showed itself to be no less abstract, a constructed totality innocent of verification. Hence, though thought stood to Vorstellung as essential to "Beispiel", the movement toward the concrete meaning "der Sache selbst" was no less a return from thought to Vorstellung than a transition from the latter to the former. At that stage of the study, no logic was at hand for the treatment of this double movement, but it was seen that thought could strive toward its "Bei-sich-sein", not in the domination of an other outside it, but only in the realization of the most intimate presence of its own "other".

The second chapter was an attempt to place these conceptions on a more solid basis by examining Hegel's transition from Vorstellung to thought in the Philosophy of Spirit. There it was found that thought, at its rudimentary levels of intuition and Vorstellung, had two "directions whence" of meaning: one was a moment of particularity, exemplified in the designation of experiences, the other was a moment of abstract formality, which could be illustrated by the manipulation of definitions within a tautologous whole. Each moment "referred" to the other, but the true meaning at any one level was not satisfied by this duality. Philosophical thought, in its search for honesty to itself, consisted in a reflection into this very duality, which "Erinnerung" constituted a fresh attitude of the subject to itself as a more concrete object. Thought appeared as a "für-sich-seiende Dialektik" that struggled to reflect on its struggle, through a process of repeated overcoming and re-instatement of the duality of formal thought and particular experience. In the "syntheses of Vorstellung", designation was raised to verification, in which the merely signified totality sought adequate realization in an experience which was thereby deepened or renewed, but which returned to opposition in the very act of achievement.

The third chapter tried to find a fitting expression for this movement in Hegel's Logic. What was required was a logic of "multiple standpoint", of a thought that reveals the presence of the totality as increasingly concrete in an experience limited to the mere complementarity of formal and particular standpoints. The Logic of Essence was chosen as forming the point where the duality at the heart of thought itself becomes explicit, not merely in the treatment of the categories of identity and difference, but especially in the self-contradictory nature of each category as a pair of coupled moments.

There, what had above been thought as "Erinnerung" appeared as the movement of "reflection", and much of the chapter was devoted to an attempt at grasping what is involved in this notion. It was to this movement that Mure referred with his view of "imperfect sublation", and in its complexities is much to be found that would supply a structure for that thought which grasps its meaning from itself precisely in a duality where meaning is only from another. For the thought which is attempted is that which is at once from each of the coupled categories in terms of the other and from the whole in its entire expression in the coupled categories. Or, in terms of the chosen illustration, it must be said (and thought) that meaning is, on the one hand, wholly in its expression, yet, on the other hand, is both more and less than its expression. It enters into its expression as a formal signification (inner, essential moment) opposed to a particular designation (outer, non-essential). In its sheer formality it is less than its full expression. But in its fundamental unity, it is more than this mere duality of essential and non-essential. Each synthesis in the dialectic of Essence is its genesis from opposed moments ("Aufhebung" as preservation); but it is no less a transcendence of this duality, an originality not accounted for by the constitutive moments ("Aufhebung" as annihilation). It is a presence to itself both in and beyond its self-alienation.

The totality that is achieved in this movement is at once a grasp of the whole by itself and a contradictory division from the level of a particular coupled category. While the first prevents it from being regarded as a merely indefinite process, the second allows of that development toward "Wirklichkeit" in which the coupled moments progress toward adequate expression of each other – a movement in which each is alternately essential in relation to the other as non-essential and each alternately presupposes and posits the other. So far as this thought is possible, the totality of the Notion – that of a Logos passing out of itself and returning to itself – demands no new "dimension" but is that totality which appears in the dual movement of Essence.

With this preparation from an examination of Hegel's thought of identity-in-difference in a section of the Logic which seems clearly conformed to it, it will now be necessary to turn to the explicit formulation of the system. The function of this chapter will be to ask in what way the "other of thought", which we have tried to understand in Vorstellung and Essence, finds expression in the triadic form of the system. For the preceding chapter may have cast some doubts upon the assumption that this Trinitarian structure was necessarily the best suited to give shape to Hegel's original ideals of a philosophical system.

As pointed out in the introduction, Hegel himself offers little on the interpretation of his system as such. The passages on the transitions of the system triad are short and metaphorical. It is for this reason that there may be special value in the source to which we shall turn in this chapter: namely those parts of the Lectures on the Philosophy of Religion in which Hegel has given detailed expression to his triadic system in the form of Vorstellung, the proximate illustration of thought.

This will form the object of the second half of the chapter. The first half will consider a preliminary question. Whether we are concerned explicitly with philosophical thought or with religion, we are in the realm of what Hegel called absolute spirit; and much of the difficulty of accounting for the movement of the system depends on a conception of what is to be understood by absolute spirit such that it can have a development. Again, it is a question on which Hegel is not as explicit as could have been wished, but it will be seen what is to be found in his treatment of the nature of religion in the Phenomenology, Encyclopaedia, and Lectures on the Philosophy of Religion.

In conclusion, it must be emphasized that all that is here sought in Hegel's presentation of religion is a "Beispiel" for his view of the system. No attempt will be made to follow the other writers on these sections of Hegel's work, whose aim has been to measure the adequacy of the conception of religion there offered. Least of all is it intended to enter the polemics over a thought that sets (or, according to some, seems to set) religion as a mere second-stage to philosophy. It is hoped that this will not be forgotten in that the cumbrous phrase "Hegel's conception of religion" will each time be shortened to the word "religion". So far as we are concerned with adequacy, it is only with that of Hegel's thought to thought itself; and the measure is no simple one.

2. ABSOLUTE SPIRIT IN THE FORM OF VORSTELLUNG

Before examining Hegel's exposition of his system in the element of Vorstellung, we must consider the preliminary question what Hegel meant by
absolute spirit and how it exists, under the form of Vorstellung, as religion.
This will be treated in four sections. The first will ask how absolute spirit is
presented in relation to finite spirit. Hegel's answer will raise the question
how there can be any further development at the level of absolute spirit: this
will constitute the subject of the second section. The third will relate the
question to the theme of the study and the preparation of the first half: it
will ask how Hegel's presentation of this development under a triadic form
may be seen as expressing the "other" of thought and the dual movement of
Vorstellung and of Essence. This will lead on to the fourth section, which will
ask how Hegel's doctrine of religion exemplifies the basic duality he admits
in his philosophical method: the two directions of the search for a final
ground.

a. Transition to Absolute Spirit

Our examination of Hegel's doctrine of religion will turn our attention to the
final stages of the Encyclopaedia (cf. appendix of categories). The Encyclopaedia is divided into Logic, Nature, and Spirit, and the latter is subdivided
into Subjective, Objective, and Absolute Spirit. Of these, the first two are
considered by Hegel the "finite" forms of spirit, whereas the third treats of
the "unity of objectivity and ideality which is spirit in its absolute truth."[1] It
is here that religion appears (preceded by art and followed by philosophy).
So it will be well to consider briefly in this section what, according to Hegel,
constitutes the absoluteness of absolute spirit in relation to finite spirit.

Finite and Absolute Spirit

In the paragraph in which he explains the division of the Philosophy of
Spirit, Hegel offers two accounts of the finitude of finite spirit.[2] Firstly, he
says, this lies in the "Unangemessenheit des Begriffs und der Realität, mit
der Bestimmung, dass sie das Scheinen innerhalb seiner ist." That is, he
continues, the finitude of spirit is not a violence external to it but a "Schein"
which the movement of spirit posits (setzt) at its interior, in order through its
sublation (Aufhebung) to realize its freedom and be absolutely revealed.

---

[1] Enc., § 385.
[2] § 386.

Those who translate "Schein" here (or elsewhere) as "illusion"[3] give full scope to Iljin's interpretation of acosmism and to all the scandal that has been taken at the notion of the "List der Vernunft".[4] It would seem fairer to Hegel, however, to try to understand his terms, not from the images of everyday experience, but from their place in the Logic – which he regarded as the ultimate criterion of interpretation. There, "Schein" is the term with which he named the opening triad of Essence, the triad which gives the motif for the whole movement of "reflection". It was this triad that we examined on pp. 93-6 above. Hence, the finitude of finite spirit would seem to be intimately connected with that "externality within the element of thought", the positing and presupposing of which constituted the movement of the Logic of Essence through its multiple standpoints.

Secondly, Hegel describes the finitude of spirit as consisting in "die Dialektik, sein Vergehen durch ein Anderes und in einem Andern zu haben".[5] Spirit in its truth, however, achieves this "Vernichtigen des Nichtigen" within itself. This might seem to contradict the previous account; for there it was emphasized that finitude was at the heart of spirit and not posited by an other. However, we have seen that the finitude of Essence was at its heart and yet involved a true externality; for the dual moments in which Essence consists are not "in sich reflektiert" but alternately dominate each other as opposites. It is only the pure "Entwicklung" proper to the Logic of the Notion that can lay claim to the complete self-possession of a movement free from a multiplicity of standpoints. The absoluteness of absolute spirit consists, for Hegel, in its being absolved from the apearance of any alien standpoint in the process of its "Erinnerung". It is, in the fullest sense, its own object.[6] There can be no standpoint from which spirit is not "bei sich".[7]

Apart from any critical attitudes toward this doctrine, it will be seen shortly that Hegel himself withdrew, in a sense, from this ideal of pure identity by setting within absolute spirit an externality and development which can scarcely be distinguished from that which we followed in the Logic of Essence. For the moment, however, it is enough to emphasize that religion, for Hegel, belongs to absolute and not finite spirit. He opens the section of the Encyclopaedia on absolute spirit with the statement that this "höchste Sphäre" may in general be designated as religion.[8] In religion, "das Denken

---

[3] E.g., W. Wallace: *Hegel's Philosophy of Mind*, p. 8.
[4] Enc. § 209; e.g., cf. Litt, pp. 219-20.
[5] Enc. § 386.
[6] RB, p. 56.
[7] RA, p. 17.
[8] Enc. § 554.

denkt sich selbst."[9] For it is in religion that most men, in fact, find the ultimate truth;[10] and he concedes it the same content as philosophy, though a different form.[11] Art, the remaining section of absolute spirit in the Encyclopaedia, was treated in the Phenomenology as a moment of religion and need not detain us here.

The "appearance" of absolute spirit as religion is described in more detail in the Phenomenology. The point of transition is that where consciousness has risen to the state of "spirit certain of itself". For there one finds not merely a thinking of many individuals "about" being, but a situation where each relinquishes the particularity of his meaning in the concrete universality of spirit revealing itself to itself. "Das versöhnende *Ja*. . . ist der erscheinende Gott mitten unter ihnen, die sich als das reine Wissen wissen."[12] This relinquishing, however, is not the loss but the achievement of true individuality, for there alone "die Verschiedenheit ist die absolute, weil sie in diesem Elemente des reinen Begriffs gesetzt ist."[13]

This affirmation of an absolute, which is no less the absolute affirming itself, was present in the preceding stages of consciousness, as the supersensuous inner being of understanding, the "beyond" of the unhappy consciousness, the controlling necessity of morality. But at all such stages the absolute was grasped only from the standpoint of consciousness: it was a totality constructed from a particular principle.[14] At none of these stages can we regard religion as in its true form, though all experience the agony of its expectation, "erwartend und drängend um die Geburtsstätte des als Selbstbewusstsein werdenden Geistes."[15] For it is only "in the deep life of spirit certain of itself" that the interiority of experience can be attained which is not merely the consciousness, but the self-consciousness of absolute spirit.

This interiority, or "self-consciousness", of absolute spirit is further presented by Hegel in two ways: as the identity of the subjective and objective aspects of religion, and – more generally – as the identity of form and content. We may conclude this section by considering each briefly.

Identity of Subjective and Objective

In the Encyclopaedia, Hegel introduces his notion of the self-consciousness

    [9] RB, p. 154.
    [10] RB, pp. 69, 110.
    [11] Enc. §§ 1, 573.
    [12] Phän., p. 472.
    [13] i.e., absolute difference can be attained only in absolute presence; cf. Dokumente, p. 320.
    [14] Phän., p. 478.
    [15] p. 525.

of absolute spirit by pointing out that religion must be studied both as found in the finite subject and as objectively issuing from the absolute spirit: that is, it forms inseparably both the subjective side of religious experience and the "objective essence" of God.[16] It was his frequent complaint that it was taught that we can know only our relation to God, not the nature of God.[17] Yet the true grasp of God's nature as spirit embraces all the subjective relations in itself.[18]

Hegel's aim was thus to replace the abstract proofs of theodicy with a religious philosophy of the concrete experience of the doctrines of religion in man's most intimate presence to himself.[19] Religion is "eine Erhebung in die Ferne, die keine Ferne ist, sondern absolute Nähe, Gegenwart."[20] Its task is to render explicit this presence to which no man is foreign, even though he admit it only in fear or hate.[21] The false structure of oppositions between spirit itself and the finite thinker will be eliminated, "je mehr der Mensch im vernünftigen Denken die Sache selbst in sich walten lässt."[22] And so far as he thus realizes in himself the nature of thought itself, so far will he realize the absolute necessity that the "an und für sich seiende Idee" should posit itself in him.[23]

Just as it was seen in the Logic that every attempt to separate identity and contradiction by setting them in the externality of "different respects" was a step out of the concrete experience of thought into an external reflection,[24] so here the final unity in opposition can be attained only in a knowledge that in no way comes from "outside".[25] "Der Geist denkt den Geist. In diesem reinen Denken ist kein Unterschied, der sie schiede; es ist nichts zwischen ihnen."[26] It is the presence that avoids all escape into different respects or into a distant future, but faces that responsibility in which "nothing" separates itself from itself. Yet it is here that the force of this "nothing" will most acutely be realized.

---

[16] Enc. § 554.

[17] RB, p. 51.

[18] p. 8.

[19] E.g., cf. H. Niel: *Hegel – Les Preuves de l'Existence de Dieu*, p. 13: "Aimer Dieu est moins penser exclusivement à Lui, que voir toutes choses avec ses yeux à Lui. . .".

(p. 23) "En nous pensant nous-même à notre place de créature, nous pouvons retrouver par l'intérieur l'acte de création par lequel Dieu nous pose dans l'être."

[20] RA, p. 17; cf. WL, II, p. 252.

[21] RB, p. 10.

[22] p. 44.

[23] p. 141.

[24] Cf. pp. 99-100 above.

[25] RB, p. 49.

[26] RA, p. 68; cf. Beweise, p. 111: God is the "denkender und gedachter Begriff".

Identity of Form and Content

The struggle of thought to think itself in the repeated frustration of division into a formal meaning opposed to the particularity of language may be seen as an effort to pass from the externality of a form opposed to its content to that interiority where the form is its own content.[27] So it is that the true subjectivity of experience is most frequently presented by Hegel as an identity of form and content.[28] "Der absolute Inhalt ist so Form seiner selbst, Wissen in sich von sich."[29] It is only thus that the question of philosophy can, in its formulation, remain within itself in questioning itself. And it is the firm grasp of this final interiority to each other of meaning and meant that is the assurance that metaphysics must be logic,[30] however great may be the appeal of models of explanation outside the "Legitimation der Sache selbst".[31]

As absolute spirit is the achievement for which subjective and objective spirit are the way,[32] the fulfilment of that growth of the multiple form and content oppositions of human experience to adequate expression in each other, then it follows that reason understands itself only in the history of its own genesis. But it is no less true that absolute spirit constitutes a transcendence of all the form-content dualities along this way, an originality for which they do not adequately "account". So, after his tortuous passage through the myriad forms of human experience, Hegel must affirm: "Die Philosophie ist keine Erkenntnis der äussern Masse des empirischen Daseins und Lebens, sondern eine Erkenntnis des Nichtweltlichen."[33] It is the result of a way that passes through all forms of the world but, even as result, reveals that it presupposes only itself.[34] And it is in this result which is no less the originating ground of itself that Hegel sets the conclusion to his lifelong struggle with the thought of facticity and destiny: "Es ist so – ein Resultat, das der Geist in sich selbst vollbringt."[35] But the conclusion is no refuge of complacency, for the opposition at the heart of thinking experience is fully felt only in the achievement of the originality of thought: "Es gibt aber Leiden, worüber man sich nicht soll trösten lassen."[36]

[27] Explicitly Enc. § 133, but the dialectic pervades the whole of Essence.
[28] E.g., Ästhetik, p. 140: "Das Denken einerseits ist die innerste eigenste Subjektivität – und der wahre Gedanke, die Idee, zugleich die sachlichste und objektivste Allgemeinheit, welche erst im Denken sich in der Form ihrer selbst erfassen kann."
Cf. also Recht, pp. 16-17; Gesch. Phil., XVII, pp. 66, 105; Phän., p. 46.
[29] RB, p. 253.
[30] Beweise, p. 91.
[31] p. 39.
[32] Enc. § 553.
[33] RB, p. 29.
[34] RA, p. 36.
[35] Beweise, p. 97. Cf. p. 123: "Das absolute Notwendige ist, weil es ist".
[36] RB, p. 180.

b. Development in Absolute Spirit

The doctrine that spirit is finally an identity of form and content, "die unendliche für-sich-seiende Form", is repeated by Hegel as he passes from art
to religion in the Encyclopaedia.[37] For this constitutes the essence of religion,
that it should be "revealed" (offenbart).[38] And he adds that any theory which
would set the ultimate nature of truth in anything other than utter self-
manifestation may be reduced to the doctrine, countered by Plato and
Aristotle, that God is envious. The corresponding paragraphs in the Logic of
the Encyclopaedia, to which the Zusatz on the envy of God has been added,
are those which criticize the view of the Notion as an inner (and hence un-
revealed) essence.[39] There it is shown that the mere inner and the mere outer
are alternating abstractions, "der als Schein gesetzte Schein des Wesens",
and that the Notion is revealed in them only so far as they progress to adequate mutual expression in the identity of "Wirklichkeit".

Religion as Development

However, with the passage to the next paragraph of absolute spirit, the
question seems to arise whether we have after all attained this identity of
inner and outer, of form and content. In spite of all previous assertions,
Hegel now speaks explicitly of the separation of form from content.[40] And
this division is set as equivalent to the presence of the absolute content in the
form of Vorstellung, such that its elements gain a separate being as presuppositions toward each other and as events that follow one another.[41]

Similarly, in the Phenomenology, after affirming that the originality of
religion consists in its transition from the standpoint of consciousness to that
of self-consciousness, Hegel informs the reader that self-knowing spirit in
religion is only "immediately" self-consciousness,[42] which immediacy
consists in that this transition has not yet been achieved.[43] It has its meaning
as spirit only "als Gegenstand vorgestellt", and develops toward overcoming
this separation.[44] Nor may it be interpreted that what is here meant is the
moment of religion in the previous forms of consciousness, whereas the true

---

[37] Enc. § 564.

[38] "Sein Offenbarsein besteht offenbar darin, dass gewusst wird, was es ist. Es wird
aber gewusst, eben indem es als Geist gewusst wird, als Wesen, das wesentlich Selbstbewusstsein ist." (Phän., p. 528).

[39] Enc. §§ 138-141.

[40] § 566.

[41] Enc., § 565.

[42] Phän., p. 474.

[43] p. 479.

[44] p. 475.

self-consciousness of religion comes only with the final stage of "revealed religion". Hegel states that religion, in its development, presupposes all these non-religious forms.[45] It must be held that the original element of self-consciousness has been attained, but that *within* this element spirit again posits itself as consciousness and has a history of forms of increasing adequacy to the element itself. Thus, although we have apparently passed the level of Essence, we face once more the problem that confronted us throughout Chapter III, of an exteriority that yet remains inside the element of thought. "Die unmittelbare Einheit des Geistes mit sich selbst ist die Grundlage oder reines Bewusstsein, *innerhalb* dessen das Bewusstsein auseinandertritt."[46]

The question is thus posed both in the Encyclopaedia and in the Phenomenology how, granting Hegel's doctrine of absolute spirit as the final sphere of self-thinking thought, there can be inadequacy and development within this sphere. The question, though it may appear merely formal and no more than an example of Hegel's habit of immediately taking back what he has given, is at heart the question which this whole study is attempting to approach: how, according to Hegel, a phenomenology can pass into an ontology and the ontology yet remain a phenomenology. Hyppolite poses the same question in the section on religion in his commentary: if the passage to absolute knowledge marks the attainment of a noumenology, how can there be a further phenomenological development?

En tant que la dialectique de la religion répond au développement de l'esprit du monde progressant jusqu'au savoir de l'esprit elle rentre dans la phénoménologie, car chacun de ses moments est un phénomène original inadéquat à la vérité intégrale; mais en tant qu'elle est une dialectique interne, un devenir du savoir de soi-même et comme une révélation de l'esprit à soi-même, elle est comme un devenir de Dieu et une véritable nouménologie. Ces deux aspects peuvent-ils se réconcilier et ne posent-ils pas le problème fondamental de la théologie hégélienne? Comment se réconcilient le point de vue de l'esprit fini, celui de l'homme, et le point de vue (si l'on peut ainsi parler) de l'esprit infini, celui de Dieu?[47]

The question of a reconciliation between the claims of ontology to speak a "discourse of being itself" and the consciousness of phenomenology that its language is one with its particular historical existence has been with us from the beginning. The concept of a development "within" absolute knowledge is not new to this study. It is, as suggested, fundamentally that problem of an exteriority within the element of thought, the notion that guided us through the chapter on the Logic. For the form and content of logical thought are

[45] p. 476.
[46] pp. 479-80.
[47] *Genèse*, p. 522.

one, in the sense that reflection there constitutes a further entry into the content and not the adoption of a position foreign to it; yet this identity allows for, indeed demands, a multiple standpoint at the interior of thought. Reflection, we saw, is no simple "Erinnerung" but a dialectic of positing and external reflection.

This chapter, then, will follow Hegel's re-statement of the problem in the context of religion and will see how this illustration "reflects" it. For religion, the proximate illustration of pure thought, is itself an exteriority at the interior of thought. Hegel describes both the perfection and the limitation of religion in saying that its actuality is the garment (Kleid) in which it is revealed to itself.[48] That is, its inner presence to itself is no less a concealing, as the garment of language hides the thought it makes possible. In its greatest intimacy, thought is present to itself only in an "illustration" of thought. In spite of Hegel's optimistic descriptions of the final achievement by spirit of a pure self-consciousness, his student is unlikely to forget the bitter duality at its heart; and though the word is scarcely Hegel's, the dual development from beginning and from result is an expression of "Verborgenheit", no less than of "Offenbarung".

Temporal Development

However one try to conceive of continued development within the fulfilment of absolute spirit, it may be noticed that there is a development which Hegel states to be possible only with this attainment. For it is, he maintains, only so far as spirit reaches its truth as self-consciousness that there can be a temporal process. "Der ganze Geist nur ist in der Zeit."[49] As was seen in Chapter II, time *as* time is for Hegel the Notion itself, and each experience of being *in* time is a manner in which the Notion passes out of itself into a form of space-time (natürliche Zeit). Just as the moments of any dialectical triad are abstractions in relation to the synthesis and cannot be experienced apart from some attainment of the synthesis, so all experience of past, future, or the false present of mere duration is possible only as an abstraction of the true present of reconciliation.[50] It is this absolute reconciliation which makes possible the Christian consciousness of redemption as an event of the past and a personal need of the future.[51] Conversely, the conviction that reconciliation has been made and needs simply to be produced for me in my particularity[52] is not to be interpreted from the moral standpoint of Kant

[48] Phän., p. 475.
[49] Phän., p. 476.
[50] Cf. p. 64 above.
[51] Phän., p. 548.
[52] RB, pp. 234-5.

and Fichte,[53] but is to be held as the experience which finds its possibility, its adequacy, and its origin in the true present.

The temporality of time would thus appear as a result manifesting itself with increasing concreteness in the passage through the many ways in which time is "vorgestellt"; again, it is a result which presupposes only itself. Similarly, in regard to Hyppolite's question about the transition to absolute knowledge which finds its place in history but is not itself a historical fact,[54] it might follow from the above that absolute knowledge, though no event simply *in* history, would be for Hegel, not the mere cancellation of history, but rather the condition of possibility for the experience of history in its historicity. To these suggestions we shall return briefly at the end of this chapter. It will be necessary first to consider how Hegel expresses the development of absolute spirit in the triadic form of the system. The next section will offer a preliminary approach.

c. The "Other" of Thought

It is with the division of form from content within their identity in absolute spirit that Hegel introduces the development of his system at the close of the Encyclopaedia: "In diesem Trennen scheidet sich die Form von dem Inhalte, und in jener die unterschiedenen Momente des Begriffs zu besondern Sphären oder Elementen ab, in deren jedem sich der absolute Inhalt darstellt."[55] He then continues with a description of the three "elements".

It will be necessary for us, in this section, to make a preliminary examination of this triadic structure: to ask how it reveals Hegel's doctrine of thought and its "other", and how this form relates to the dual form of Essence. As Hegel's description of the three elements of religion in the Encyclopaedia is repeated in greater detail in his Lectures on Absolute Religion, which will constitute the subject of the second half of this chapter, it may be of value to draw on another source for this preliminary examination, the Phenomenology.

The Three Elements of Religion

It is in the section on revealed religion that Hegel describes the content of spirit in the achieved religious consciousness as a movement of three "moments" or "elements". We shall study the passage in some detail.

Dies Element des Denkens ist die Bewegung, zum Dasein oder der Einzelheit herunterzusteigen. Die Mitte zwischen ihnen ist ihre synthetische Verbindung, das

---

[53] p. 258.
[54] Cf. p. 5 above.
[55] Enc. § 566.

Bewusstsein des Anderswerdens oder das Vorstellen als solches. Das dritte ist die
Rückkehr aus der Vorstellung und dem Anderssein oder das Element des Selbst-
bewusstseins selbst. Diese drei Momente machen den Geist aus.[56]

Before continuing with the quotation, it will be well first to clarify which are
the three moments which constitute spirit. A later sentence will be of
assistance: "Die Vorstellung macht die Mitte zwischen dem reinen Denken
und dem Selbstbewusstsein als solchem aus." Thus it would seem clear that
Hegel understands the three elements as those of thought, Vorstellung, and
self-consciousness itself ("as such"). The nature of the second remains,
however, ambiguous, for the movement of the first is to "Dasein oder Einzelheit", and Vorstellung is here only a medium. The duality reappears when
the third element is described as a return from Vorstellung (which is "Anderswerden") *and* from "Anders*sein*".

An interpretation may be offered which would see this apparent ambiguity
as fundamental to an understanding of the triadic form of the system. This is
usually explained as consisting of Idea, Nature, and Spirit, where the latter is
held to cover both finite and absolute spirit. But here, the third element is
self-consciousness itself: that is, absolute spirit and not finite spirit as such.
The second is both the pure "Anders*sein*" of nature and the medium which
stands between it and both first and third elements, namely the "Anderswerden" of Vorstellung, or finite spirit.

This would perhaps help to substantiate the duality in the system noticed
(among others) by Iljin,[57] according to which the transition from the Idea
(Logic) is a double one, passing into both the Philosophy of Nature and
empirical nature itself. Here, taking the former in the wider sense of Vorstellung, we interpret it as including the whole experience of finite spirit as a
medium between the pure, autonomous, categorial thought of the Logic and
the sheer "Aussersichsein" of empirical being, which as such cannot enter
into spirit. If a philosopher can think only at a level he experiences, under
pain of merely imposing a classification not drawn from experience,[58] then
nature exists for the philosopher as it is taken up into the experience of finite
spirit, forming with it that dialectic of which the essential is the dual standpoint of "an sich" and "für sich", because this is the realm where experience
is not to be identified with the thought of experience.[59] That is, if this interpretation be acceptable, then what is thought in the second element, that of

[56] Phän., p. 533.
[57] *Die Philosophie Hegels*, p. 351.
[58] Cf. pp. 45-6 above.
[59] Hegel's reference to Vorstellung as "synthetische Verbindung" may perhaps be interpreted as referring to this externality of imposed unity in contrast to the inner unity of the
"concrete": cf. p. 57 above.

Vorstellung, is fundamentally the dialectic of experience which Hegel presented in his phenomenology, so far as distinguished from the movement of the Logic (first element) and from the absolute spirit of the third element.

That the first element is to be identified with the element of logical thought which we considered at length in Chapter III can hardly be doubted. The difficulty comes with the attempt at a profounder understanding of what this is in relation to the other elements, and why its movement is not simply within itself but is a transition to Vorstellung. This is the problem of the whole study.

The identification of the third element with absolute spirit is likewise only a beginning of the difficulties. In this regard, the question may be posed as follows: if spirit is in its true nature the self-consciousness of spirit, then how can one say that this third element is but one of the three moments of spirit? A following sentence from the quotation may help to clarify the question:

Seine [i.e., des Geistes] ausführliche Bewegung ist also diese, in jedem seiner Momente, als in einem Elemente, seine Natur auszubreiten; indem jeder dieser Kreise sich in sich vollendet, ist diese seine Reflexion in sich zugleich der Übergang in den andern.

Spirit thus enters whole into each of its moments, which as such are opposed and derive their meaning precisely as moments in this opposition. The thought which seems here to be prescribed is that which can adopt not only the standpoint of each of the opposed moments but also that of the true totality which expresses itself in them and yet constitutes a single movement of spirit, as these develop from abstract opposition to full actuality in each other. In other words, what is described would appear to be that thought of a multiple standpoint, for which we sought logic and illustration in Chapter III. And the reference to Essence is supported by the choice of the word "Reflexion". For we saw that as each of the coupled moments attained an inner reflection into itself, it reached *eo ipso* an adequate reflection in the other.

This interpretation would at least abolish the naive view that each element advances in isolation to its own final stage and then makes an inexplicable transition to the lowest stage of another.[60] But the triadic form has not thereby been reconciled with the dual thought that was examined in the first part of the study. A further sentence from the quotation may help:

Sein Auseinandertreten in der Vorstellung besteht darin, auf eine bestimmte Weise zu sein; diese Bestimmtheit aber ist nichts anderes, als eines seiner Momente.

[60] It is a false construction to represent "Begreifen und Begriffsbestimmung und dann eine Realisation diesem gemäss". (RA, p. 54).

And Hegel adds later that Vorstellung, although only one of the determinations, has nevertheless the character:

die synthetische Verbindung zu sein, über alle diese Elemente ausgebreitet, und ihre gemeinschaftliche Bestimmtheit.

These sentences would seem to present the other face of what was described in the previous quotation. There, attention was on the unity of spirit in its multiple standpoint. Here, emphasis is placed on the necessary multiplicity within the unity. Spirit is an "Auseinandertreten". That is, no less than being a concrete unity of all moments, it is in each as a "privileged" standpoint, at the expense of the others. And this thought "at the expense of" another[61] is here identified by Hegel as the thought of Vorstellung.

How is it, then, that Hegel can say that Vorstellung is not merely one of the three elements ("das Vorstellen als solches"), but also the common characteristic of all? We have seen that its own element is that of phenomenological thought in the dual standpoint of "an sich" and "für sich". But so far as any element represents at once the true presence of spirit and the privileged standpoint of a moment of spirit, then its thought must be no less a duality of "an sich" ("für uns") and "für sich". There appears in it "ein phänomenologischer Anteil".[62]

Relation to the Duality of Essence

With these suggestions we may return to the two questions posed above: how is the fundamental duality of experience to be reconciled with the triplicity of form, and how is it that the self-consciousness of spirit can be represented as one element of spirit, seemingly on a par with the other two?

In Chapter III, it was stressed that whereas Hegel described the transition from the Logic of Being to that of Essence as involving a new "dimension" of thought, which alone made possible the conception of a totality,[63] the transition from the Logic of Essence to that of the Notion postulated no further dimension. For the form in which the third book of the Logic thinks the whole, as passing out of itself and returning to itself, is precisely that totality which is thought by the contradictory division of Essence, so far as the coupled categories, which are the principle of an increasingly adequate whole, reach the stage of "Wirklichkeit".[64] That which the Subjective Logic thinks is fundamentally that which the Objective Logic achieves in its final stages; but it substitutes a triadic for a dual form.

[61] Cf. p. 33 above.
[62] Cf. pp. 37 and 84-5 above.
[63] pp. 78-9 above.
[64] Cf. pp. 89-91 above.

The Notion, then, regarded in its genesis in Essence, expresses itself in the radical duality of an inner, formal, essential moment and an outer, particular, unessential moment. It is, in its genesis, the dialectic of these opposed moments. At each stage it is an identity that thereby breaks into a further such division. In terms of the chosen illustration, its course is that of philosophical meaning in the repeated duality of a purely formal signification opposed to the particularity of its expression. Every achievement of an interiority overcoming this division shows itself to be no less of a formality opposed to its particularity. Without losing sight of the bitter experience of thought in its development that it represents, and excluding all images of simple sequence, we may perhaps speak of an "element" of formal thought, an "element" of particular experience, and an "element" of reconciling meaning.

It is, then, provisionally suggested – and the suggestion will be examined in Hegel's doctrine of Absolute Religion in the second half of this chapter – that the three elements of the above quotation from the Phenomenology, and similarly the three "spheres or elements" of religion in the Encyclopaedia, may also be thought in this manner. Spirit is in its true nature the self-consciousness of absolute spirit (third element); but this, for all its identity of form and content, is achieved only in a radical duality. The formal moment (first element) is a logical thought which, though identical with spirit and hence all experience, is nevertheless in every attainment of this identity the realization of itself as a thinking opposed to the world of experiences in which it is verified. The moment of particularity (second element) is the complex element of Vorstellung which, so far as opposed to logical thought, is that mere immersion in finite experience which grasps at meaning in illustrations and in designation rather than in the inner comprehension of its own development.

The original experience, thus, and the only one which truly has a history, is the experience of self-conscious spirit in its genesis from thought and from Vorstellung as abstract, but constitutive, elements. It is only from this situation that inadequacy and development can be grasped as truly interior,[65] that finitude can be known as a "Scheinen innerhalb seiner", a predicament rather than an illusion.[66] For though this "third" element is that thought of experience which is the experience of thought, both thought and experience are its "other": it is present to itself, not in dominating them to a forced unity, but in a self-alienation that is no less a difference than an identity. The

[65] Cf. pp. 158-9 above.
[66] Cf. pp. 151-2 above.

"nothing" that separates spirit from itself[67] is itself, without any refuge in an "insofern" outside itself. For whereas each moment can retreat outside its element, outside spirit there is nothing but itself. The revelation of self to self, in which Hegel sets the final character of absolute spirit, is no simple presence. A more religious thinker might have called it an awful presence, but Hegel, following an old tradition, described it as death.[68]

It is freely to be acknowledged that the terms and metaphors of this attempt to understand the form in which Hegel presented his system fall themselves before that duality of meaning and language to which they refer. Many commentators have written on the three "syllogisms" in which Hegel epitomizes his thought at the end of the Encyclopaedia,[69] and which are likewise expounded in the preceding section on religion as "the three syllogisms that constitute the one syllogism of the absolute self-mediation of spirit."[70] But few have approached them with any apparent sense of the deep concern for the standpoint of experience that Hegel elsewhere shows.

In conclusion of this section, brief reference may be made to one who has attempted to disengage this concern from the confident formalism that covers it. It is the thesis of J. Van der Meulen[71] that the undue formalism of the traditional interpretation of Hegel comes largely from accepting too readily the division of the dialectic into triads, and neglecting the "Herstellung der ersten Unmittelbarkeit" which, Hegel himself points out, establishes a "unit" of four terms, so far as one yields to the desire to count.[72] Renewed attention, he maintains, to the duality of the traditional synthesis, by which it is both a result and an immediate beginning, will bring to light "die vielfach verborgene Zweideutigkeit des Hegelschen Logos" and make possible an interpretation of the system of Idea, Nature, and Spirit that will free Hegel's thought from the "gnostic remains" in it.[73]

These suggestions offer a further formulation for much of what we have tried to think throughout this study as the "dilemma" or "predicament" of thought in its effort to reflect upon itself. The attainment of the interiority of meaning arises only in a reinstated duality of thought and expression, presence falls to immediacy and futurity, the concrete identity of positing and presupposing retreats to the complacency of the "insofern". This is the

---

[67] RA, p. 68; cf. p. 154 above.
[68] E.g., cf. Phän., pp. 29, 69, 545.
[69] Enc. §§ 575-7.
[70] § 571.
[71] *Hegel: die gebrochene Mitte* (1958).
[72] WL, II, p. 497; cf. pp. 65-6 above.
[73] *Heidegger und Hegel*, p. 186.

"Ohnmacht der Vernunft"[74] which is present in every act of thought expressed by the Logic, so that the transition to Nature (Vorstellung) is ever
realized. In the terminology of Van der Meulen, "dieses vierte Moment ist
die sich im Geist bekundende Wurzel der Natur."[75]

d. Spirit as Result and as Origin

The previous section made a preliminary examination of the triadic structure
of Hegel's system, as illustrated by the three "elements" of revealed religion
in the Phenomenology. An attempt was made to understand it in relation to
the dual structure of Essence.

In this concluding section, the doctrine of the three elements will be referred to the duality which Hegel explicitly admits in the discussion of his
philosophical method: that is, at the level of the Notion itself. This, as was
seen at the end of Chapter III,[76] is the double movement of starting "from"
the ground and returning "to" the ground. Philosophical thought must "develop", and can do so only as a movement that is at once from the totality
(as abstract) toward its self-particularization and from particulars toward the
totality.

"Offenbarung" and "Erhebung"

In the realm of religion, this is the double (and yet single) movement by
which the objective essence of God is revealed to man ("Offenbarung") and
man raises himself to God ("Erhebung"). In an earlier section, these two
aspects of religion, and Hegel's affirmation of their final identity, have already been encountered.[77] It is not, however, an identity which is immediately affirmed or easily understood. God appears as a particular "Gestalt"
in the "Äther des Denkens" or "Element des Allgemeinen".[78] Opposed to
this, yet corresponding to it, is the religious consciousness in its particularity,
"Das Bewusstsein in seiner Einzelheit. . . mit seinen Bedürfnissen, Zustän-
den, Sünden usf., überhaupt nach seinem ganzen empirischen, zeitlichen
Charakter". Thus, in his treatment of the religions of history, Hegel presents
for each the "metaphysical notion", or logical category in which God is
there revealed,[79] and a corresponding "Vorstellung" by which this notion is
embodied in subjective religious attitudes.

---

[74] WL. II, p. 251.
[75] *Heidegger und Hegel*, p. 132.
[76] pp. 108-13 above.
[77] pp. 153-4 above.
[78] RB, p. 155.
[79] For a list of the logical categories with the religion that is thought to correspond to
each, cf. Lasson, *Einführung*, pp. 116-8.

"Offenbarung" is thus the process through which the merely universal appears to consciousness: "Offenbaren heisst. . . dies Urteil der unendlichen Form, ihr sich Bestimmen, für ein anderes zu sein."[80] "Erhebung" is the process by which the subject lifts himself above the particularities of his situation to grasp the universal: "Diese Erhebung ist Hinausgehen über das Sinnliche, über das blosse Gefühl in die reine Region, und die Region des Allgemeinen ist das Denken."[81]

At each stage of religion, the two "moments" achieve a partial identity in the cult of that religion, where the theoretical and the practical are united.[82] But it is only religion in its absolute form where the objective side is completely revealed in the subjective.[83] "Diese absolute Religion ist die Offenbare, die Religion, die sich selbst zu ihrem Inhalt, Erfüllung hat."[84]

In this sense one may then say that God's self-consciousness is in man and man's self-consciousness is in God; but the understanding of such propositions, Hegel warns, demands "gründliche Spekulation".[85] They can not be understood "from outside", from the standpoint of Spinoza's philosophy of substance.[86] For such an attitude would reduce the concrete identity of identity and non-identity to one of the abstract terms that are reconciled in it. The identity of revealed religion is such that we must think development in God and in the world as the same and yet as "ganz verschieden".[87]

How this balance is in fact maintained in the three elements of absolute religion will be for the rest of this chapter to see. For the present, it is sufficient to be able to say that the "final identity" is no simple domination of the multiplicity "within" it. It is the result of a development and is constituted by a "continuing" development. It is no mere ideal of the future, but it sinks to an abstract present unless its identity be thought at once from a universal seeking particularization and from particulars seeking universalization.

Logic and Phenomenology

Thus, the identity of revealed religion is the process of the self-consciousness of spirit. The diversity which prevents this from falling to an abstract identity is the fact that this process is "ein Strom mit entgegengesetzter Richtung".[88] The final identity which "results" from the full course of finite

[80] RA, p. 35.
[81] RB, pp. 193-4.
[82] p. 226.
[83] RA, p. 5.
[84] p. 19.
[85] Enc. § 564.
[86] RB, pp. 168-9.
[87] p. 186.
[88] p. 170.

forms is itself the absolute origin of all these forms. To view it only as result is one-sided. "Der Gang aber, durch den der absolute Geist als nur Resultat... erscheint, ist zugleich einseitig."[89] Yet it is no less one-sided to view it only as origin, to see it in abstraction from the entire course of finite dualities that "account" for it. The conclusion presupposes the way, and the way shows that it has always presupposed the conclusion.

This mutual presupposition of result and origin may be seen as that which makes the three elements of absolute spirit to be three, and not simply one. As the previous section showed,[90] spirit is the basic unity of its own self-consciousness, but is equally merely one element among three. It is the identity of the first and second elements. Nevertheless, in its identity with the first element it becomes a logic defined in its opposition to the particular experiences of the second element. In its identity with the latter it must likewise include a certain determination "against" the former. A thought of identity which excludes these real oppositions would affirm spirit as origin to the exclusion of spirit as result.

In practice, then, one may perhaps join Kojève in speaking of Hegel's triadic system as "un système qui se décompose nécessairement en deux parties, à savoir en une *Logik* et en une *Phänomenologie des Geistes*."[91] It is a Logic which, though in a true sense the whole of experience and of the system, is no less one element within the whole, which presupposes and draws meaning from the full range of the forms of consciousness. It is equally a Phenomenology which, though it no less covers the whole system, presupposes the full thinking of the Logic.

This mutual presupposition is, indeed, exactly that to which the most common objections against Hegel's system may be reduced. As Hyppolite expresses it:

On accusera la *Phénoménologie* de comporter un au-delà de la description de l'expérience qui en rend ensuite possible la genèse, et la *Logique* de supposer au début ce qui n'est vraiment démontré qu'à la fin. C'est en d'autres termes le mode de pensée hégélien lui-même qui est en cause, cette pensée circulaire, ou cette finalité du Soi.[92]

Hence, if it is the "ruse of reason" to set the fundamental difficulty as the

---

[89] p. 174.
[90] pp. 162-4 above.
[91] *Introduction à la Lecture de Hegel*, p. 427.
   Cf. Hyppolite, *Etudes sur Marx et Hegel*, pp. 191-2: "C'est pourquoi la *Phénoménologie de l'Esprit* et la *Logique* hégélienne sont l'une et l'autre le Tout de la philosophie, mais sous deux aspects différents."
[92] *Genèse*, p. 567.

principle of system,[93] then the fact that phenomenology is a concealed (or parenthetical) logic of a "für uns", and that each step of logic no less hides its phenomenological moment, is itself the principle of the movement and experience of spirit. This basic movement, which is for Hegel "das Durch-laufen der Bewegung der Sache",[94] appears in systematic form as a double paradox: we remain within the experience of the Phenomenology only by passing out of it into a non-phenomenological grasp of the totality, and we attain the interiority of logical reflection only in a complex act of which one moment is an external reflection that is the original "voraus" of the spatio-temporal element of Vorstellung.[95]

3. SYSTEM IN THE FORM OF VORSTELLUNG

a. The Notion of System

If Hegel's aim in philosophy was to think the identity of experience and the thought of experience, little need be added here on his notion of system as a form of thought identical with its content, where "Methode ist der sich ex-plizierende Begriff."[96] It will be our purpose for the rest of this chapter to examine that section of Hegel's Lectures on the Philosophy of Religion in which he presents the triadic form of an achieved system in the guise of that religion which has attained "die absolute unendliche Form, das sich Wissen-de überhaupt".[97] It is the religion which Hegel terms "absolut", "offenbar", "vollendet", and which he identifies historically with Christianity. Though the form of an achieved system may give the appearance of a presupposition-less beginning, the system of absolute religion must not, Hegel warns, be thought in abstraction from the process of historical religions which con-stitute its genesis.[98] It is only as the culmination of the historical process of "Offenbarung" and "Erhebung" that the adequate form of religion is achieved, such that "die Sache selbst ist in der christlichen Religion voll-bracht."[99]

The mark of a religion as absolute is that it can have no standpoint where spirit is not "bei sich", for its doctrine and the experience of its doctrine are one.[100] That dogma should be verified in experience means that to reflect

[93] Cf. pp. 105-6 above.
[94] RB, p. 122.
[95] Cf. pp. 101-2 above.
[96] RB, p. 62; cf. Enc. § 14; WL, II, p. 486.
[97] RI, p. 235.
[98] RA, p. 184.
[99] RI, p. 241.
[100] RA, p. 17.

upon it is thereby to enter more truly into it, not to set oneself at a stand-point outside it. Theology is the witness of spirit to itself.[101] Thus, of the fundamental doctrine of absolute religion Hegel writes that "the Trinity is not only present in Vorstellung, but actuality is perfectly united to it."[102] And Descartes' assertion that we must believe what is revealed to us by God, though we can not understand it, is contrasted unfavourably by Hegel with Jacob Böhme's realization that "the mystery of the Trinity is ever born within us."[103]

It is in this identification of the thought of experience and the experience of thought that Hegel grasps the actuality of the divinity in the believer, in a way that penetrates all the deceptions of imagination,[104] and frees doctrine from a mere objectivity to which a variety of religious aspirations may come as to an ill-fitting garment.[105] For any religious belief or philosophical truth will, in the act in which its meaning is grasped, appear no less in the duality of formal meaning and particular expression. Thus, identity of system as ex-pressed and as lived can be had only where the system itself shows forth this fundamental unity in division. But it was to this grasp of the presence of thought to itself only in its alienation that Hegel dedicated his life of thought. "Ich bin, und es ist in mir für mich dieser Widerstreit und diese Einigung. . . Ich bin nicht einer der im Kampfe Begriffenen, ich bin beide Kämpfende, ich bin der Kampf selbst."[106]

It was in the system which he represented, in the religious element, by the doctrines of the Trinity and Incarnation that Hegel sought to express his ex-perience of this fundamental identity-in-difference. It is for the rest of this chapter to examine how this insight found formulation in the three elements of the absolute religion – and hence in the triadic system which they illu-strate.

b. The Three Elements

Hegel's warning, in his Logic, that the divisions of his work are an external addition after the completion of the process of thought[107] imposes itself upon the student of his system of absolute religion. It will be our task in this section merely to explain briefly the divisions and headings which have come down to us, for it is upon a more detailed study of the thought itself that any interpretation of the system must be based.

[101] p. 24.
[102] Gesch. Phil., XIX, p. 115.
[103] p. 352.
[104] Phän., p. 527.
[105] p. 526.
[106] RB, p. 241.
[107] WL, I, p. 36.

The manuscript which Hegel composed for his lectures of 1821 divides "die vollendete Religion oder offenbare" into the following three sections: "a) Abstrakter Begriff, b) Konkrete Vorstellung oder vielmehr Bestimmung, d.i. Entwicklung der Idee, c) Gemeinde, Kultus." The middle section is again divided into three sections, but no titles are added: they treat of the Trinity, nature, and finite spirit.

The division found in the notes of Hegel's students and in the Collected Works is still tripartite, but differs in that the Abstract Notion is excluded from the division, forming a mere introduction. Hence, the three parts become: a) the Trinity, b) nature and finite spirit, c) "die Gemeinde". The two editions of the Philosophy of Religion in the Collected Works[108] entitle these three parts "das Reich des Vaters, des Sohnes, des Geistes". The terms are not to be found in the manuscript, nor, with one exception,[109] in the notes; but as no record survives of the lectures of 1831, it is not excluded that Hegel may have introduced them then. The notes all give the same division but speak of the three realms as three "Elemente", "Böden", "Sphären".[110] The terminology of the notes and the movement of thought itself clearly point to this division as fundamental. We shall therefore follow it, rather than that of the manuscript, and refer to the three "elements".[111]

Hegel stresses that this division, as we think it, is not simply to be equated with the division as a truly adequate form of the self-thinking of the system. "In dem wir diesen Unterschied, diese Scheidung machten, haben wir es mehr empirisch getan, den Unterschied empirisch aufgenommen von uns her."[112] That is, the division into three "vorhandene Böden" is made on the basis of our empirical grasp of distinctions.[113] In thinking them, it is thus our task to appreciate the distinctions as the original manifestation of the standpoints of spirit itself, as "das Tun, die entwickelte Lebendigkeit des

---

[108] 1832, by Marheineke, and 1840, by Bruno Bauer.

[109] "Reich des Geistes", in one set of notes for 1824.

[110] The Encyclopaedia speaks of the three "Elemente", "Sphären", "Momente", "Schlüsse". (§§ 566-71).

[111] A similar situation is to be observed in Hegel's treatment of the Determinate Religions. In his manuscript of 1821, the three subdivisions are: a) nature religions, b) Jewish and Greek religions, c) Roman religion. Absolute Religion is thus set outside this triad, forming the synthesis of Determinate (finite) Religion as such and the Notion of Religion. But with the repetitions of the course, so far as can be judged from the notes of students, Roman religion joined Jewish and Greek to form the antithesis to which Nature Religion was the thesis and Absolute Religion the synthesis. Thus, the Notion of Religion is again dropped, so that the triad represents three actual religious attitudes.

[112] RA, p. 29.

[113] which, in so far as it sets the distinguished elements "nebeneinander" is itself the external division of Vorstellung. (Enc. § 18).

absoluten Geistes selbst."[114] Spirit is entire in each of the moments, as moments,[115] yet is fundamentally the very process of movement through them, which process Hegel terms "die göttliche Geschichte".[116] Our aim is therefore to think that place which is grasped only *from* various standpoints yet is nevertheless the origin of all such standpoints.

The first element is clearly represented as that of pure thought, of the Logic. It is "das Element des Gedankens. . . die Form der Allgemeinheit. . . das Denken seiner selbst. . . die ewige Idee Gottes für sich selbst. . . die ewige Idee auf dem Boden des Denkens überhaupt. . . Gott in seiner Ewigkeit vor Erschaffung der Welt, ausserhalb der Welt. . . raumlos, ausser der Zeit. . . rein nur als Denken."[117]

The second element is opposed to the first as that in which "die Idee ist nicht für uns als denkend, sondern für den endlichen, äusserlichen, empirischen Geist. . . für die Vorstellung im Elemente des Vorstellens."[118] As we saw in the corresponding development in the Phenomenology,[119] this element, as that of "Trennung, Anderssein", splits into the duality of nature ("heaven and earth") and finite spirit in reaction with each other on their way to reconciliation.[120] This way "legt sich auseinander in Vergangenheit, Gegenwart und Zukunft,"[121] so that we can speak of it as "die Geschichte der göttlichen Idee am endlichen Geist".[122]

The third element is that of reconciliation, in which spirit is present in the religious communion, and the process of reconciliation is the cult. "Das dritte Element ist die Gegenwart." This, however, is itself a duality. So far as it remains opposed to past and future, it is a mere "Jetztsein". So far, however, as it becomes a true "Dritte", it becomes "eine Gegenwart, die sich erhebt, wesentlich versöhnt, sich durch die Negation ihrer Unmittelbarkeit zur Allgemeinheit vollendet, eine Vollendung, die aber noch nicht ist und so als Zukunft zu fassen ist, ein Jetzt der Gegenwart, das Vollendung vor sich hat."[123] To this view of the temporalities of the element of spirit we must return in the final section of this chapter.

After expounding the general characteristics of the three elements, Hegel

[114] RA, p. 30.
[115] p. 56: "Dies sind die drei Sphären, in denen die göttliche Idee zu betrachten ist, in deren jeder sie ganz, aber unterschieden nach der Bestimmung des Elements ist."
[116] RA, p. 65.
[117] pp. 28-31, 56, 65-6.
[118] pp. 28, 31.
[119] Cf. pp. 160-1 above.
[120] RA, p. 30; Enc. § 568.
[121] RA, p. 66.
[122] p. 95.
[123] p. 66.

adds: "das Element, in dem, die Bestimmung, in der wir sind, ist der Geist,"
and from this standpoint it is our task to comprehend how the Idea is
present in each of the elements and comes to Vorstellung.[124] For we have
seen that the standpoint of any one element, at the expense of the others, has
the duality of Vorstellung.[125] Thus, the thought of the first element is at
once a thought opposed to an experience outside it, "nur Denken", and a
thought that is all experience, the thought of spirit in its process through the
elements:[126] a dual standpoint, the difficulty of which, Hegel adds, led to
many heresies.[127] It is this difficulty which will dominate our attempt at
understanding, as we consider each of the three elements in more detail.

c. The Element of Thought

In examining Hegel's description of the three elements of absolute religion
as an illustration of his system, we must pose two questions for each. Firstly,
what sphere of thought or experience is represented by this element? Secondly, what is its relation to the other elements?

The two questions are naturally in close connexion. Yet for the first element, it may be best to consider the answer to the first question as clear and
put the whole weight of discussion on the second question. For the element
of "pure thought, in the form of universality, outside time and space"
evidently represents the Logic. Yet the question of its relation to the other
elements sets us immediately at the heart of that paradox of the system with
which this study began.

Transition in Thought and from Thought

The first element of absolute religion is the Trinity. It is sometimes maintained that the Trinity is, for Hegel, the whole system: that is, the First Person
represents the Logic, the Second the created world, and their reconciliation
is the Third Person. However, Hegel is himself at pains to deny this, stressing
that the transitions of the Trinity are prior to the creation of the world. That
is, Logic is – in one sense, at least – "complete" in itself apart from the
transition to nature.

The Trinity is in itself a life of thought, actual, for itself, with a "reines
Anderswerden" such that it is "in dieser Entäusserung nur bei sich".[128] This

---

[124] p. 67.

[125] pp. 161-2 above.

[126] RA, p. 62.

[127] p. 64; a difficulty which Hessen sees also as the basis for the division of Hegel's
followers into "right" and "left": Hegels Trinitätslehre, p. 36.

[128] Phän., p. 534.

self-alienation remains within the divinity;[129] it is "offenbar, aber noch nicht zur Erscheinung gekommen".[130] It is the thought of thought, in which man's highest activity consists.[131] The notion of God as spirit, in which the whole development of religious thought is to be found,[132] cast its reflection in certain triadic dogmas in the determinate religions, but it is only in the Christian thought of the Trinity that the true notion of spirit is revealed,[133] and the thought of thought is attained in the religious element.[134] This is the thought of God as "Geist im Elemente des Gedankens. . . das Mysterium Gottes. . . die absolute Tätigkeit, *actus purus*," which in his infinite self-division and generation of a son remains in absolute subjectivity and does not pass to the finite world.[135] And at the beginning of his treatment of the element of Vorstellung, Hegel states that though this second sphere, being the same absolute act as the first, does not have that simple independence from it which is commonly represented, we must be careful to avoid a false interpretation, "als ob der ewige Sohn des Vaters, der sich objektiv seienden, sich selbst gegenständlich seinden Göttlichkeit, dasselbe sei als die Welt physisch und geistig, und als ob unter jenem Sohne nur diese zu verstehen sei."[136]

Hence, if we grant that the first element represents the "thought of thought" which is the Logic in its concrete form, and in its independence from all "illustrations" in the world, then the problem of its relation to the other elements is posed in its most acute form. The question why there should be a "transition" from the pure categories of thought itself to a phenomenal, spatio-temporal embodiment is thus represented by Hegel as the religious question why God, in the complete self-sufficiency of his life as Trinity, should create the world of nature and finite spirit.

Though this question was, in some sense, always present to the religious consciousness, Hegel emphasizes that it could not be posed in its profundity until the fullness of time, when "die Idee vollständig reif war in ihrer Tiefe,"[137] and spirit had reached a sufficient comprehension of its subjectivity to

---

[129] RB, p. 173.
[130] RA, p. 65; cf. p. 182; Beweise, p. 28; Enc. § 161 Zusatz.
[131] RA, p. 69.
[132] RB, p. 51.
[133] RA, pp. 58-9; RN, p. 154; Ästhetik, p. 346.
[134] Gesch. Phil., XIX, p. 13: "Das Denken, das sich selbst denkt, der νους, der sich selber zum Gegenstande hat. . . diese konkrete Idee ist wieder hervorgekommen, und in der Ausbildung des Christentums, als das Denken auch in ihm aufging, als die Dreieinigkeit gewusst."
[135] RA, pp. 56-7; in the margin of Hegel's manuscript, this section is indicated as "Absolute Idee der Philosophie".
[136] RA, pp. 85-6; cf. Berlin, pp. 187-8.
[137] RA, p. 185.

realize the profound opposition between subjectivity and objectivity as such.[138] The ancients never came "zu dieser Entzweiung, die nur der Geist ertragen kann," and it remained for those raised to the thought of the Trinity to reach that grasp of a true totality which makes it possible to question thought and being as such in their infinite opposition.[139]

In the first part of this study it was often suggested that Hegel does not ask us to think the whole of the Logic and *then* to make a mysterious transition to the lowest category of nature: that every stage of logical thought is equally an externalization in a language and a history that are as much productive of the thought as produced by it. Far from being compelled to abandon this suggestion, we find here its truest sense. Just as the religious consciousness always believed in a transition from God to the world, but this belief reached its profoundest form only in the Christian awareness of the complete interiority of God's presence to himself – so we may accept the fact that every particular level of thought is "already" an externalization, but we are now confronted with the true "origin" or "final stage" of all such externalization, where thought *as such*, in its complete interiority and independence, must nevertheless pass to its "other".

The Ontological Argument

This question is identified by Hegel with the thought underlying the ontological argument for God's existence. For the true interiority of thought is a function of its historical position, and the manner in which any given religion proposes a "proof" of God's existence is a reflection of the categories of thought attained by that religion.[140] The thought of the ontological argument thus became possible only well in the Christian period.[141]

Indeed there is, for Hegel, a sense in which the ontological argument, as the final stage, is the only true one;[142] and it is at this historical "standpoint" that he finds himself and sets his own thinking.[143] His presentation of the argument is thus a restatement of his metaphysical position rather than a "proof". The final obscurities of the one must therefore remain with the other, and the comments that follow make no claim to lift them.

The ontological argument is, in effect, presented as a summary of Hegel's whole philosophical attempt to return to the originality of experience as one with the thought of experience. It may be seen, therefore, not so much as an

[138] RB, p. 219.
[139] RA, p. 46.
[140] RB, p. 73.
[141] RB, p. 219; Beweise, p. 172.
[142] Beweise, p. 172.
[143] p. 176.

attempt to lead to new knowledge as an effort to dissipate the constructions of common sense which distort the knowledge one has. "Es ist blosse Meinung, wenn man das Sein vom Begriff entfernt zu haben glaubt."[144] For the particularity and subjectivity of "Meinung" represents thought as simply opposed to an objective reality, and it is the task of philosophy to reveal the original and fundamental objectivity of thought: "Begriff ohne Objektivität ist nur ein leeres Vorstellen, Meinen."[145]

Yet this purpose, as clear as it may be in its general statement and in the broad lines of its execution, involves at once the basic question of the double direction and presupposition of philosophical thought. In simple terms, the "argument" must begin with its result, with what it has to prove. For to begin merely at the standpoint of common sense, or at any stage of thought below the final one, is to begin with thought as opposed to being and hence to arrive at an identity in terms of these merely abstract extremes. This, Hegel points out, can offer no more than a mere ideal of future attainment: an age that starts simply with Kant's supposition of a thought "beside" a sense-concrete, such that one "denkt *auch*", can hope for no more than a concept of God as "*nur* ein Begriff".[146] If the concrete notion is to be attained, it must be there already at the beginning. Even Anselm did not fully realize "inwiefern der Begriff selbst seine Einseitigkeit aufhebt."

Hence it is the nature of the ontological argument that "am Begriffe selbst, vom Begriff aus und zwar durch den Begriff zur Objektivität, zum Sein übergegangen werden soll im Elemente des Denkens."[147] Hegel affirms thus what common sense must take to be a double paradox. The Notion can reveal its own inadequacy to itself; and one can make the transition "to being" while remaining "within the element of thought". The matter may be expressed in another way. For Hegel, a grasp of the true identity of thought and experience is not primarily a task of *overcoming* the status of "nur Denken" in opposition to experience; it is rather the process by which thought and experience *manifest* themselves as "only" thought and "only" experience in relation to the "element" in which they are present *as such*, the element of "spirit" which is their concrete identity.

This re-statement does not solve the many questions that arise in its regard, but it makes clear the scheme under which the first element of absolute religion must be thought in relation to the other two. The element of thought is originally one with the element of spirit (the "third") and hence with the

[144] p. 175.
[145] RA, p. 42.
[146] p. 51.
[147] p. 47.

system as a whole; but this original identity is realized only in the act by
which the first element is opposed to the second and hence grasped as but
one sphere of the whole. As was seen in the analysis of a corresponding section of the Phenomenology,[148] thought develops in revealing itself as both
identical with the self-consciousness of spirit and but one moment within
spirit, in a relation of "Reflexion" with the moment of Vorstellung.

Thus, Hegel's effort to remove the constructions of common sense and
arrive at the originality of thought and experience may be seen as based on an
affirmation of the true "measure" or "criterion" that philosophy must
accept. This is no measure applied to thought, but a measure that is revealed at the interior of thought. It is only in measuring itself in its inadequacy to its true nature intimately present to it that thought shows itself as
mere thought.[149] And it is in this notion of a purely interior measure that we
understand the true subjectivity of thought that took so long to develop in
history, as opposed to the mere subjectivity of "Meinen": "Es ist doch die
konkrete, totale Subjektivität des Menschen, die als Massstab vorschwebt,
an dem gemessen dann das Begreifen nur Begreifen ist."[150]

So it is that the thought of thought is the concrete identity of thought and
experience only in revealing itself as but an illustration of thought, as a
"mere" thought opposed to a "mere" experience. Hence Hegel's supreme
paradox – or insight – that the final identity is grasped as such only in
realizing the most intimate duality. Between thought and its thinking there
stands "nothing", yet it is only in this presence that inadequacy can truly be
revealed.[151]

Relation to Essence

That what is here expressed is not fundamentally different from the thought
of the Logic of Essence may briefly be shown. There it may likewise be said
that the process begins with the result. For one does not start with an inner
(essential) moment *as opposed to* an outer (non-essential) and progress to a
distant actuality (Wirklichkeit), in terms of these. Actuality is present "from
the beginning", and the movement of the dialectic is a progressive realization
of its presence in the duality of the moments; for it is in their inadequacy to
actuality that they *are* moments, opposed to each other. Opposition, we may

[148] pp. 159-64 above.
[149] "Die Unendlichkeit des Geistes ist sein Insichsein, abstrakt sein reines Insichsein,
und dies ist sein Denken, und dieses abstrakte Denken ist eine wirkliche, gegenwärtige
Unendlichkeit, und sein konkretes Insichsein ist, dass dies Denken Geist ist." (Beweise,
p. 116).
[150] RA, p. 52.
[151] p. 68; cf. p. 154 above.

say, follows from inadequacy, not vice-versa. Or, in terms of the illustration employed, the awareness of final philosophical meaning is present from the beginning, and it is in its inadequacy to this that the meaning of any particular stage grasps itself as a "mere signification" opposed to the language with which it is no less identical.

The final identity of the coupled moments is no mere ideal, for it is truly present from the beginning. Nor is it a mere identity (or difference) on the model of the identity (or difference) attained at any stage of the process. It is originative of the stages rather than derived from them. "Es geht durch seinen Prozess hindurch, und aus diesem kommt nichts Neues hervor: das Hervorgebrachte ist schon von Anfang."[152]

So far as the result is truly the beginning and shows itself as such, then it "posits" all the stages of the way. So far, however, as one makes any stage, as such, one's beginning, this will remain an unsublated presupposition. This will be so, in the ontological argument, if one's beginning has not already overcome all the attitudes of common sense. And this is, in fact, the reproach that Hegel makes to Anselm, who held that "das Sein für sich und der Begriff für sich Einseitige sind."[153] That is, the form of his argument so presents its opening conceptions that they remain simply independent and yield a merely subjective grasp of the identity of notion and being: a unity in terms of an unsublated starting-point.[154]

The result, Hegel maintains, was shown historically. Anselm's argument produced a merely abstract identity of thought and being. But one unsublated presupposition can always be met with its equal and opposite: to abstract identity, abstract opposition may simply be opposed. And so it was. Anselm, Descartes, Leibniz, and Spinoza drew their model of identity from an abstract thought opposed to being. "Modern thought", writes Hegel, argues to a surviving difference of thought and being on the model of a difference drawn from an empirical concrete determined merely in its opposition to thought.[155]

Result and Origin

The question must nevertheless remain how the "result" *can* truly sublate the "beginning": whether, in fact, the two attitudes illustrated above do not have a certain inevitability, such that Hegel's own attitude stands to them as but an attempted synthesis, proper to his time.

[152] RA, p. 72.
[153] Beweise, p. 175.
[154] RA, p. 43.
[155] p. 52.

The question may be posed in terms of the paradoxical position of the first element. On the one hand, this is identical with the third element and hence with the whole system. This identity is present from the beginning of one's philosophical progress. But it is there present only abstractly. And so far as it is abstractly present, it exists as the first element in opposition to the second. One's progress will then be "from" the first "to" the second, and vice-versa. As Hegel puts it, our "Erhebung" to God may be expressed in the form of proofs; but these form a duality – from thought to being and from being to thought[156] – such that the process in its truth must embrace the two.[157]

One is left, then, with the suggestion of Kojève[158] that Hegel's attempted thought of a result that is the origin must in practice always split into a Logic and a Phenomenology, each presupposing the other. The fact that the result is present at the beginning makes of the process a logic. The fact that the beginning must manifest itself as a result makes of it a phenomenology. Yet only so far as each "justifies" the other, may Hegel be said to support his claim to posit his presuppositions.

Again, however, this final harmony is achieved on the basis of a radical duality at its centre, which is not simply "dominated" by the circularity of the result. As suggested in an earlier chapter,[159] though Hegel consistently rejected any ineffable "beyond" his system, the price he paid was – knowingly or not – to transfer the ineffable to the "heart" of the system. Whether the traditional problems of "transcendence" may be re-stated (avoiding the language of a "Jenseits") within the horizon set by Hegel's basic metaphysical attitude is a question, the formulation of which would go far beyond the scope of this study.[160]

d. The Element of Vorstellung

In our examination of Hegel's presentation of the three elements of absolute religion for such light as they may throw on the interpretation of his system, we have seen that the first element treated of the doctrine of the Trinity and the question why the complete sufficiency of this "thought of thought" should be "complemented" by transition to the world as its "other". We

[156] Beweise, pp. 75 ff.
[157] p. 154; cf. RA, pp. 44-5; Enc. § 50.
[158] Cf. p. 167 above.
[159] pp. 109-10 above.
[160] "Mais l'être vers quoi la réalité humaine se dépasse n'est pas un Dieu transcendant: il est au coeur d'elle-même, il n'est qu'elle-même comme totalité."
(Sartre: *L'Être et le Néant*, p. 133).

must now turn to this second element, which we have followed Hegel in calling "das Element des Vorstellens",[161] and ask what Hegel reveals there of the nature of the "other" into which thought passes. The doctrines of absolute religion which Hegel discusses in this section are those of the Fall and the Incarnation.

The "Other" of Thought

The "other" into which thought passes can not be interpreted in a way that would imply a reversion to stages which preceded the true subjectivity of absolute religion. The realm of experience to be examined is still that which has "die ewige Wahrheit vor sich".[162] Yet whereas this was grasped in the first element in a timeless thought, here the experience is of this thought as outside itself in a past, present, and future.[163]

This lapse of thought from its "timelessness" to a self-externality is represented – in the medium of the latter – by the narration of the Fall.[164] This, as showing the lapse from natural unity to the original guilt of thought, is for Hegel the moment of division, of judgment, in all forms and levels of experience.[165] But though it is universal, its depth is proportional to the power of thought. The possibility of evil depends on the penetration of experience.[166] Here, at the level of absolute religion, the experience of "original sin" is at its profoundest. For what is here represented is not the "other" of any stage of thought, but the alienation of thought as such. It is the experience of that deepest division made possible by the mature subjectivity of the ontological argument. Here we have "die ganze Idee... in dieser Entfremdung".[167] Thought as thought is opposed to itself.

It was seen in Chapter I that the element of Vorstellung is characterized by its appeal to the familiarity of sheer fact.[168] And Hegel's earliest concerns were with the positivity of experience.[169] Yet this problem became for him more profound in proportion as facticity ceased to be a merely external "shock" and assumed the interiority of a self-opposition. Here, it could be said, in the appearance of the second element from the first, Hegel presents what must be for him the origin of all facticity. This must, in his system,

[161] RA, p. 31.
[162] p. 91.
[163] p. 66.
[164] pp. 102-129.
[165] Cf. Phil. Gesch., pp. 412-3; and the Zusätze to Enc. §§ 24, 246, 405.
[166] "Je tiefer der Geist, desto ungeheurer in seinem Irrtum... Nur das an sich Tiefe kann ebenso das Böseste, Schlimmste sein." (RI, p. 238).
[167] RA, p. 85.
[168] Cf. p. 29 above.
[169] Cf. pp. 124-7 above.

finally be that inadequacy of thought to itself which constitutes its transition to another. Thought is present to itself only in an illustration of thought. This is its original guilt, and it is only through the realization of guilt that the need and possibility of reconciliation can arise. So it is only in and through the deepest appreciation of the alienation of thought in its expression that the final identity of spirit is achieved.

The Need of Reconciliation

Much of this study has been concerned with Hegel's notion of synthesis, which he suggested in the different meanings of the word "Aufheben": every synthesis is as much a preservation of its opposed terms as a suppression of them in a simple identity. This thought was developed in Hegel's early meditations and represented by the religious notion of "reconciliation". So it is that the second element of Hegel's system finds an illustration close to the "origin" when it is presented in the absolute religion as the believer's search for reconciliation through the life and death of Christ.

In his youth, Hegel expressed his early experiments with Kant's philosophy by writing a life of Christ as the incarnation of a purely moral religion.[170] As was seen in the previous chapter, this ideal of a purely moral "Vernunft-religion" was superseded by a greater realization of the place of positivity at the heart of experience. And when, at the close of his career, Hegel returned to a contemplation of the life and death of Christ in his Lectures on the Philosophy of Religion, these were enriched by his life-long thought of the categories and forms of spirit as expressing all phases of man's struggle for identity-in-opposition.

For the believer, the history of Christ on earth is now the presence to man of the history of spirit itself.[171] In re-experiencing this life, the individual believer "fühlt den Schmerz des Bösen und seiner eigenen Entfremdung, welche Christus auf sich genommen hat."[172] He realizes thus the "guilt" of his alienation and the need of reconciliation. And this realization of his need is itself the way to its resolution: "Die Spitze der Entäusserung ist dies Moment der Rückkehr selbst."[173] For the presence of Christ to him is no mere memory from which he draws example, but a true "Erlebnis" of the self-offering of God.[174]

What the believer finds in the presence of Christ is the identity of the divine and human nature: more exactly, he experiences the process of their ident-

---

[170] Cf. pp. 124-5 above.
[171] RA, p. 156.
[172] p. 173.
[173] p. 95.
[174] Berlin, pp. 185-6.

ity.[175] Though this movement, Hegel warns, is that which is proper to the "Phenomenology of Spirit", it must be remembered that we are here at the highest stage of religion and have not to re-trace the path of lower forms.[176] Although a more or less concrete grasp of the truth of the Incarnation is to be found in all religions,[177] the central truth of the absolute religion is that the life of the Trinity is revealed to us by the presence of the Son of God in the world.[178] The need and possibility of reconciliation are at their profoundest; it is both absolute objectivity and infinite subjectivity that are demanded.[179]

Hegel's explicit reference to the "Phenomenology of Spirit" supports the suggestion of a previous section that the second element corresponds basically to the movement of experience portrayed in that work.[180] This is the movement of particular standpoints ("für sich") which are accompanied by a view from the totality ("für uns") that is always "behind the back" of the former. The second element of absolute religion, however, can not simply be identified with this movement of a "für sich" and of a merely parenthetical "für uns". For it is an element of absolute religion, where the identity of subjective and objective, of form and content, is attained. Hence, the truth that the life of the Trinity is revealed to us by the presence of Christ must mean that the divine nature (pure thought, the "für uns" of the Phenomenology) is no longer hidden from us, disclosed only in parentheses to a privileged observer: it stands open to our sight.

It is, however, precisely to our sight that it is open, in the presence of immediacy.[181] The identity of divine and human nature is grasped "from the side of" human nature, interpreted "in terms of" that structure of particular, temporal experiences that form the standpoint of the "für sich".

Hence the paradoxical, but suggestive, result: the experience finally represented by the second element of absolute religion, the profoundest alienation of pure thought, is a situation whereby absolute truth ("für uns") is present as such to the individual thinker ("für sich") who, despite this achieved identity, is nevertheless held in a persisting separation by the position from which he thinks. He has lost the state of innocence and is fully aware of the role he plays as a role; yet he is powerless to step out of it and completely embrace the truth. It is in this impotence "within" the presence

---

[175] RA, p. 135.
[176] p. 89.
[177] RN, p. 6.
[178] RA, p. 170.
[179] p. 130.
[180] pp. 160-1 above.
[181] Phän., p. 531.

of the final reconciliation that the believer comes in the revealed religion "zur tiefsten Entzweiung, dem gewussten Negativen".[182]

Much of this description remains metaphorical. Yet it may serve to suggest an approach to Hegel's doctrine of the "List der Vernunft",[183] which could make it less objectionable. For this term indicates that duality of "für sich" and "für uns", whereby the "world spirit" seems to be represented as hiding from itself the way it has come, in order later to "discover" itself therein. Litt terms this the "Selbstüberlistung der Idee"[184] and quotes a Zusatz to the Encyclopaedia Logic: "Die Idee in ihrem Prozess macht sich selbst jene Täuschung, setzt ein Anderes sich gegenüber und ihr Tun besteht darin, diese Täuschung aufzuheben."[185] The objection to such a representation touches the heart of Hegel's conception of phenomenology. Yet it may be that the final self-identity of truth is no simple opposite to what we experience as "delusion". If the concrete presence of truth is to be the identity of identity and non-identity, then the latter moment must be no less at its heart than the former. And Hegel's presentation of the second element may serve to give just emphasis to this aspect of the whole, which is too easily lost in our ready thinking of its final identity on the model of the abstract identities we find at hand.

Transition to Spirit

The concrete whole has been attained from two different "directions" in the first and second elements of absolute religion. Both elements are identical with it, but abstractly and with the partiality of their "standpoint". If the whole be termed the identity of thought and experience, then it is grasped in the first element by a thought abstractly opposed to experience, and in the second element by an experience abstractly opposed to thought.

This is schematically expressed, but what is implied has always been present in this study – as in any study of a philosopher. Even the most faithful attempt to enter his thought demands a certain distance from the expression he achieved, and this distance is an interpretation in terms of our own experience. Similarly, even when we try to realize our "own" thought, we do so only in a certain "distance" from it, or interpretation of it in terms of a language and history in some way foreign to it. The more profoundly we realize the claims of a thinking whose content is purely its own thought, the more keenly we feel the inadequacy of our own attempts to reach this final

---

[182] RA, p. 164.
[183] Enc. § 209.
[184] *Hegel*, p. 219.
[185] Enc. § 212 Zusatz.

reconciliation in the illustrations of our particular "intuitions". We seek the experience of thinking but construct a psychology of thought. And in realizing this, we realize how – just as the first element was revealed as "only" thought by the self-measurement of thought as spirit – so the second element is revealed as "only" experience by the self-measurement of experience as spirit.

The full realization of this need of an absolute reconciliation is itself the way of reconciliation and the transition to the third element, the element of spirit. It is only in death, "die höchste Spitze der Endlichkeit", that Hegel can represent this:

Das zeitliche, vollkommene Dasein der göttlichen Idee in der Gegenwart wird nur in Christi Tode angeschaut. Die höchste Entäusserung der göttlichen Idee: "Gott ist gestorben, Gott selbst ist tot" ist eine ungeheure, fürchterliche Vorstellung, die vor die Vorstellung den tiefsten Abgrund der Entzweiung bringt.[186]

This death of the Son of God is not merely a natural death but a death of dishonour, and the Cross symbolizes the Kingdom of God as a denial of the security of "Staatsleben und bürgerliches Sein".[187] It is a death to all the forms through which the individual consciousness has passed and in which – as "presuppositions" – it found its support and its meaning. "Alles Geltende der Welt ist ins Grab des Geistes versenkt."[188]

With these forms must pass those very categories of identity and opposition which have united and separated the first and second elements in their development. "Das Sein der Welt ist. . . nur dies zu sein: zurückzukehren in Ihren Ursprung."[189] And this "origin" is the element of spirit, in which the other elements "result", and yet from which they, their identity and their difference, must derive their meaning.

e. The Element of Spirit

To accept Hegel's basic thesis that "truth can be only where it makes itself its own result,"[190] is to renounce for all time any definitive interpretation of the notion of "Geist" and hence of the system itself. Throughout this study it has been stressed that no category or form of the system is a merely static "model of explanation" which is simply "applied" for the understanding of other categories or forms: verification is always a changing (and "sublation") of both measure and measured. In regard to the system-triad of Idea, Nature, and Spirit, this difficulty is magnified in two ways:

[186] RA, pp. 157-8; cf. p. 167 and Phän., p. 523.
[187] RA, pp. 161-2.
[188] p. 166.
[189] RA, p. 94.
[190] Enc. § 212 Zusatz.

Firstly, the system-triad is the concrete whole, revealed as the result that is the origin of all its stages. Hence the commentator must abandon the claim to any final understanding of it on the model of any particular triad of logic, nature, or finite spirit through which he has passed on the way. Though the totality is one with its genesis, each stage is no more than an illustration.

Secondly, there is at least one sense in which this originality of the origin seems to be complete. Every triad along the way was comprehended in an act that went beyond it to a greater whole; each synthesis was the concrete totality of its moments only at the expense of "falling" to a fresh immediacy as the thesis, or first moment, of a further triad.[191] But the final triad, the system itself, can not be so understood. There is no new dimension into which to pass. And this is a situation that is radically original – one might even say, "un-Hegelian". So much so, as we have seen, that Hegel's early "Systemfragment" spoke of this final synthesis as a "reality beyond all reflection."[192]

So far as we accept the triadic form in which Hegel formulated his system, the synthesis of the system itself is "Spirit", and Logic and Nature are the moments reconciled. It has already been seen that, just as this form is a violence to the dogma which inspired it,[193] so it does not in fact represent what Hegel expounded when he illustrated his system in the form of the three elements of absolute religion.[194] The second element is not merely nature, but nature as taken up in the experience of finite spirit. The third element is absolute spirit, in the sense that it is the progressive reconciliation of abstract thought and merely finite experience. The burden of interpretation is thus to understand what Hegel means by this "situation" of reconciliation, and how it is the identity of the other two elements, yet respects their difference. It remains for us, therefore, to examine the third element of absolute religion, in terms of its situation and its identity.

The Situation of Philosophy

Religious thought in the second element, we have seen, was a grasp of the final reconciliation of thought and experience from the side of the latter: the union of divine and human natures in Christ was mediated in its immediacy. The believer could pass from this realm only in that self-measuring of spirit by which the whole realm was recognized as "only" experience. "Seine Grenze wissen heisst, sich aufzuopfern wissen."[195] And this self-sacrificing,

---

[191] Cf. pp. 65-6, 164 above.
[192] Nohl, p. 348; cf. p. 128 above.
[193] pp. 140-1 above.
[194] pp. 160-1 above.
[195] Phän., p. 567.

which the believer achieves in his "Erlebnis" of the death of Christ, is itself the realization of – or "transition to" – the element of spirit. This is represented, in religious terms, by the true interiority of the presence of the Spirit of Truth in the "Gemeinde";[196] and what is here portrayed is the situation of the third element, for the religious communion is the "Boden des Geistes".[197] It is the standpoint where the first and second elements are identified in their original opposition.

Wenn wir erstens die Gemeinde mit dem vergleichen, was wir bereits gehabt haben, so hatten wir zuerst die ewige Idee im Elemente des Denkens betrachtet, zweitens im Elemente der Entäusserung, in der Darstellung einer sinnlich äusseren, unmittelbaren Weise. Wir haben dies so betrachtet, und es war für uns. Aber wer sind wir? Wir sind nichts anderes al die Gemeinde selber.[198]

Thus, as we saw in the general introduction to the three elements, Hegel identifies the "privileged" position of the philosopher of religion with the standpoint of the third element.[199] His task is that of the believer at this level: to comprehend how spirit, in its fundamental self-identity, is present in the elements, in their opposition. And so far as he achieves this task, he passes from a division of the elements that is merely "vorhanden", imposed by the philosopher, to the self-division which is the process of spirit itself.[200] In this way he comes to the "absolute Bedeutung des Geistes", the actual presence of the Spirit of God in the religious communion, as opposed to the abstract presence of the Trinity (first element, as such) and of Christ (second element).[201]

The "absolute meaning" of spirit is thus an attainment of meaning from itself precisely in a duality where meaning is from another. It is the "freier Geist" which is thought *and* Vorstellung,[202] yet which in both these elements, those of the Trinity and of Christ, constitutes "derselbe Verlauf und Prozess der Explikation Gottes".[203] For though the third element is a transition "from" the first and second, it is no mystical presence that rises simply above them, or denies their difference. The life of the religious communion is rather the "ewige Wiederholung" of the life of Christ[204] and of the thought of the Trinity.[205]

[196] RA, pp. 168-9.
[197] p. 182.
[198] p. 189.
[199] pp. 171-2 above.
[200] RA, pp. 29-30.
[201] p. 180.
[202] RA, pp. 65-6; cf. Enc. §§ 159, 481-2.
[203] RA, p. 167.
[204] p. 208.
[205] p. 173.

It is in the phrase "eternal repetition" that we have the inner contradiction of the element of spirit as origin and result, as a completion that is yet a development to completion. Whereas the first element was outside time, and the element of Vorstellung was dissipated into a past and a future, the experience of the Church is that of an "errungene Gegenwart".[206] "Das Jetzt des Genusses zerrinnt in der Vorstellung teils in ein Jenseits, in einen jenseitigen Himmel, teils in Vergangenheit, teils in Zukunft. Der Geist aber ist sich schlechthin gegenwärtig und fordert eine erfüllte Gegenwart."[207] Yet this "absolute presence" is not the mere timelessness of the first element. The final stage is neither a merely future ideal nor a simply achieved and static situation "from" which one can think. It is rather the original experience of the "temporalities" of Vorstellung and of the "eternity" of thought, such that only spirit in its completion can truly be said to experience time.[208]

Thus, we find that the religious communion, far from being a synthesis beyond development, "ist innerhalb ihrer ein ewiges Werden."[209] This is not, however, a mere infinite process, as in Kant's representation of an eternal struggle.[210] It is, in one sense, achieved; its doctrine is complete. Yet in another sense it must repeatedly create its belief, give expression to its teaching. The Sacraments express man's need to be born again in the Spirit, to recognize the truth in which he is.[211] Far from this being a present that could be confused with the timelessness of the first element, Hegel speaks of a "Konzentration der Gegenwart zum Tode".[212]

This "concentration of the present to death" may perhaps be seen as a symbolic representation of that inner conflict of spirit as origin and as result. This is, in a sense, a conflict that bears upon every particular synthesis of the system, so far as it must reveal itself as the true source of its moments while not ceasing to be their result. Yet, as mentioned above, it is only in the synthesis of the system itself that this conflict is realized in its most acute form. For every particular synthesis achieves itself by a certain escape into the abstraction of an "insofern": that is, it fails to realize its fully concrete contradiction, and the abstraction of its escape constitutes the "Wiederherstellung der ersten Unmittelbarkeit" which makes it the first moment of a further triad.[213] Rather than being the "living result" of its own triad, it falls

---

[206] p. 201.
[207] p. 215.
[208] Phän., p. 476.
[209] RA, p. 202.
[210] p. 206.
[211] p. 205.
[212] p. 177.
[213] Cf. pp. 164-5 above.

to the "lifeless repose" of an external attitude; yet "dieses scheinbare Ende, der Übergang der lebendigen Dialektik in die tote Ruhe des Resultats ist selbst der Anfang wieder nur dieser lebendigen Dialektik."[214] This may be seen as the basis of that fundamental presupposition of Hegel's system, according to which one remains within the experience of the Phenomenology only by passing out of it into an alien "für uns", and according to which the interiority of logical movement manifests a "phänomenologischer Anteil" at its heart. The element of Vorstellung reveals, in its own development, its passage out of itself into the dimension of pure thought, and the element of thought reveals its passage into that of experience.

Yet "outside" spirit there is nothing but spirit, no "new dimension" in which it can find an "insofern" and escape from the concrete realization of the contradiction at its heart. It is the "final unity". But this would be falsified, made subjective, formal, "positive", should it be interpreted as an identity in any way "beyond" the difference of the moments it reconciles. The "profoundest need" of man is not satisfied by a synthesis of his finite dualites in terms of the identity of the absolute as only abstractly present to him: the "need" of philosophy is for a reconciliation of this abstract presence itself with the dualities of man's particular experience.[215] The situation of philosophy, as suggested in the third element of absolute religion, re-states Hegel's early ideals of the "equilibrium" of a philosophical system, and poses again the problem of thinking the final identity as a true "Indifferenzpunkt".

The Final Identity

It is this difficulty of experiencing spirit as both absolute presence and particular duality, as both "allgemeiner Geist" and "das Fürsichsein des einzelnen Individuums",[216] which has – according to Hegel – given rise of the different churches.[217] For it becomes apparent that the Kingdom of God "hat in sich schon Gott und sein Reich, die Gemeinde,"[218] and the problem is the thinking of the "and" whereby spirit is but a moment of spirit. It is the problem, shown forth in the experience of the religious communion, of that "Offenbarung" and "Erhebung" which Hegel thought in the proofs of God's existence. "Die Frage ist allein, wie es anzufangen sei, aufzuzeigen, dass etwas von sich selbst anfange."[219] The showing forth of a result "from"

---

[214] Beweise, p. 156.
[215] Differenz, p. 49; cf. pp. 129-30 above.
[216] RA, p. 207.
[217] pp. 212-3.
[218] p. 150.
[219] Beweise, p. 147.

particular experience must be reconciled with the derivation of experience "from" the result as a beginning.

This is the problem which accounts for the fact that the absolute experience of the third element is nevertheless a historical development. The question of this relation between system and history will be touched upon in the following section. Here, merely one example will be given of Hegel's treatment of the experience of the religious communion.

The total self-offering which is the achievement of the third element, in relation to the elements which thus passed into it, is represented by Hegel equivalently as death and as love.[220] In the latter, Hegel returns to the first principle of reconciliation which he developed at Frankfurt.[221] In those early writings, the emphasis was set mainly on the union achieved in love. Here, with his lifelong experience of the "suffering of God in the world",[222] Hegel gives greater scope to the fact that this is a union of opposing personalities, that this reconciliation is the possibility for the experience of true difference. The thought of spirit as return from alienation in the Trinity is expressed in the relation of Persons, such that "der Gegensatz absolut zu nehmen sei."[223] Love is the basis of life in the religious communion, the infinite power to retain oneself "in diesem schlechthin Andern".[223] And in the life of faith, love is the "unendlicher Schmerz" in which Christ is "in einer unendlichen Ferne, Hoheit, aber in unendlicher Nähe."[225] Little can be based directly upon such metaphors, but there is no doubt that Hegel found in the basic religious conception of complete union in total otherness both illustration and inspiration for his thought of a final identity.

If one may employ spatial language to say that the duality of thought and experience is "within" the final identity, then one must no less qualify this statement by adding that the point of reconciliation is not "beyond" but "at the heart of" this duality. For the element of spirit is a continued realization of "die Entzweiung, die nur der Geist ertragen kann".[226] And to the extent that the believer realizes his situation in its full concreteness, "he repeats in himself the process of spirit", which is at once the thinking of the "universal idea" (i.e. the Trinity: first element) and its "appearance" (i.e. as the life of Christ: second element).[227]

---

[220] RA, pp. 158-9.
[221] Cf. pp. 33-4, 126-7 above.
[222] Cf. Iljin, p. 379.
[223] RA, p. 71.
[224] p. 176.
[225] p. 180.
[226] p. 46.
[227] pp. 194-5.

So far, then, as absolute religion be a valid illustration of what Hegel wished to convey in his system, it may seem that the triad of Idea, Nature, and Spirit is a not entirely happy formulation. In this sense, the suggestion was hazarded in the previous chapter[228] that his early ideals of philosophical system might have found a truer – and more acceptable – expression if Hegel had perhaps stayed closer to that formulation of Schelling he once defended: of a system which reveals the absolute only in the complementarity of two "parallel" sciences, each a "relative totality" that both pressupposes and interprets the other. Yet if Hegel's final identity is in any way to be likened to Schelling's "Indifferenzpunkt", then such an analogy must pass far beyond the mystical "night" of a transcendental intuition. Hegel's vast effort was to provide a scheme for the thinking of such an intuition. And this, if our interpretation has not gone completely astray, is to be found pre-eminently in the Logic of Essence. It was in this respect that it has often been repeated that the transitions of the system can neglect their moment of "Reflexion" only at the risk of falling to a view of the system as a simple "Übergang" of Idea to Nature, and Nature to Spirit.

In his doctrine of religion, Hegel has often been accused of "rationalism" in his rejection of "mysteries".[229] The charge is probably justified. Yet its proof is no easy matter. For his system has – whether he wanted it or not – transferred mystery from a future "beyond" to the heart of his thought. Hegel's "rationalism" consists, at least partially, in a vigorous and life-long rejection of the merely "residual unknown" of an indefinite future. His "romanticism" consists in the metaphysical deception, or perception, of setting the original mystery as the principle of his dialectic. His system is the showing forth of this principle in its presence and in its originality.

f. System and History

With the element of spirit the system of absolute religion is completed. Yet the synthesis of the system-triad has shown itself to be a "final stage" which, precisely in its reconciliation of the other two elements, is an "ewige Wiederholung". It is not with a hymn to the final achievement of the thought of thought that Hegel closes the Lectures on the Philosophy of Religion, but with remarks on the incompletion of philosophy.[230]

If spirit is the achieved totality, yet the philosopher must renounce a final

---

[228] p. 135 above.

[229] E.g., RB, p. 206: 'Dann ist nichts verborgenes mehr in ihm; was Gott ist, hat er zur Erscheinung gebracht."

[230] RA, p. 231.

understanding of it, then the question of the place of history in such a philosophy is not easily avoided. This concluding note is no attempt to develop, or even to suggest, an interpretation of Hegel's philosophy of history. It will merely return, in the light of the reflections on the structure of absolute religion, to the question posed at the end of Chapter III: what is philosophy that it should be not merely a development (Entwicklung) but a history?[231]

There it was seen that Hegel identified philosophy and its history in all except that the former is "rein im Elemente des Denkens", whereas the latter is burdened with "geschichtliche Äusserlichkeit"; yet the "In-der-Zeit-Sein" which constitutes this externality is no less within the element of thought.

In the examination of Hegel's doctrine of absolute religion, we saw that he identified the standpoint of the philosopher with the third element and described his task as that of thinking the presence of spirit in the different elements in a way that overcomes the imposition of his own divisions and allows the manifestation of the process of spirit itself in its moments.[232] This task is to be realized only so far as the philosopher thinks and experiences the situation he is in, avoiding the abstract constructions that come with any one-sided beginning. That which is truly real is the philosopher's situation in the element of spirit; that question is true which is a question of the place from which it is posed.

Yet it is fundamental to the interpretation proposed that this original situation is honestly attained only in the "dishonesty of construction". Hegel finds that philosophical thought, as opposed to mathematical or empirical, is an inseparably dual movement from beginning to result and from result to beginning. Its truth is in the untruth of presupposition. The pure description of experience can proceed only with presupposition of a logic outside it, and the pure thought of logic reveals its reliance on an alien experience. But in both elements, that which is foreign develops within the element itself, in its inadequacy (as "mere" thought or "mere" experience) to the element of spirit in which both are originally identified and opposed.

Hegel's statements on the relation between philosophy and its history would seem to accord with these conceptions. For the history of philosophy consists primarily, not in outward circumstances, but in that historicity of expression which manifests itself at the heart of a philosophical thought trying to formulate its problem. Though thought posits its expression, it no less finds its origin in means of expression that bear, indeed are, the possibilities

[231] Cf. pp. 102-5 above.
[232] p. 185 above.

and limitations of a historical position. This is the "Grenzpunkt der Vorstellung" which determines the "umschriebener Horizont von Gedanken"
in a given age.[233] The historicity of philosophy is thus the externality of Vorstellung which manifests itself at the interior of the element of thought as the
hidden presupposition of its pure development.[234]

The concern of the philosopher is therefore not with a pure thought in abstraction from the history of thought, nor with a thought that is simply opposed to its history. The task Hegel set those who would understand the
Logic of Essence was that of thinking the essential, neither as a pure interiority from which its opposing moment is banned, nor as simply determined in relation to the non-essential, but as the actuality which draws its
meaning purely from itself only in the duality in which it, as essential, is
opposed to its non-essential moment. Hegel's system may – it is maintained –
be interpreted as an attempt to express analogously the situation in which the
philosopher finds himself, and to which he must be true. For this situation,
to be at once truly philosophical and truly historical, must be a re-thinking
of the logic of philosophy, neither in abstraction from its history nor in
simple opposition to it, but as a system which draws meaning from itself only
in the mutual positing and presupposing of its pure thought and its history.
And if the situation of the philosopher has been described as a "concentration to death",[235] then it is thus that he experiences both the absoluteness
and the relativity of his thought: actuality is present in his thought so far as
this thought is a realization of its "Grenzpunkt" and its "umschriebener
Horizont" as a mere stage to that actuality.

History would, therefore, have a double meaning. Firstly, it would constitute, in many different forms, what we have examined throughout this
study under the title of Vorstellung, the non-essential "other" of pure
thought. Secondly, it would be the originality of the philosopher's situation,
that self-division of spirit itself in its thought and experience which constitutes the standpoint of his time.[236] So, in his discussion of absolute religion,
Hegel distinguishes between the "äusserliche Geschichte" of the element of
Vorstellung[237] and the "göttliche Geschichte" which is the process of spirit
through the three elements,[238] the process which the believer attains so far as

[233] Beweise, p. 91.

[234] Cf. the comments of Chapter III on the Objective Logic as Hegel's re-thinking of the
history of philosophy: e.g., p. 73 above.

[235] Cf. p. 186 above.

[236] Or, as Hegel would perhaps express it, the time that is fulfilled in the thought of the
philosopher. "Erst als die Zeit gekommen war, ist der Geist sich offenbar geworden."
(RB, p. 74; cf. Phil. Gesch., p. 410).

[237] RA, p. 31.

[238] p. 65.

he abandons the one-sidedness of his "beginning" and is true to the situation of the "Gemeinde".[239]

In this double sense of history is a more than accidental relation to the double meaning of time that was discussed in Chapter II.[240] For the consideration of history with which Hegel concludes his Phenomenology is made in terms of his doctrine of time and space. The Notion is time itself, and it appears "in" time so far as its expression in inadequate to itself.[241] Similarly, history is spirit externalized "in" time as a succession of spiritual shapes,[242] whose process toward adequate revelation is a dialectic of the true interiority of time and its spatial embodiments.[243] The process of spirit, in its originality, is thus attained only in its genesis through the historical situations of thought and experience, "the recollection and the Golgotha of Absolute Spirit", from which realm there "foams forth to God his own infinitude".[244]

Hegel's awareness that his own thought constituted a new epoch[245] and, in a sense, the "end of history" is not incompatible, in this account, with his consciousness that philosophy is a continuing development, of which his thought was but a stage.[246] For every true grasp that a philosopher makes of his situation is the attainment of the originality of spirit and of all history, "a new stage of existence, a new world, and a new embodiment or mode of spirit".[247]

In his youth, Hegel wrote:

Das wahre Eigentümliche einer Philosophie ist die interessante Individualität, in welcher die Vernunft aus dem Bauzeug eines besondern Zeitalters sich eine Gestalt organisiert hat ... Jede Philosophie ist in sich vollendet, und hat, wie ein echter kunstwerk, die Totalität in sich. So wenig des Apelles und Sophokles Werke, wenn Raphael und Shakespeare sie gekannt hätten, diesen als blosse Vorübungen

---

[239] p. 194.
[240] Cf. pp. 47-8 above.
[241] Phän., p. 558.
[242] p. 563.
[243] p. 564.
[244] An adapted quotation from Schiller, with which Hegel concludes the Phenomenology. Kojève regards the alterations as significant, and concludes: "La PhG s'achève donc par une négation radicale de toute transcendance." (*Introduction*, p. 440).

It may be of interest that the same quotation occurs fourteen years later in Hegel's manuscript on absolute religion (p. 132), this time without the two alterations on which Kojève comments. If the changes in the Phenomenology were of any significance, one might then have to conclude that Hegel had been converted to an affirmation of transcendence. But it would be more satisfactory to hold that he was attempting a thought of considerably more subtlety than could be set in the categories of mere denial or affirmation of transcendence which his progeny imposed on him from left and from right.

[245] Phän., p. 15.
[246] Recht, pp. 16-17.
[247] Phän., p. 564.

für sich hätten erscheinen können . . . so wenig kann die Vernunft in früheren Gestaltungen ihrer selbst nur nützliche Vorübungen für sich erblicken.[248]

So it is that a system of philosophy can rightly present itself as a "logic"
complete in itself only so far as the logic is equally but one element of the
system, drawing its ability to formulate its problem from the thought of its
predecessors and submitting itself to its death before the revitalized thought
and Vorstellung of its successors.

Hegel's consciousness that his philosophy of "spirit" was but a thought in
transition was not altogether occluded by his recognition that the materials
of his age had come to an original self-expression in his system. And it is
with these words that he concludes his manuscript of the religion in which
nothing more remains hidden of God or creation:

Yet, as we have remarked, philosophy is but partial. It forms a sacred priesthood
which lives in isolation, withdrawn from the business of the world, and guarding
its possession of truth. What transpires outside this seclusion is no concern of
ours.[249]

---

[248] Differenz, pp. 43-4.
[249] RA, p. 231.

CHAPTER VI

THE SYSTEM IN THE ELEMENT OF THOUGHT: CONCLUSION

I. CIRCULARITY AND CRITICISM

The "circularity" which Hegel frequently emphasized as the form of his thought at once supplies him with a ready escape from criticism and leaves him peculiarly open to it.

On the one hand, it becomes impossible simply to isolate from his whole system any part of it, and to submit this to a norm of "verification" which appears "from outside". Hegel would concede that any part, so isolated, is abstract and needs criticism; but that the only criticism to which it may justly be subjected is the self-criticism of the whole. From the closed circle formed by Hegel's dual movement of explanation there is no escape.

On the other hand, by thus identifying his philosophy, as a whole, with the whole of experience, Hegel himself applies a norm of verification before which the judgment of inadequacy is so clear as to render its pronouncement a banality. If "the force of mind is only as great as its expression",[1] Hegel's mind remains one of the most forceful to have set itself before the full extension of experience. Yet the record of his efforts, which he finally left in 1831 to his followers in the history of philosophy, rests a highly "abstract" and "subjective" identity of experience and its thought.

This study has, as already carefully stressed, treated of Hegel's exposition of religion purely as an illustration of his system. It has avoided all reference to the question of adequacy to religious experience as such. However, even allowing for the "self-criticism of the whole", Hegel's inadequacy in this realm is manifest. The awe and anguish that turn for expression to the doctrine and sense of original sin find but a faint echo in the negativity of Hegelian thought. In his choice of terms here, Hegel has supplied his critics, old and new, with a telling reproach.[2] Though there is today a certain re-

[1] Phän., p. 15.
[2] For example, cf. McTaggart: *Studies in Hegelian Cosmology* (1901), pp. 151-176, and Schmidt: *Hegels Lehre von Gott* (1952), pp. 201-11.

vived interest in Hegel as "religious thinker", he remained, for all his opposition to the "Aufklärung", much a child of its light.

It is indeed, Hegel's historical position at the synthesis of rationalism and romanticism which helps to explain both his immense influence on so many radically different mentalities and his failure truly to satisfy any one of them. If, as it seems, one must speak of finally irreconcilable attitudes in philosophy, Hegel will win the genuine sympathies neither of those who incline to the "analytical" nor of those tending to the "intuitional". He was too much a romantic to set his guide, even in the Logic, purely in the self-justifying movement of any "strenge Wissenschaft"; the voice of inspiration came always "from behind the back". Yet he remained too much a rationalist to refrain from the mere imposition of categories, and to submit himself in true sympathy to the movement of the thing itself.

Nevertheless, if it is the measure of a great thinker that no one has shown himself capable of assimilating and criticizing his thought as a whole, this is a test before which Hegel eminently succeeds. The era that is well termed post-Hegelian has explored, by development or by reaction, a multitude of ways which he opened to thought. But it is singularly barren of any profound attempt to ask in what the limit, or "subjectivity", of his thought finally lies. Nor is this surprising. For Hegel may well mark the culmination of a certain form of thinking, which runs deep and wide in man's efforts to rise to philosophy. To criticize this thought is to go beyond it. And that is a task which perhaps only Heidegger has so far seriously set himself.[3]

The aim of this study has been far more modest. Its concern has been, not with the limits history put upon Hegel's thought, but rather with Hegel's claim to have put some limit upon history. It is difficult to believe that any serious philosopher, least of all one steeped in the history of philosophy, can honestly have believed that his own thought marked the "end" of that history. Yet the apparent claim to completion made by Hegel's system puts a severe demand upon any commentator who is concerned to reconcile it with sanity of historical perspective.

No such demand is set in commenting upon a philosopher who assumed a simple duality between his philosophy and the experience or facts of which it was an "explanation". To apologize for Hegel by implying that he really meant no more is to evacuate from his philosophy that fundamental insight which dated from his earliest meditations and remained with his final

---

[3] whatever opinion be held of the success of his attempt. There are few places in which he explicitly takes a position in regard to Hegel. But Hegel is, for him, the climax of that subjectivism in which metaphysics has developed, and to study Heidegger without clear reference to Hegel is to miss a basic orientation of his thought.

lectures. No interpretation can simply deny that Hegel claimed for the philosopher a final "Bei-sich-Sein", a radical unity of the form and content of thought, of philosophy and experience. It was his affirmation of a true interiority, or absolute, even in the most casual human experience. To meditate the absolute, one must begin "absolutely".

To concede this, however, is not necessarily to allow that Hegel's system must represent an unequivocal account of all reality from the point of view at which it is perfectly achieved. Dogmatism of this sort is certainly to be found. But it is far from an adequate account of Hegel's meaning, complex and ambiguous as it was even at the end. This study has sought an understanding of this meaning which will leave his basic insight and yet allow Hegel some sense of occupying a place in the history of philosophy rather than of setting an end to it.

Metaphor must prevail in any summary. Yet it may be said that Hegel's affirmation of a final unity, while certainly a denial of all that he considered to be an "external" – and hence false – duality, nevertheless allows, and demands, a profounder realization of the duality "at the heart of" this unity. This is that sense of "depth" in the reconciliations of experience which led him first to seek the culminating stage in faith rather than in thought; which forced him to define it as the identity, not merely of different elements, but of identity and difference; and which inspired him to find in the final interiority of thought to itself an exteriority by which it is "nur Denken". It is, indeed, this intimate duality, paradoxical as it seems in its expression, which may offer some approach to the no lesser paradox that is manifested by every metaphysician who affirms truths as absolute and yet historical.

The traditional account of Hegel's position, we have seen, tends to emphasize the "domination" of all duality "within" the pure identity of the final stage. This study has formed no denial of this account or of its terms. It has tried, however, to stress the need to avoid all over-simple understanding of those terms. Interpretation may not bow completely before criticism in looking for the persistence in Hegel's thought of some faithfulness to his youthful rejection of "domination"[4] and of some awareness that the "inner" is but one of the dual categories of Essence.

Such an interpretation involves an attention to themes which Hegel himself, at least within the hearing of his opponents, was little inclined to put at the centre of his exposition. It is not suggested, for example, that the explicitly formulated problem of thought and language drew Hegel's attention in the way in which it may that of a contemporary commentator. He was cer-

[4] Cf. pp. 127, 130-1 above.

tainly aware of the difficulty with which meaning achieves itself in language,[5] and at one point concedes that the greater concern he showed for the passage from Vorstellung to thought than for the equally essential transition of thought into Vorstellung was determined by effectively polemical reasons.[6] Yet it was not with explicit concessions that the first part of this study was concerned, so much as with the *basis* Hegel's thought – and especially his Logic – gives to one who would express this duality which language sets at the heart of his profoundest "meaning". If words make the problem, they no less prevent any unambiguous solution; yet Hegel's Logic may make possible a statement of the question that would be of interest, if not value, even today.

The second part of the study has applied this question of the "other" of thought, which is yet at its heart, to the traditional paradox of the system, whereby logical thought is the whole and is yet opposed to its "other" in nature. The first chapter considered the origins of this paradox in Hegel's early religious meditations; the second analyzed the expression he gave it in his mature account of the "absolute religion". It remains for this chapter to expose the formulation Hegel gave to his system in the "element of thought", when, at the close of the Encyclopaedia, he explained it in relation to his doctrine of the syllogism. Then, in conclusion, some of the themes of this study will be drawn together in terms of its title.

2. SYSTEM AND SYLLOGISM

If Hegel's lectures on the absolute religion supply but an example of his system, it is only in the closing words of his Encyclopaedia that he ventures to expose the system professedly stripped of all illustration, in the "element of thought". The exposition remains, however, in terms of a lower stage of the dialectic, that of the syllogism. To account for this choice and to understand the final "triad of syllogisms", a word of reference to the nature of the "Subjective Logic" is necessary.

a. The Doctrine of the Syllogism

Hegel's doctrine of the syllogism forms the culmination of the first part of the "Logik des Begriffs"; the part, that is, which portrays the general movement of the Notion. It has already been seen that the Logic of the Notion con-

---

[5] E.g., Berlin, p. 196: "Wissen, was man sagt, ist viel seltener, als man meint, und es ist mit dem allergrössten Unrecht, dass die Anschuldigung, nicht zu wissen, was man sagt, für die härteste gilt."

[6] Berlin, pp. 318-20.

stitutes at once the third part of the triple division of the Logic (Being, Essence, and Notion) and the second part of its double division (Objective and Subjective Logic).[7] The "standpoint" of transition from Essence to Notion is said by Hegel to have two "sides".[8] From the first, the Notion appears as the "ground" into which Being and Essence pass. From the second, it is the ground from which developes the reality which had thus vanished into it.

That is, the Objective Logic was the demonstration, by means of a criticism of all former metaphysics, that philosophy is not merely a thought "about" experience but is finally constitutive of experience. The Logic of Essence retraces, in the element of thought, the path of the Phenomenology, and thus overcomes a presupposed subjectivity (merely "external reflection") to establish the true objectivity of thought ("determining reflection"). But this path can no less be viewed "from the other side" as the progressive self-constitution of a truly self-conscious subject. The Logic that develops from this standpoint is thus called the Subjective Logic. Its general movement culminates in the syllogism.

The process of alternating standpoints which characterized the Logic of Essence is here "overcome", and it is in the self-development of the Notion that the traditional interpretation of Hegel finds its logical verification. The question remains, however, whether in dividing the Objective Logic into Being and Essence and in designating the Subjective Logic as their "synthesis", Hegel was not imposing a triadic form false to his original (and perhaps truer) thought.[9] It was nevertheless this triadic division which prevailed. In the Encyclopaedia version of the Logic there is no mention of Objective and Subjective Logic, certainly no suggestion that they constitute alternative standpoints.[10]

As the ground from which the full reality is to appear, the Notion must develop completely from itself. In its most general form, Hegel represents this as the self-particularization of mere universality to form the "individual", or "concrete universal".[11] This scheme provides him with a basis for re-

[7] Cf. pp. 71-4 above.
[8] WL, II, p. 229.
[9] Cf. pp. 140-1 above.
[10] Though Hegel is there at pains to stress the difficulty of the transition from Essence to Notion (§ 159). That is, if the movement of the Notion is not to be "complemented" by that of Essence, the latter must – with all its complexity – be "aufgehoben" without loss. Else the Notion will be a merely abstract totality.
[11] The three moments of the Hegelian Notion ("Allgemeinheit", "Besonderheit", "Einzelheit") are better understood from the ideal of perfect self-development than from their connotations in formal logic. Hegel himself introduces them as corresponding to the three most general moments of Essence (identity, difference, and ground), but with the

thinking the science of formal logic. It is to be no longer a mere codification of the various ways of thought, as simply "given", but a self-manifestation of thought itself.

Formal logic is traditionally divided into the doctrine of the notion as such, of the judgment, and of the syllogism. Hegel interprets them as the stages of explicit self-development. A man may be viewed in his abstract universality, in the particular ways in which this can be expressed, or as an individual whose particularity adequately incarnates the universal. Any one of the three considered in abstraction from the others is a mere notion. But so far as there is awareness of one *as* universal, or particular, or individual, it must be in explicit relation to the others. And this relation is at once the original division ("Urteil") and original identity. Hence the doctrine of the judgment is no mere classification of forms of affirmation. It must trace these portentous first steps of the self-conscious subject, rising to awareness of the paradoxical truth that "the individual is the universal", and thence through the other forms of identity and opposition.

Hegel tries thus to understand the many forms of judgment, which Kant simply presupposed.[12] Yet the triplicity of the notion is inadequately grasped in its self-expression as subject-copula-predicate. The forms of judgment show, for Hegel, a progressive growth in the concreteness of the copula, until it becomes one of the three terms of the Notion, mediating the other two. The syllogism is therefore that higher stage of self-awareness in which, for example, "the individual, because particular, is the universal".

The understanding of the various forms of syllogism as progressive stages of self-development is made to depend on the middle-term. This is that moment of the Notion in function of which the whole is grasped. True development will therefore require that each of the three moments should in turn present itself as the whole and the mediating ground ("das Ganze und der vermittelnde Grund").[13] Hence the three figures of the syllogism.[14]

The manner in which the whole is grasped in function of the middle-term will vary. This latter may incorporate the two extremes merely externally and thus remain a purely abstract totality. Or it may grow toward a true

advance that each perfectly contains the others (Enc. § 164). The merely self-identical genus particularizes itself in the "difference" of its species; but the species exhausts the genus and remains universal, and this self-grounding is concrete totality or "individuality".

Whether such a self-development is truly intelligible, or remains a "mere ideal" projected from the imperfect dual development of Essence, is a question which the critic of Hegel – and perhaps also his interpreter – may well pose.

[12] Cf. Enc. § 42, § 171 Zusatz.

[13] § 187.

[14] which Hegel interprets in the order: a) Individual-Particular-Universal, b) Universal-Individual-Particular, c) Particular-Universal-Individual.

unity of the extremes. This growth is the basis for Hegel's understanding of
the three types of syllogism (qualitative syllogisms, syllogisms of reflection,
and syllogisms of necessity), in each of which the three figures are to be
found. But even in the most concrete type, the true totality can be attained
only through the three partial views in which each moment acts as middle-
term: that is, through a triad of syllogisms ("Dreiheit von Schlüssen").[15]

"Everything is a syllogism."[16] With these words, Hegel reminds the reader
that he is not simply repeating the rules for thinking about experience. He is
trying to map the course of that self-development where experience and its
thought are one. Yet even within this fundamental movement of the Subjective Logic we see a re-formulation of that which appeared so clearly in the
Logic of Essence as the complementarity of partial standpoints. Each
"syllogism" remains a biased situation, needing to be offset by others in a
"triad of syllogisms". So is it with the system as a whole.

b. The Triad of Syllogisms

The three final paragraphs of the Encyclopaedia expose briefly the triad of
syllogisms in which the whole system finds its expression. If it is just to see
any isolated syllogism as representing, through its middle-term, a particular
situation of thought or experience, then these concluding paragraphs must
constitute Hegel's final – yet still obscure and ambiguous – outline for the
thinking of a philosophical standpoint.

In the triad of syllogisms, each of the three parts of the system assumes
successively the role of middle-term. Hence, the three syllogisms appear as
follows: a) Idea-Nature-Spirit, b) Nature-Spirit-Idea, c) Nature-Idea-
Spirit.

The first syllogism adopts Nature as its standpoint, having "das Logische
zum Grunde als Ausgangspunkt" and connecting it with Spirit as the other
extreme.[17] Here the claim of the middle-term to totality is at its most external.
Because the syllogism is "in the Idea" (i.e., what is thought is the whole
system as such, not any part of it), this is not the mere externality of independent moments. Yet the mediation "has the external form of mere transition" ("des Übergehens"). "Das Logische wird zur Natur, und die Natur
zum Geiste."

It is not at once evident what situation for the thought of the system is here
described. It would not be sufficient to maintain, as some commentators

[15] Enc. § 198.
[16] § 181.
[17] § 575.

have, that setting Nature as the middle-term designates simply the attitude of natural science. Hegel's reminder that the syllogism is "in the Idea" implies that he is representing a strictly philosophical attitude. What this may be is suggested by Hegel himself in two other places where he discusses the system as a whole.

At the beginning of the Philosophy of Spirit, Hegel describes the three ways in which the Notion is revealed.[18] The second and third correspond respectively to the second and third syllogism above. The first is presented as the "immediate transition of abstract Idea into Nature".

In his introductory lectures on the philosophy of religion, Hegel discusses the two methods of approach to the "whole system of philosophical science".[19] The second corresponds clearly to the method of the second syllogism above. The first is an "abstract observation" which grasps the Idea as the "essence" of Nature and Spirit, but in such a way that the movement of thought remains distinct from the reality "about" which it is exercised. Hegel identifies the attitude with that of Spinoza and Schelling.

If these two passages serve in any way as a commentary to the first syllogism, then this will represent the standpoint, not merely of natural science or empirical thinking, but more fundamentally of a dogmatic metaphysics. It is the attitude of one for whom the circularity of the system means that the Logic achieves itself, then passes – by a merely external transition – into Nature and is subsequently "observed" as the essence of the various stages of Nature and Spirit. At the level of the system triad, the standpoint of "Nature" is that in which "the method is in the position of a tool."[20]

The second syllogism presents its philosophical attitude less obscurely.[21] Hegel states that it is the standpoint of Spirit, which presupposes Nature and unites it "mit dem Logischen". It is the syllogism of "reflection", where philosophy "appears" as a subjective knowing which is itself the way for the realization of its true end. The corresponding passage from the introduction to the Philosophy of Spirit states that it is a reflection which is both the positing of nature as its world and the presupposing of nature as independent. The passage cited from the Philosophy of Religion explicitly identifies this situation and dual movement with that of the "Phenomenology of Spirit". Yet this approach to "philosophical science" is no less incomplete than the first one: if the first remained a formal withdrawal from, and manipulation of, experience, the second errs on the side of a mere immersion in finite experience.

[18] Enc. § 384.
[19] RB, pp. 168-71.
[20] Cf. WL, II, p. 487.
[21] Enc. § 576.

The reconciliation of these two standpoints is thus set by Hegel in the third syllogism.[22] This has the Idea as its middle-term, "die sich wissende Vernunft". The syllogism is indeed itself "the Idea of Philosophy", and its self-division ("sich-Urteilen") into the first two syllogisms determines these partial attitudes as "its own manifestations". And with this affirmation of final harmony, the system, as presented by the Encyclopaedia, closes.

c. The Mediating Syllogism

It might seem disrespectful to suggest that the ending would have been more impressive had not the reader become accustomed to finding such a "final closing" at every stage of his weary route. But each time a new turning, a fresh "immediacy", appeared and the way stretched onward.[23]

The point is not merely rhetorical. Hegel was certainly a victim of his own constructions. Yet he was also struggling with words and forms to express a presence of the absolute within finite experience which would fall neither to a mere dogmatism nor to a simply external duality. The problem has been presented throughout this study as that of continued development within fulfilment,[24] which is, as Hyppolite pointed out, the problem of finite and absolute viewpoints.[25]

"Spirit is actual," Hegel wrote, "in so far as it runs through the three elements of its nature."[26] The movement sets a high ideal of philosophical balance. All hesitation in any one element at the expense of the others places the philosopher in a "subjective" position where he measures the whole from one of its parts. Yet this prohibition to rest seems to apply as much to the third, or reconciling, element as to the other two. So far as it adopts the attitude of a final identity, it is reduced to one of the extremes it must reconcile. The true totality becomes an abstract identity.[27]

Hence every synthesis on the way falls to a fresh immediacy, owing to its incapacity to realize the true duality at its heart.[28] But the synthesis of the system can yield to no further stage. Thus, if it is thinkable, it must be by a realization of its intimate "sich-Urteilen" that does not simply dominate the partial standpoints which are "reconciled" in it. The system of syllogisms,

[22] § 577.
[23] Cf. p. 66 above.
[24] E.g., cf. pp. 30, 144-5, 156-8 above.
[25] Cf. p. 157 above.
[26] Phän., p. 546.
[27] E.g., cf. pp. 87-8, 142 above.
[28] The experience of the divine presence, Hegel stresses in one of his book reviews, is not to be had apart from the "recognition of the opposition in unity and of the unity in opposition". (Berlin, p. 208).

for all its triadic harmony, presents a view of philosophical "situation" basically similar to that of the Logic of Essence.

3. THE PLACE OF THE LOGIC IN THE SYSTEM

If Hegel's own representation of his system in the "element of thought" manifests so clearly, if unwillingly, the "Grenzpunkt der Vorstellung", then the conclusion of this study can be under no illusion of saying the final word. What has been attempted has been to draw attention to some of the shadows that nevertheless lurk in the apparent clarity of the thought which "absolute spirit" achieves of itself. Shadows may be designated but can not be illuminated. Hence this conclusion will but point to some of those which have been found here and there in the study.

a. System

Any contemporary attempt to understand what a metaphysician is trying to do must include some appreciation of what the systematic formulation of thought meant for him.[29] What approach has been suggested for Hegel?

The Need of System

"The final purpose of the world is accomplished, yet is ever accomplishing itself. . . And this balance between the 'is' and the 'ought' is no fixity without process."[30] So Hegel expressed, in the lectures at the end of his career, that need for reconciliation between absolute presence and finite duality which he considered the deepest meaning of both religion and philosophy.

Chapter IV was a sketch of the way in which Hegel's youthful meditations on this, the profoundest of needs, determined the ideals he set for a philosophical system to satisfy it at that point where presence and duality are at their most intimate, in thought. Yet it was also suggested that the influence of the doctrine of the Trinity on the final form of his system may have diverted him from more apt philosophical expression of these aims. The question how the ideals may have retained some of their purity "under" this form was posed at length, in Chapter V, by an examination of Hegel's interpretation of "absolute religion".

The Thought of Totality

The introduction supplied one point of approach to a criticism or appreciation of systematic thought, by emphasizing contemporary difficulties about

[29] Cf. p. 16 above.
[30] Enc. § 234 Zusatz.

that thinking of totality which is central to traditional metaphysics.[31] Hegel, it was suggested, may finally stand condemned for his inadequacies in this task, but the understanding of what he attempted is more complex than many critics seem to suppose.

Hegel was himself a critic of the superficial assumption of totality, and denounced the unthinking use of the word in philosophy.[32] Indeed, it may be said that for him the primary function of a philosophical system was to make possible the gradual manifestation of a true totality through the repeated overcoming and reappearance of the extremes formed by merely abstract identity (or totality) and simply finite duality (or incompleteness). Chapter II offered an approach through Hegel's psychology of a repeated "recollection" from dissipation in an inadequately particularized thought and in the mere "Meinen" of experience, toward a truer philosophical meaning. Chapter III examined the appearance of totality in the three books of the Logic, and implied that whereas "Being" may be below totality, and "Notion" above its verification, the movement of "Essence" supplies a fruitful attitude toward a metaphysics that is conscious of both its fulfilment and its limits. This provided a basis for what may have perhaps remained ambiguously a criticism and an interpretation of the form of the system in the second part.

The Transitions

The original problem, however, that was posed by the authors quoted in the introduction was that of the legitimacy of the transitions in Hegel's system.[33] The question is traditional but yields easily to an over-simple imagery. Hegel's own understanding of the transitions of his system was ambiguous: certainly at Jena, probably at Berlin. It was, however, the aim of the authors quoted to find in his thought a meaning that would apply no less to the embarrassment in which a contemporary metaphysician finds himself.

A way to the question was sought in the Logic, where Hegel's thought of transition itself was seen to have various levels, termed (according to the three books of the Logic) "Übergehen", "Reflexion", and "Entwicklung". With reservations again toward the first and third, a more detailed study was made of the movement of "internal" and "external" reflection. This, it was hoped, would make possible a less superficial understanding of the transitions in the system and of the ambiguous situation of the Logic.

---

[31] E.g., pp. 2-3, 8 above.
[32] Cf. Berlin, pp. 383-9.
[33] summarized on pp. 14-15 above.

b. Logic

The metaphysician, as opposed to the student of any special science, finds himself in the situation that the method, or "logic", of his thought must be justified by that thought itself. For Hegel, this dilemma stands at the centre of his system, though he may have been more concerned to use it than to worry about it.

Ambiguity and Autonomy

The problem appeared first in the introduction as the question whether the Logic develops purely from itself before passing into the "Realphilosophie" or whether it draws its meaning from its "illustrations" in this realm.[34] Historically, there was certainly a duplicity in Hegel's own interpretation of his Logic in his early efforts at system.[35] It seems, however, to have been a duplicity of which he was aware, and which he "allowed" for the interpretation of his system.

Before broaching the question of the Logic as a science, this study tried to find in Hegel's doctrine of meaning and language an illustration of, and some justification for, this duality. His rejection of an "ineffable" simply beyond language is not incompatible with a deep sense of that externality of language which is at the heart of meaning: indeed, his dialectic may be seen to spring from the embarrassment of a thought that is present to itself only in the alienation of its expression. Chapter III was basically an examination of Hegel's logical treatment of the duality inherent in a meaning that is at once the whole, positing and existing in its language, and but a part, a "mere essential" opposed to a language which it presupposes. The question was, thus, whether this situation, so aptly fitted to the Logic of Essence, could justly be found in Hegel's understanding of the relation of Logic to System.

Explanation and Verification

If the transition of thought, or of Logic, to its "other" is no mere "Über-gehen" but a "Reflexion", then greater subtlety is demanded than the interpretation implies which sees the Logic as an autonomous whole that simply finds or determines its verifications in experience.[36] The metaphysician can not follow the scientist in "explaining" by means of fixed models; nor, however, can he simply retreat from verification. Logic is absolved from simple dependence on an experience "outside" it, but it must submit itself to a struggle for progressive recognition in its "other".[37]

[34] pp. 8-9 above.
[35] pp. 140-1 above.
[36] pp. 88-9, 123 above.
[37] pp. 18-19, 59-60 above.

Thought and Experience

It was some such notion of verification that was implied by the search of the authors quoted for a "parallel" movement of Logic and "Realphilosophie".[38] Hegel's early development suggests that this search may not be vain,[39] and Chapter V was devoted largely to an examination of the traces of such a movement in Hegel's own illustration of his system.

So far as it is present, this movement means an admission of one of the commonest objections against Hegel, that his Logic and Phenomenology presuppose each other.[40] The admission, however, suggests the value of a profounder investigation of this identity-in-opposition of thought and experience in Hegel. He himself spoke of Logic as "timeless", of finite experience as "in time". Yet the Notion is "time itself". Hence the true presence of the absolute is neither in a timeless thought, nor in an experience set to a merely future ideal: it is in a thought-experience of which these are but abstractions.

The paradox of a Logic that is at once the whole and but a part of experience is thus a systematic expression of the need for reconciliation of a standpoint that is simply accomplished and a standpoint that is ever accomplishing itself. It poses the question of the place that the philosopher holds.

c. Place

At the close of his article on Hegel's attitude before existence, F. Grégoire presents a "character sketch" of the philosopher.[41] Independent of all particular affections, Hegel would feel at home only in confronting the "whole" as such, with a sympathy that is serious and intellectualized. Yet he would find no inspiration in contemplating the horizon of the ocean or the silent distance of the stars.

Hegel would certainly not want his thought to be lightly classified under the traditional headings of "transcendence" and "immanence". Yet he has been interpreted, by some, as claiming a position reserved for the Absolute; by others, as pursuing a rigorous anthropology that excludes all thought of transcendence. It is understandable how both interpretations have risen. This study, however, has sought in Hegel a more nuanced sense of philosophical situation, and has tried to see how Hegel suggests this in terms of the basic paradox of the place of his Logic in his System.

[38]   pp. 9, 121-2 above.
[39]   pp. 135, 140-1, 144-5 above.
[40]   pp. 167-8 above.
[41]   Etudes Hégéliennes, pp. 47-50.

The Situation of Man

As he speaks of simply observing (zusehen) the movement of the Notion, so Hegel writes of the philosopher as "looking back" on the path traversed.[42] Consideration of the origin of Hegel's system, however, emphasizes the need for caution in interpreting such expressions. While affirming a "final unity" in opposition to the philosophy of a mere "ought", Hegel rejects just as firmly any such unity that involves a standpoint beyond the terms of the human predicament with which he starts. And it was much the purpose of Chapter V to show that, whereas Hegel clearly sets the standpoint of the philosopher in the third "element" of his system, this is itself no simple "domination" of the first two elements; it is a delicate situation that carries the task of experiencing the first two elements no less in their opposition than in their identity, without falling to a subjective position that is simply one with either of them. Only so far as he achieves this does the philosopher avoid "Meinung" and take upon himself a true "Ernst um die Sache".

"Der Mensch ist Geist und Bewusstsein, Vorstellen."[43] To disengage from Hegel's thought his "philosophy of man" would present a task radically different from the one which other philosophers demand. To have concentrated, as this study has done, on the second category of each triad as the "definition of the finite"[44] (i.e., Vorstellung between Anschauung and Denken, Wesen between Sein and Begriff), may be one-sided. Yet it may also be a not unjust approach to the double meaning of the word "Geist" ("mind" and "spirit") which Kroner presented as the whole "secret of Hegel".[45]

Man's "Element"

If it is acceptable that Hegel set himself no unequivocally divine standpoint, it may nevertheless be held that he so identified himself with the place of man as to close any opening to a "transcendence" of the human order.

The question is made especially difficult by the fact that so much of the traditional religious thought of "transcendence" has been expressed in the language of a "Jenseits". This study has avoided any attempt at a re-statement of the problem, in terms of which Hegel could fairly be judged. Mere

---

[42] Enc. § 573.

[43] RB, p. 245.

[44] Enc. § 85. Hegel states that, while the categories of the Logic may be looked upon as definitions of the absolute, the second of each triad may not be so termed, for this is a "definition of the finite".

[45] Cf. his introduction to the English translation of Hegel's *Early Theological Writings*, pp. 23-4. The ambiguity, which is clear in English, is well shown by the dilemma whether to translate Hegel's book as "Phenomenology of Mind" or "Phenomenology of Spirit".

suggestions have been offered at various places. It has been pointed out, for instance, that Hegel's thought of "Vernunft" grew out of the religious grasp of a "non-positive faith", and that the final stage was at first presented as a "reality beyond thought". Hegel's subsequent efforts to mediate the "transcendental intuition" with a dialectical thought put an end to such expressions. Yet the problem may not itself have been so radically altered. The very necessity of development in thought – of a dual and mutually presupposing development from beginning to result and from result to beginning – leaves the concrete whole an "undominated originality", an "element" of spirit which is no mere "beyond" to the stages of its genesis, but which is not adequately accounted for by any summation of those stages.

In his comments on Hegel's philosophy of religion, Hyppolite asks whether this tends more in the direction of Feuerbach's anthropology or of a mysticism similar to that of Jacob Böhme.[46] Neither extreme, he maintains, could be defended as such: Hegel was no mystic, yet he equally refused the complete reduction of God to man.

Both comparisons are instructive. That with Feuerbach and his progeny has often been studied. But if an adequate appraisal of Hegel's thought of religious transcendence were to be made, then a profound examination of his relation to the Lutheran mystic would be necessary.[47] Hegel was much inspired by Böhme, even though he found the manner of expression barbarically unphilosophical. He devotes a long chapter of his "History of Philosophy" to this mystic, in whose thought he found a deep grasp of the unity of opposites and an inwardness "of experiencing and knowing and feeling in his own self-consciousness all that formerly was conceived as a Beyond."[48] In Böhme, this was not irreconcilable with a profound religious sense of the transcendence and personality of God. Yet his difference from Hegel may perhaps be set fundamentally in the fact that in making the identity of opposites the principle of his speculation, Böhme realized this to be an incomprehensible mystery: in its "light" he "explained" all, yet did not thereby render it intrinsically intelligible. Hegel likewise made the identity of opposites his principle of explanation, but for him the light this principle cast on all else was no less the light by which it illuminated itself, the pure intelligibility of "Vernunft".[49]

The difference may, from one point of view, be regarded as slight. From

---

[46] *Genèse*, pp. 523-5.

[47] None yet exists. The most detailed study of Böhme, by H. Grunsky, makes only passing reference to Hegel. The various studies by E. Benz of the relation between the German mystics and Idealism have concentrated on the later thought of Schelling.

[48] Gesch. Phil., XIX, p. 300.

[49] Cf. pp. 108-10 above.

another standpoint, it is that which sets a definitive gap between Hegel and those contemporary philosophical attitudes which served to introduce this study.[50] Facticity is for Hegel no final barrier; he makes it his principle of explanation.

The History of Man's Thought

How, finally, may the interpreter set himself in sympathy before Hegel's apparent claim to put an "end" to the history of thought with his system?

Much must be left to the indulgence freely allowed for the exaggerations of all innovators, particularly in their polemics. Yet the history of thought is no mere catalogue of succeeding ideas. There remains a sense in which thought can take its place in that history only by assuming an absoluteness which sets an "end" to it. If Hegel held that limits must be revealed from within, then that may be supposed to have been his attitude to his own historical situation.

He was certainly never very explicit on the subject. But so far as he held that thought could be present to itself only in the externality of its expression, there may be sufficient ground for the reflections on this question which have been suggested.[51] At least, if criticism may take over from interpretation, we may say that Hegel himself exemplifies the truth that thought is but an illustration of thought. He may himself have been lacking in "respect for the antinomy" in his final triad, and may have lost his balance of "is" and "ought"; but subsequent history shows that his own system exhibits well (if unintentionally) the surviving complementarity of the first and second syllogisms. He brought clearly to light the dilemma of ontology and phenomenology, and one may well hesitate before throwing the first stone.

Heidegger sees in the relation between Hegel's "Logic" and "Phenomenology" a culminating instance of the fundamental ambiguity of metaphysics.[52] One need not go so far in order to see in Hegel a notable example of thought manifesting its limits. Few philosophers have entered so fully into the effort to drive thought to its extreme of independence. Few have shown so clearly, if unwillingly, that their thought does not stand on its own legs.

---

[50] pp. 2-3 above.
[51] pp. 102-5, 189-93 above.
[52] *Holzwege*, p. 179.

BIBLIOGRAPHY

A. HEGEL: EDITIONS USED, AND ABBREVIATIONS IN FOOTNOTES

	Date	Edition	Abbreviation
Theologische Jugendschriften	1790-1800	Nohl	Nohl
Dokumente zu Hegels Entwicklung	1790-1800	Hoffmeister	Dokumente
Differenz des Fichteschen und Schellingschen Systems	1801	Glockner, I	Differenz
Über das Wesen der philosophischen Kritik	1802	Glockner, I	PK
Wie der gemeine Menschenverstand die Philosophie nehme	1802	Glockner, I	—
Verhältnis des Skeptizismus zur Philosophie	1802	Glockner, I	Skept.
Glauben und Wissen	1802	Glockner, I	GW
Über die wissenschaftlichen Behandlungsarten des Naturrechts	1802-3	Glockner, I	BN
Jenenser Logik, Metaphysik und Naturphilosophie	1802	Lasson	JL
Jenenser Realphilosophie I & II	1803-6	Hoffmeister	JR, I & II
Phänomenologie des Geistes	1807	Hoffmeister	Phän.
Philosophische Propädeutik	1808-11	Glockner, III	Propäd.
Nürnberger Schriften	1808-16	Hoffmeister	Nürnberg
Wissenschaft der Logik	1812-16	Lasson	WL, I & II
Enzyklopädie der philosophischen Wissenschaften	1817, 1827, 1830	Nicolin	Enc.
Grundlinien der Philosophie des Rechts	1820-1	Hoffmeister	Recht
Vorlesungen:	1818-31		
Geschichte der Philosophie		Glockner, XVII-XIX	Gesch. Phil.
Philosophie der Geschichte		Glockner, XI	Phil. Gesch.
Ästhetik		Bassenge	Ästhetik
Philosophie der Religion		Lasson	
Begriff der Religion			RB
Naturreligion			RN
Religionen der geistigen Individualität			RI
Absolute Religion			RA
Beweise vom Dasein Gottes			Beweise
Berliner Schriften		Hoffmeister	Berlin
Briefe		Hoffmeister	Briefe

B. WORKS ON HEGEL

The following list contains only those books on Hegel that have been studied in connexion with this dissertation.

Extensive bibliographies up to 1945 may be found in the works of NIEL and HYPPOLITE (*Genèse*). They may be supplemented in certain respects, and brought up to 1958, by that of VAN DER MEULEN (*Die gebrochene Mitte*). The best bibliography for studies of Hegel's philosophy of religion is that of SCHMIDT. For the older commentators, ILJIN's thirty-page appendix is of interest, as he indicates the opinions each defended on important questions of interpretation.

P. Asveld — La Pensée Religieuse du Jeune Hegel (Louvain, 1953)
J. Baillie — The Origin and Significance of Hegel's Logic (London, 1901)
E. Caird — Hegel (London, 1893)
E. Coreth — Das dialektische Sein in Hegels Logik (Wien, 1952)
G. Dulckeit — Die Idee Gottes im Geiste der Philosophie Hegels (München, 1947)
J. N. Findlay — Hegel: A Re-Examination (London, 1958)
H. Fischer — Hegels Methode (München, 1928)
K. Fischer — Hegels Leben, Werke und Lehre (Heidelberg, 1901)
J. Flügge — Die sittlichen Grundlagen des Denkens: Hegels existentielle Erkenntnisgesinnung (Hamburg, 1953)
H. Glockner — Hegel (Stuttgart, 1929 & 1940)
F. Grégoire — Aux Sources de la Pensée de Marx: Hegel, Feuerbach (Louvain, 1947)
— Etudes Hégéliennes (Louvain, 1958)
T. Haering — Hegel, sein Wollen und sein Werk (Leipzig, 1929 & 1938)
N. Hartmann — Hegel (Berlin, 1929)
J. Hessen — Hegels Trinitätslehre (Freiburg/Breisgau, 1922)
J. Hyppolite — Genèse et Structure de la Phénoménologie de l'Esprit (Paris, 1946)
— Introduction à la Philosophie de l'Histoire de Hegel (Paris, 1948)
— Logique et Existence (Paris, 1953)
— Etudes sur Marx et Hegel (Paris, 1955)
I. Iljin — Die Philosophie Hegels (Berne, 1946)
A. Kojève — Introduction à la Lecture de Hegel (Paris, 1947)
R. Kroner — Von Kant bis Hegel (Tübingen, 1921 & 1924)
G. Lasson — Einführung in Hegels Religionsphilosophie (Leipzig, 1930)
T. Litt — Hegel: Versuch einer kritischen Erneuerung (Heidelberg, 1953)
G. Lukacs — Der junge Hegel: über die Beziehungen von Dialektik und Ökonomie (Zürich, 1948)
J. Mc Taggart — Studies in the Hegelian Dialectic (Cambridge, 1896)
— Studies in Hegelian Cosmology (Cambridge, 1901)
— A Commentary on Hegel's Logic (Cambridge, 1910)
J. Möller — Der Geist und das Absolute (Paderborn, 1951)
G. R. G. Mure — An Introduction to Hegel (Oxford, 1940)
— A Study of Hegel's Logic (Oxford, 1950)
H. Niel — De la Médiation dans la Philosophie de Hegel (Paris, 1945)
H. Ogiermann — Hegels Gottesbeweise (Rome, 1948)

E. Ott	– Die Religionsphilosophie Hegels (Berlin, 1948)
E. Schmidt	– Hegels Lehre von Gott (Gütersloh, 1952)
W. T. Stace	– The Philosophy of Hegel (London, 1924)
J. H. Stirling	– The Secret of Hegel (London, 1865)

J. Van der
  Meulen   – Heidegger und Hegel (Meisenheim, 1953)
              – Hegel: die gebrochene Mitte (Hamburg, 1958)

J. Wahl   – Le Malheur de la Conscience dans la Philosophie de Hegel (Paris, 1929)

W. Wallace   – Prolegomena to the Study of Hegel's Philosophy and especially of his Logic (Oxford, 1874)

B. Wigersma
  (editor)   – Verhandlungen der Hegelkongressen (1930, 1931, 1933)

Appendix

Main Divisions of the *Encyclopaedia* (showing the categories discussed)

I. LOGIK
- Sein
  - Qualität
  - Quantität
  - Mass
- Wesen
  - Wesen als Grund der Existenz
    - Die reinen Reflexionsbestimmungen
      - Identität
      - Unterschied
      - Grund
    - Die Existenz
  - Erscheinung
    - Das Ding
  - Wirklichkeit
- Begriff
  - Der subjektive Begriff
    - Der Begriff als Solcher
    - Das Urteil
    - Der Schluss
  - Der objektive Begriff
  - Die Idee

II. NATUR

III. GEIST
- Der subjektive Geist
  - Anthropologie (Seele)
  - Phänomenologie (Bewusstsein)
  - Psychologie (Geist)
    - Der theoretische Geist
      - Anschauung
      - Vorstellung
        - Erinnerung
        - Einbildungskraft
        - Gedächtnis
      - Denken
    - Der praktische Geist
    - Der freie Geist
- Der objektive Geist
- Der absolute Geist
  - Kunst
  - Religion
  - Philosophie

The Logic of Essence in the *Wissenschaft der Logik* (categories discussed)

WESEN
- Das Wesen der Reflexion in ihm selbst
  - Schein
    - Das Wesentliche und das Unwesentliche
    - Der Schein
    - Die Reflexion
      - Die setzende Reflexion
      - Die äussere Reflexion
      - Bestimmende Reflexion
  - Reflexionsbestimmungen
    - Identität
    - Unterschied
    - Widerspruch
  - Grund
- Erscheinung
- Wirklichkeit